AF564902

Women in India

Women in India

FARHAT JAHAN

ANMOL PUBLICATIONS PVT. LTD.
NEW DELHI - 110 002 (INDIA)

ANMOL PUBLICATIONS PVT. LTD.
4374/4B, Ansari Road, Daryaganj
New Delhi - 110 002
Ph.: 23261597, 23278000
Visit us at: www.anmolpublications.com

Women in India

First Published, 2004

ISBN 81-261-1989-6

PRINTED IN INDIA

Published by J.L. Kumar for Anmol Publications Pvt. Ltd., New Delhi - 110 002 and Printed at Mehra Offset Press, Delhi.

Contents

Preface

Women in India has been a subject of concern in India for decades. The scholars, academics, sociologists and even politicians have been pondering over the issue and searching for a readymade solution for an overall emancipation and empowerment of the female folk in this country. However, little has been done in concrete terms.

No body can deny that the Women—the better half of our population have a definite role to play in our social framework and they have been doing so for years now. Still, they are a neglected lot, even today. They are being treated as the 'worse half of the society'.

Our civilization is claimed to be five thousand year old, (or even older than that) and our family life has evolved and developed for all these ages, but, in spite of all the cultivation of civility and development of social life women have not achieved their rightful place in our community or society. No doubt, today they have a strong presence in all walks of life, but proportionately (women make almost half of the populace) they are nowhere. At best, we intend to give them a thirty per cent quota in polity. But again it seems to be a distant dream.

Interestingly, empowerment of women is guaranteed by the constitution and guarded by law of the land, but, ironically most of it is on paper alone. In practice what we find is not more than an eyewash. There is a strong case for women's empowerment, as a subject, to be researched about and written on. Hence, this study.

The undersigned has made all efforts to make this research based study, a comprehensive one, as it covers all genuine aspects of the topic and discusses all core issues at length. Hopefully, this modest endeavour would be accorded due recognition.

Editor

WOMEN IN INDIA
(Emancipation & Empowerment)

1

Introduction

India is a developing country, which depends very much on its vast potential of human resources, if these resources are properly tapped the country is bound to progress efficiently, effectively and rapidly. Women form the most important part of the human resources of the nation and they may contribute very substantially in building a strong, powerful and affluent nation. They can, however, make their best contribution when they are properly educated and are able to explode the myths, which have kept them in a state of backwardness and neglect. In the present chapter we are trying to project the type of education which is needed in future for Indian women in view of their socio-phychological make up.

Today too much theory based on little reality exists. Men talk of morality while all the time degrading their women. The reformists talk of abstinence to reduce population while they themselves might have fathered more, than half a dozen children. The harmony in family life is preached while subjugating the women in the name of old ideal of Pativrata. The quarrels between the husband and wife may involve much cruelty yet the divorce may be very much condemned. There is an urgent need to cry a half to this type of duplicity in talks and action. For example, when there is genuine discord between husband and wife or there is much cruelty involved in their relationship then divorce is the only viable solution. It will injure the ego of the children much less than their upbringing in a daily quarrelsome situation. But this point of no return in the relationship between husband and wife will not come up if both respect each other's individuality and live together with mutual trust, faith, desire and love. In a stable marriage alliance consideration of each other's viewpoint is desirable and Indian men and women have the capability of developing such consideration.

There is enough scientific evidence available, which shows that since birth onwards girl child receives rejection; unequal, indifferent and discriminatory treatment as compared to male children. Access to food and other household assets allocation of domestic duties, participation in community and neighbourhood activities, school education, etc. reflect serious gender based differences and inequalities.

Modern scientific techniques like amniocentesis and ultrasound have been widely misused as "sex determination test" for selective elimination of the female foetuses. Between 1978 and 1983, 78,000 female were aborted in India, following sex determination tests. A Mumbai-based survey in 1984 revealed that out of the 8,000 foetuses aborted following such tests 7,999 were female. Many State Governments have framed or are framing legislation against this practice. But still there is a danger that secretly such tests will continue to be conducted and female foetuses aborted. The tradition of having a male child is so deep-rooted that the women themselves do not hesitate in destroying their pregnancies if the tests reveal that the baby to be born is a female. Proper education is needed to discourage this tendency. It has been noticed that many educated women also indulge in the practice of destroying foetuses hence our emphasis is on proper education by which we mean an education, which frees the woman from gender biases.

Conservative cultural values, coupled with assumption of domestic responsibilities dictate the girl child's withdrawal from formal education in our country the female literacy rates are very low. These are 39.4 per cent according to the 1991 census. The drop out rate for girls in the school is estimated at 55.5 per cent at the primary stage and 77.7 per cent at the middle school stage. There is thus great need for having a crash programme for women education.

It is unfortunate that in spite of Indian women getting all those legal rights which are being demanded by the women of some developed nations they are having quite difficult time in keeping themselves from the old fossilised traditions. The mother cult may be one of the reasons for their remaining tradition oriented. Though that which is motherly is represented as noble, it has its drawbacks as well in those situations in which the women cannot think of any other thing except being mothers. The motherhood syndrome is incompatible with modern woman's development and exists because of cultural conditioning. According to Evelyn Reed: "The subordination of the women is not the result of a predetermined biological handicap i.e. child bearing." She considers that attribution of inferior status of women to her faulty biology is a false preposition.

Self-reliance, self-esteem and a reality-oriented approach to life must be the goal of Indian women. Some people may take exception to this suggestion because of the fear of loss of domestic harmony but unless the women are able to assert their will the family and the social life will remain in a state of disharmony.

After independence India framed planning, strategies and techniques to steer the nation's economic development towards attaining a socialist pattern of society. The first five-year plan was launched in 1950-51 and thereafter nine more five-year plans besides some yearly plans have already been adopted. In each of these plans women's development issues, especially their economic, educational and health issues, have received considerable attention and various welfare measures were taken to ameliorate their conditions. The result of all these measures is that the status and position of the Indian women have much improved. But as we have repeated again and again in this book there is much, which has still to be done.

The Draft of the National Policy on Empowerment of Women released by the Ministry of Human Resource Development seeks to eliminate all forms of violence against women as also to abolish discrimination against the girl child. It commits the government to ensure that women are not denied of their human rights and fundamental freedom. This policy also seeks to provide equal opportunities for power sharing and decision-making to women at all levels and processes in public and private sectors. All these are highly desirable goals. But these alone would not be sufficient unless the government policies and its mechanism are supplemented by a social will, a wave and a movement by women themselves for achieving these goals and for promoting rational attitudinal changes.

The National Policy on Education (NPE) 1986 has given very important recommendations for women education. It has paid attention to the basic issues of women's equality. In the section titled 'Education for Women's Equality' the Policy states:

> "Education will be used as an agent of basic change in the status of women. In order to neutralise the accumulated distortions of the past, there will be a well-conceived edge in favour of women. The national education system will pay a positive role in the empowerment of women. It will foster the development of new values through redesigned curricula textbooks, training and orientation of teachers, decision makers and administrators, and the active involvement of educational institutions--- women's studies will be promoted as a part of various courses and educational institutions encouraged to take up active programmes to further women's development.

The removal of women's illiteracy and obstacles inhibiting their access to, and retention in, elementary education will receive overriding priority, through provision of special support services, setting of time targets and effective monitoring. Major emphasis will be laid on women's participation in vocational, technical and professional education at different levels. The policy of nondiscrimination will be pursued vigorously to eliminate sex stereotyping in vocational and professional courses and to promote women's participation in non-traditional occupation, as well as in existing and exerged technologies".

The above recommendations have given very important guidelines for the futuristic education of the women. The government definitely took interest in implementing the policy framework and so there were developed "Programme of Action" in 1986 and 1992. Also a National Perspective Plan for Women's Education 1997-98 to 2000 AD was drawn. The National Perspective Plan formulated some important specific objectives for women education so that women may also participate actively in the social cultural, economic and political areas. These important objectives were to be obtained by 2000 AD. These objectives included elimination of illiteracy and universalisation of elementary education, substantial vocalisation and diversification of courses at secondary level, making education as an effective means for women equality, making necessary intervention in the content and processes of education to inculcate positive and egalitarian attitudes, providing non-formal and part-time courses to women to enable them to acquire knowledge and skills for their social, cultural and economic advancement, and to provide impetus to women to enroll themselves in various professional degree courses so as to increase their number in medicine, teaching, engineering and other fields substantially. To achieve the above mentioned and some other objectives the National Perspective Plan made important recommendations that awareness needs to be generated among the masses regarding the necessity of educating girls so as to prepare them to effectively contribute to the socio-economic development of the country, to strengthen their role in society and to realise their own capacities for improving and minimising drop-outs and wastage of girl students.

The Revised Plan of Action (1992) has laid down suitable strategies for implementing the above mentioned targets.

In spite of all endeavours made so far for promoting women education, we still find that for every 100 boys there are only 62 girls in primary schools, 43 girls in middle schools, 36 girls in secondary schools and 31 girls at different stages of higher education. According to the 1991 census female literacy is 39.4 per cent compared to 63.8 per cent for males, the total number of female illiterates is 197 millions which is more than male counterparts by 70 millions, even though the female population is less than the male population by 32 millions. There are rural urban disparities, and among rural women, literacy is about half of the urban female literacy.

The above figures lead us to conclude that more intensive efforts are needed to educate our women specially those who are living in the rural areas or the slum areas in the towns. Since most of these women who are illiterate and do not go to the school the programmes for educating them may be accompanied with the programmes of improving their financial conditions. The programmes for the poverty alleviation should be intensified. It may be emphasised that the success of any scheme of education depends to a great extent on it being productive both in the material as well as social sense. Actually education should lead to social, economic and moral development. An educated person must be able to earn more than an uneducated one. The national education system will play a positive, interventionist role in the empowerment of women. It will foster the development of new values through redesigned curricula, textbooks, training and orientation of teachers, decision-makers and administrators, and the active involvement of educational institutions. Women's studies will be promoted as a part of various courses and educational institutions encouraged taking up active programmes to further women's development.

The removal of women's illiteracy and obstacles inhibiting their access to, and retention in, elementary education will receive overriding priority, through provision of special support services, setting of time targets and effective monitoring. Major emphasis will be laid on women's participation in vocational, technical and professional education at different levels. The policy of nondiscrimination will be pursued vigorously to eliminate sex stereo-typing in vocational and professional courses and to promote women's contribution effectively towards bringing desirable social change and be honest, sincere and affectionate individual. For our women such education is required which may help them in getting gainful employment and in improving their financial position.

From the above discussion it may be evident that the government is very much aware of the need of providing education to the women of the country. In the recent decades it has made some genuine efforts to bring the women on the national scene by giving them incentives, providing for their education schools and colleges, giving free education to the girls up to a particular stage, developing centres of women studies, opening various avenues of employment to them, providing non-formal centres for their vocational training. It is very much desirable that no discrimination is made on the basis of jobs meant exclusively for males or for females. The interest of the student should be the main consideration. From the lower classes onwards the attention of the students should be directed towards creating social awareness and motivating them for higher achievements in all the areas of concern to them. India needs good housewives as well as efficient women workers. Education for women must be organised around these two powerful needs.

It is to be noted that the outlook of the women has changed considerably during the last four decades. Much of it is due to the expansion of education that has taken place in the country. The young women of today are neither afraid of moving out of their homes nor are as dependent on their parents or husbands as were their mothers and grand mothers. The woman wants to be economically independent. She has realised the importance of education and is quite conscious of the need of raising the standard of living of the family through her engagement in the world of work. The educated women are prepared to fight for their rights and to assert their individuality. Hence web may say that the educational efforts made so far have yielded positive results. These efforts are now required to be intensified. Certain changes in the educational system are also needed so that the women learn to be self-reliant, are able to develop self-esteem and become caring, loving and the source of amity and goodwill in the family. The following are some suggestions regarding the changes to be brought about in the educational system:

1. All out efforts should be made to implement the constitutional directives of compulsory elementary education up to 14 years of age. Education should be free up to this age for both boys and girls.

2. The girls should be taught the same subjects as are being taught to the boys, which means that if home craft is taught to the girls it should also be taught to the boys. The physical education should be given to both boys and girls. At the onset of puberty the girl's menses begin. At this age some training in personal hygiene may be given exclusively to the girls.

3. From the lower classes onwards the attention of the students should be directed towards social evils and in them social awareness should be created. They should also be motivated for higher achievements in all the areas of concern to them. As said earlier India needs good housewives as well as efficient women workers. Education for women must be organised around these two powerful needs.

4. The girls should be encouraged to join technical, managerial, professional institutions of higher learning so that they can compete with boys in the job market.

5. The methods of teaching should be so planned that they inculcate the habits of thinking freely and expressing their views freely.

6. The curricula of all the subjects, which are taught to the school children, should be free from sex bias.

7. The education of the school children must include co-curricular activities in which both boys and girls should participate and learn to take independent decisions.

8. In our educational institutions the courses in the maintenance of inter-personal relationships be introduced. Some of these courses must be compulsory for both boys and girls.

9. Some special courses for girls in mother craft, in the home economics and household affairs should be introduced. Some of such courses may also be open for boys.

10. Non-formal system of education must be strengthened. It should be available to all those girls who are unable to join the formal system of education. Education from the elementary to postgraduate levels must be available through this system.

11. A network of adult literacy centres must be established throughout the country. In these centres the education for social change must be stressed. The women must specially be prepared to fight against social evils and to rise above their mythical existence.

12. A network of counselling centres must be set up. These centres must be equipped with to give educational, vocational and personal counselling. Special emphasis should also be placed to marital and family conselling. Each big school must have adequately trained counsellors. Counselling is very much needed at the adolescent stage to both the boys and girls. Our educational system must be able to fulfil this need.

13. Precaution should be taken in teaching those topics, which involve the status and position of women. It will all depend on the teachers how they present an

episode where the women are depicted as serving their husbands. It may be taught in terms of inferior position of the women or it may be taught as an ideal example of love and affection. The teachers training colleges or colleges of education should pay special attention towards the teaching of such lessons by their teacher trainees so that the myths regarding women perpetuated in our society for centuries are exploded and the modern outlook is inculcated.

14. The educational institutions must also provide placement services so that the boys and girls are not only prepared for jobs but are also able to be placed in jobs.

15. The emphasis on the education of the girls must be specifically on making them strong so that they are able to reverse their image of being delicate and unfit for jobs requiring tough exterior.

The above are some of the suggestions which have emerged out of the discussions made in the different chapters of the present book. Many useful and worthwhile suggestions have been made by various commissions and committees, plans and policies. We have refrained ourselves form repeating them, as they are available in the from of reports in full details. In planning or the futuristic education they may all be taken into consideration.

In conclusion we may say that the Indian women have always been quite strong. They have always been in the forefront of the struggle for the betterment of the mankind. They have been great support to their male counterpart. It is their power of resilience that in spite of the persistent efforts of the male to enmesh them in the web of myth they have never lost their composure and cool and today they are bravely facing the challenges of their subjugation.

2

Historical Background

Through the ages, the woman has been the subject of study – from the ancient to the modern times. Comments on the nature of women their ambitions and aspirations, desires and wishes, birth and upbringing, relations with husband, paramour, children and other relatives have been the subject of discussion, comments, conversations and investigations throughout the history of mankind. The woman has been branded as a mysterious creature as well as a devoted mother and self-sacrificing wife during various periods of time through which the human civilization has evolved out from its primitive roots to an advanced scientific and technical culture.

The changing status and position of the woman in different periods and in different civilizations have very greatly influenced her upbringing and education. If during one period of time or in one civilization she was brought up as a prized possession of the parents, in some others she was completely neglected and was accepted only as a provider of sexual pleasure to man and as a producer of his offspring. As a provider of pleasure and producer of children, her education was completely neglected but whenever and wherever she was given high prestige in society, her education became the primary concern of the social order. Thus, the education of the woman has been completely limited to her sociological status and psychological make up. In the present book the focus is on the social psychological dimensions of a women education in India.

For better understanding of the socio-psychological dimensions of women education in India one may look into the background out of which the role, position and education of women have emerged from the past to the present. In the following pages the authors have presented a brief description of women's role, position and education in the religious and historical perspectives. The authors have confined their description mainly to the Indian women but have also focused attention on the women in the West in the context of their struggle for emancipation and empowerment in order to visualize its influence on the Indian womanhood.

Indian Angle

Ironically, very little information is available about the civilization in pre-Aryan India. However, opinion of some, archaeologists is that the non-Aryans had originated in India as early as around 2500 B.C. and were of mixed origin and diverse ethnic composition. Later, their intellectual bent of mind influenced the Aryan thought process. The law of karma, reincarnation, animal veneration, female or earth-mother goddesses, deity worship and male and female fertility symbols might have been imbibed by the Aryans from them.

It seems that to begin with the Aryans overwhelmed the non-Aryans, suppressed their religion and culture and imposed their own values. However, as time passed the Aryans became progressively Indianized, they absorbed the customs of the original inhabitants and modified their religion assimilating the existing culture. The Aryans' own religious and social customs were fused with theirs and Indianized by the native people. Thus, fusing together of incoming concepts and prevailing customs became the tradition of India and of Hinduism.

The Aryans produced vedic literature. The philosophies of Vedanta and Upanishads are their contributions.

Aryan family life was stable. The society was founded on the institutions of home and family. The women were assigned prestigious position in the social order. The Rig Vedic expression "the wife is the home"-shows how domestic life was woven around the woman.

The pre-vedic society was basically matriarchal. It worshipped a goddess of earth-mother type. The Aryan society was patriarchal but the worship of the goddess prevailed. Earlier the mother goddess was worshipped in the form of icons but the Aryans almost replaced the icons with matronly women real mothers who were human and humane. The mother was given a high status in all the spheres of life.

There was attached great importance to the goddess Aditi who typified the motherhood. She was considered the ideal mother like Maat of the Egyptians and Themis of the Greeks. Her function has been described to tenderly the living beings.

Rig Vedic Aryans loved their wives and children. They had a desire for male child but the birth of a daughter as potential mother was also accepted and welcomed. However, in Rig Veda no desire for a daughter is expressed, while in Atharva Veda the birth of a daughter is even deprecated. In Upanishads there are prescribed certain rituals to be performed by a man who wants a learned daughter to be born.

In the Rig Vedic period the son and daughter were not discriminated in their upbringing. The son was to take to the profession of the father, while the daughter was to inherit the glory and honour of her mother. The wife as mother was given the dignity and respect in the household. She was expected to perform duties which were both of celestial as well as terrestial in nature. She participated in all sacrifices instituted by her husband.

Women were educated both in the spiritual as well as temporal subjects. They were given training in the religious lore, in the historical tradition and mythology. They were also given training in the fine arts as well as in the military science in certain cases. As a qualification for marriage, the education of a girl was considered as important as that of a boy.

The education of the women mainly centred round the acquisition of language and literature, the fine arts and the military science. The ancient literature records that there were scores of women, eligible to become Rishis and composed very effective poetry. The name of Ghosa, the wife of the great seer Kaksivan can be mentioned. In Rig Veda she has been mentioned many a time. Two long, hymns, 39 and 40 of the tenth mandala stand to her credit. Lopamundra is another lady Rishi who is credited with having composed a hymn jointly with her husband Agastya.

Music was a necessary equipment for women of the period. Songs were sung on all important occasions and functions. Dancing as an art was also learnt by the women. The women were also trained in self-defence. They knew how to use bow and arrow.

The paternal and maternal tie was very strong among the early Aryans. The father was respected as the earner and protector, the mother was loved for providing daily nourishment and maintaining the household. The daughter was caressed and fondled by her parents and brothers who gave her lavish presents at the time of her marriage. She was considered the breath and life of the family.

The women had liberty of movement. There was no Parda. Indo-Aryans recognized the truth embodied in the dictums, "Ignorance is weakness," "Knowledge is power".

The number of Upanishads is estimated to be around fifty. In most of them, we do not find any reference to women. It is only in Chandogya and Brihadaranyaka Upanishads that we find that women were admitted into philosophical groups and were allowed to discuss the highest spiritual truths of life. They enjoyed a position on a par with men. The men and women were considered as the 'two wheels of the same chariot'.

From the account of this period we find that women were free from social constraints. Girls were free to choose their own husbands. They married only after attaining puberty. The women were even exalted to the position of goddess and given different celestial names like Prithvi, a vague personification of the earth, Usha, the goddess of dawn, Ratri, the spirit of night, etc.

The concept of Ardhanarishwara was propagated. The concept was that of a figure image of half Shiva and the other half as Parvati. This image signified the interdependence of men and women. It conveyed the message that separately men and women are incomplete. Only jointly they are complete. The figure image depicted the masculine and the feminine functions of the Supreme being.

It may be noted that in the Upanishadic texts woman was not eulogized as a person in herself but first and foremost her role as wife and mother was given high status and value. The women were idealized and glorified as mothers. The girl as a potential perpetuator of a family line was valued as much as a son.

Since Rig Vedic age education of women was given much importance. There is evidence that the discipline of brahamacharya was also required to be observed by the girl. The stage of brahamacharya in all probability may be the period of studentship of the girl preceding her married life. The girls were taught that marriage was not for lust, but for perfect domestic life and for producing illustrious progeny. They were given training in the art of house-keeping and house management. Their education was to prepare them to conduct themselves properly in the married life. They learnt the art of some handicrafts, the elements of hygiene, physiology and nutrition.

The pattern of education in the Upanishadic period became more philosophical in nature. The men and women shifted their attention from Vedic ritualism to more intricate problems of life. The women engaged themselves freely in debates and philosophical symposia.

Education helped the women to become more balanced and lead a regulated good life. It was directed towards the development of their natural virtues and latent capabilities and aimed at all round development of their character and personality. Eminent women scholars of this period, like Sulabha, Vadya, Maitreyi and Gargi made significant contributions to the advancement of knowledge.

A description of status, position and education of the women of ancient India is incomplete without the mention of Manu's views. *Manusmriti* (about 200 B.C.) prescribes duties and obligations of a woman. For Manu, woman is a perpetual minor and has to lead whole of her life under the guardianship of either the father, the husband or the son.

Manu prescribes that the wife must always worship her husband as God even if he is debauch, immoral and lacks good qualities. It is the bounden duty of the wife to obey and follow the dictates of her husband. The woman's salvation lies only in the devoted service to her husband. He refers to her duties in the following words:

> "She must always be cheerful, clever in the management of her household affairs, careful in cleaning her utensils, and economical in expenditure"

Manu favoured only the domestic and religious education for women. He also favoured the giving of training in music and dance to the woman in order that she may be able to please her man.

The society in the Epic period was completely patriarchal and patrilineal, so the husband was considered the senior partner in the home. But the wife was also given the dignity in the household because of her vocation of motherhood. Her virtues were recognized. Her abilities in the maintenance of the household were appreciated. She was considered to be a true friend of man given by God. She was man's half, his religious partner, giver of joy and sons.

The epics *Ramayana* and *Mahabharata* contain the description of women who presented ideal conduct and models for the womenhood to be adopted by the lesser mortals. But these models also have ingrained in themselves the subordination of the women. Thus the epics trace the story of the rise and fall of the status of women in Hindu society. Mentioned below are a few highly revered and illustrious ladies who form the central theme of these epics.

The foremost among all the ladies mentioned in epics is Devi Sita. Sita is a paragon of virtue. She is an ideal wife who serves her husband with complete devotion, who is an embodiment of the spiritual sublimity of feminine character. She suffers great hardships but remains unperturbed by them. Her only wish is to serve her husband with all her capabilities. She has to suffer the ordeal of fire but at no occasion she expresses any doubt in her loyalty, fidelity, devotion, love and sacrifice for the well being of her husband. She is learned. She can quote moral tales and smrities. She had religious education.

No doubt the ideal of Sita has inspired Indian women for ages. But in the modern times some are raising doubts about the complete subordination to the husband eulogised in the character of Sita. For educationists, it is a dilemma. Should the women education be directed towards the flowering of the women as devoted as Sita to her husband or teach them for independent outlook. For a proper answer all the aspects of Sita's personality as portrayed in the epic have to be carefully examined. One thing stands out that as Sita had her own will and determination and even when she had to undergo torture her determination did not waver.

She was one of the strong-willed women of the Epic Period. She possessed not only physical charm but also a brilliant mind. She was exposed to the brutalities of men when she was forced to discard her clothes before the men of the Kauravas court. But she did not lose the balance of her mind and reasoning power. The arguments presented by her in the Kaurava court were so perfect that nobody except Vidura and Vikarna possessed the courage to reply to her question. In the midst of her humiliation, she still showed good manners and saluted those Kuru elders who did not dare to check the evil. She was deeply learned and had comprehensive knowledge of old traditions, history and the Puranas. She did not hesitate in condemning her husbands when they failed in the performance of their duties. She did not tolerate her insult and inspired even a peace loving man like Yudhistira to war.

Draupadi presents to us an ideal of womanhood who was learned, iron willed, revengeful, intolerant towards undignified behaviour, loving and affectionate and also forgiving. She was a perfect wife, wise counsellor and dear companion to her husbands.

Among the other learned ladies of the Epic period we may name Gandhari, Kunti, Kaushalya, Sumitra, Kaikeyi, Gautami, Sulabha, Mandodri, Trigata and many others.

Gandhari was the noblest of mothers. She had understanding, judgment, intellect and good sense. She remained attached to the cause of justice and righteousness even when her sons were on the verge of being annihilated and their empire destroyed. She had a high sense of justice, possessed great intellectual qualities and depicted in her conduct both human virtues and frailties. She was jealous of Kunti's motherhood and had a longing for a daughter and son-in-law in order to attain Heaven. She spent her life in penance, self denial and righteousness. But she had weaknesses which make her character real and thus presents ideals which are attainable by ordinary human beings.

Kunti was an ideal wife and mother. She was also of strong will. She taught her sons to die gloriously in war than live in infamy. She was an unwed mother of Karna whom she threw in the river. But her love for her son was irresistible, sublime and pure. Kunti presents an ideal of womanhood which is unflinching in love, righteousness yet not so bold as to face the hostile society for her begetting a son out of wedlock.

The three queens of king Dashratha-Kaushalya, Kaikeyi, Sumitra were well-versed in household affairs but were also involved in the state craft. They had many virtues but also sufferred from human frailties. Kaushalya was the ordinary human being but served her husband, as a slave, friend, sister, wife, and mother. Sumitra was calm, steady and balanced. For her the path of duty and righteousness was more important than any material possession. Kaikeyi was dominating, bold and resourceful. Her life shows that she was over-ambitious and wished, to control the kingdom through her husband, and, later through her son. She is by and large portrayed as a negative character.

There are many other women whose lives and exploits are presented as the ideals of Hindu womanhood. These ladies were highly cultured and were prepared to sacrifice personal good for the social good. The education of the Indian women, particularly the Hindu women has been very greatly influenced by the ideals propagated through the study of their lives and exhortations. However, in the modern times some questions are being asked about the ideals so propagated. In the various chapters of this book we will examine these doubts and try to arrive at some conclusions regarding their validity in the twenty-first century.

Buddha inculcated in his followers a reverence for learning. He conveyed the Dharma or Truth to his first disciples at his teaching sessions at Varanasi. These disciples became the first members of the Sangha. Among his first Upasikas or followers there, were two women. Initially, he was reluctant to incorporate women into the Sangha and this attitude resulted in the subsequent neglect of female education by his followers.

Buddha believed that seven factors lead to wisdom: inner mindfulness, searching of the norms, energy, zest, serenity, concentration, and mental balance. These thoughts were installed in the young Buddhist males but were ignored in the case of sisters of the Sangha. As indicated above Buddha initially was averse to the admission of women into his Sangha system but later on agreed to the formation of the order of the nuns-these nuns were imparted religious and spiritual education. A life of celibacy, austerity and strict mental discipline was expected of them. The education for the women was also introduced at the later stage in order to help them to acquire the knowledge that would enable them to lead a fuller life. But the end of Buddhist era in India also resulted in the end of female education for many generations.

In Jainism, there was given great importance to self-denial, restrains of passion and a life of renunciation. A life of restraint and devoid of passion was expected from men and women. The women were also admitted into monasteries and given full facilities to get the best possible education. The Jaina system of education had depth, was universal in nature and applicable to all alike, irrespective of caste, creed or sex.

The spiritually trained Jaina women attained a high degree of academic education and involved themselves in preaching their faith of universal love and brotherhood. They dedicated themselves to social service.

Jainism was divided into two main sects-Digambaras and Shwetambaras. The Digambaras were of the opinion that women were incapable of attaining salvation and so did not admit them into their order. The Shwetambaras, on the other hand, made no distinction between the sexes and freely admitted aspirants of both the sexes into their order.

Theoretically, Jaina believed that man and women both had the right to attain perfection or perfect liberation of the highest order. But in practice Jaina felt that there were very few women who had the strength of mind and body to endure the hard life of an ascetic. The women were considered weak and so unfit to undertake a course of self-mortification and self-effacement. Thus in the spiritual order women had secondary position.

Sikhism considers woman as worthy of respect as man's helpmate and a partner in his domestic life. Women are not looked upon as evil or perpetrator of sin, nor simply the objects of men's pleasure. A woman's roles as mother, wife, sister and daughter are praised and the qualities which the women are expected to develop are love, obedience, contentment and sweet temper.

Sikhism advocated equality among all the human beings. The social equality of the women is ungrudgingly recognised. The militant brotherhood of the Sikhs, the Khalsa founded by Guru Gobind Singh in the seventeenth century was open to both sexes and all classes. The women were initiated into the Khalsa by taking the name of Kaur and were expected to perform the same duties as men.

Since in Sikhism the equality of sexes was recognized, very few restrictions were put on womens' education.

Christian Angle

In Christianity, women are considered as the harbinger of evil. No doubt Catholics give a high respectful place to Virgin Mary but both Protestants and Catholics feel that the women brought the evil to the earth. The fall of Adam is attributed to the evil design of Eve. Hence the pious and saintly Christians like St. Bernard, St. Antony, St. Bonaventure, St. George the great, all cursed women. The woman was described by them as the organ of the devil', 'a scorpion ever ready to sting', 'the poison of an asp', 'the malice of the dragon' and 'the instrument which the devil uses to get possession of our souls'.

The position of the woman in the Jewish faith was very low but in Christianity it was further lowered. They charge her with the crime of disobeying God, causing the fall of Adam and her guilt being transmitted to the whole mankind so that every child is born in sin. Since God had to send, Jesus to be sacrificed because of the first crime of the woman, so she is considered responsible for the crucification of Jesus. The Christian saints and priests considered women to be unclean and so gave much importance to a life of celibacy. It is because of this attitude that the Christian women were denied those rights and privileges which Christian men enjoyed. It is only in twentieth century that the movements of women liberation have resulted in their recognition as equals to men. The women had to wage a severe and persistent battle to achieve those rights which should have been their on the basis of their recognition as a part of humanity.

It is true that women have now been given rights. But they obtained these by their own struggle and by the slackening of the hold of priests over western societies and laws.

Education, historically, was the sole privilege of the rich and the priestly class. The priests dominated the transmission of knowledge throughout Christiandom. They controlled the access to institutions of learning. In all the Christian countries education was the monopoly of the religious orders. The governing priests did not consider the education of women essential. They were of the view that women were incapable of absorbing the same amount of education or the same in-depth knowledge as men. Besides this they thought that women's minds were weaker than men's and did not require that intellectual exercise which the men needed. They had spread the myth that women should be restrained from speaking in church and from getting education.

The Christian priests' disregard for women education was rooted in their belief in women's inferiority. This disregard was further reinforced by the fear of female emancipation. They were afraid that free education may lead to the deployment of women's full potential.

This in their view was going to upset the natural order between men and women and God and women and the church. They emphatically pointed out that the women are modest, obedient and docile and as such do not require as thorough an education as men do.

Later the missionaries started giving education to women but they segregated boys and girls and prescribed different courses of study to the two sexes. The boys were taught useful subjects in the vocational, mechanical and scientific spheres. The girls were taught domesticity, cooking, knitting, etc. The idea was that boys should be prepared for life outside home and the girls for life inside the home.

As we have already pointed out that the situation has very much changed now in almost all the Christian countries but still the stigma attached of being a woman has not been completely wiped out. And whatever women have achieved in raising their status and position and in attaining prestige has been the fruits of their own struggle for emancipation and empowerment.

Islamic Angle

In Islam straight forward directions regarding the status and the position of the women have been laid down. It is the only religion in which the universal laws for all walks of human life are laid down including that for women. There are directions regarding social and political rights of women. There are laws regarding their claims to property and their privileges for the custody of children and their religious duties.

Islam gives equality to women in relation to men in many respects. It makes a case for the dignity of women. In holy Quran it is mentioned that "women are the twin halves of men". "The world and all things in it are valuable but the most valuable thing in the world is a virtuous wife", God enjoins upon you to treat women well for they are your mothers, daughters and aunts".

There are also many aspects which present seeds of discrimination between men and women. Islam gives rights of inheritance of property to women as a daughter, a wife, a mother, a sister and in some cases even to more distantly related. But when a man has a son and a daughter both, the share of the daughter is, half that of the son.

The inequality between men and women is also evident in Islam when we find that women are put in seclusion in Islam. They are put behind parda and debarred from any male company besides their immediate and near relations. Other areas of discrimination are man's right of divorce, the right of men to practice polygamy, have four wives at a time and similar other provisions like "the testimonies of two women are equal to one man". Parda system isolated women from the outer world and confined them to the four walls of their house.

In the holy Quran the women are exhorted to be modest, chaste, lead a life of decorum and decency which was interpreted by the religious leaders in terms of putting the women in Parda, put a veil or burkha on their bodies. This resulted in losing their right to participate in communal activities. Thus Islam differentiated between the man's world and the woman's world.

In early Islam, female education was highly restricted. Only in the families in which the father was educated, the girls learnt to recite the verses of Quran. But her learning was totally dependent on the approval of the father.

In the medieval period women education was by and large ignored. The women were excluded from public gatherings or in any intellectual deliberations. The result was that most of the women remained illiterate and unlettered. Some females had access to tutors and libraries but they were not engaged by men-folk in any intellectual discussion. Hence they could learn through their own individual efforts. By and large women remained in status as inferior, unequal, submissive and ignorant beings. Females were denied access to learning. They were also excluded from the mosques where most of the education occurred. They could not attend the Kuttabs and the Madrasah.

Some of the women who were fortunate to receive education usually came from affluent, prestigious families that could afford to hire private tutors and successfully face the criticism of the community for educating their females.

It is worth noticing that despite Islam giving equality to sexes and permitting men and women to acquire success, education and honour and in spite of it giving equal religious and spiritual rights, the Islamic clergy interpreted it in terms of equality in their own natural sphere of being men and women. They propagated that the roles of men and women are different and so they have to be isolated from each other. While man needs education woman has to stay at home and involve herself in house keeping for which the training in the house craft is only needed, which can be provided in the home itself.

Centuries Long Journey

Above we have described the role, status and education of Indian women as determined by the religious order to which they belonged. Let us now look into the status, etc., of the Indian women in historical perspective.

We have already emphasized that from the very beginning of the history of civilization society has been male dominated and the status and the position of the woman depended on how man conceived her in his relationship with her. In India the Rig Vedic society was founded on the home and family and so assigned a place of importance to her. The Rig Vedic sages focus the domestic life on the sentiments centred round the women. The women of the Vedic and Brahmanic literature. The learned lady was held in high esteem.

In the Epic age the woman was considered to be a true friend of man. She was regarded as man's half, his religious partner, giver of joy and sons. Through her man was able to attain immortality. Sita, Savitri, Damyanti, Draupadi born in royal families and in luxury followed their husbands to the wilderness of the forests and endured a life of much hardships along with them. They embodied in themselves extreme love, devotion and selfless service to their spouses. They served without expectations of any return from them. Women of this period were also ideal mothers and true teachers of their offspring.

There is evidence that the Muslim invasion brought about the deterioration of women's position. Restrictions on her rights and freedom were imposed. Muslims adherence to Polygamy and Parda also influenced the Hindus. Restrictions of the rights and privileges of the women were imposed. The women were considered inferior to men and so began to be ill-treated. The women, both among Hindus and Muslims were confined to their homes and their duties, rights or obligations all were interpreted in terms of devoted wife and sacrificing mother.

The position of the medieval Muslim women, according to Muslim law was somewhat better than that of contemporary Hindu women. But in practice it was similar or in many instances inferior than Hindu women because of the rigidity of the Parda system and the denial of education to Muslim women.

There is no authentic account of the prevalence of education among Muslim women of various classes and masses. However, it seems that the majority of Muslim women were illiterate and those few who were educated learnt through oral and non-formal instructions. There were ladies of the noble families who had the privilege of learning the religious texts and various arts and crafts but those they learnt by their own persistence and in their own homes. History reveals that there were highly learned and accomplished Muslim ladies like Razia Sultan, Chand Bibi, Nur Jahan, Jahanara, etc. These ladies could learn and attain dominance by sheer strength of their personality. Thus, we may conclude that during Muslim period while the women from royal families enjoyed much respect and freedom and were interested in learning, the women of lower and middle strata of society were largely ignorant and illiterate.

New Age

At the advent of the British Empire the status and the position of the Indian women were very low. From the ideological point of view women were considered a complete or inferior species. They were inferior to males having no personality, no significance. From the social point of view they were kept in a state of utter subjection, denied any right, suppressed and oppressed.

The customs of polygamy, the parda, the denial of woman's rights over property, child marriage, Sati Pratha and denial of remarriage to widows - all these practices in this period resulted in the development of a very weak personality of the woman. She was not only considered an inferior by the male members of the society but she in herself became rooted to the idea that she was weak, helpless, subordinate and inferior - a non entity, a slave. Hence women themselves became great perpetuators of tyranny on the women over whom they could exercise their sadism. So dowry demands, forcing of the widows to burn or to lead a life of misery and toil, a dominant mother-in-law and subservient daughter-in-law, all such acts were initiated, perpetuated and committed by the women or in connivance with the women.

The British influence was in the positive direction. The close contacts with western cultural tradition, literature and education affected very deeply the minds of the Indian leaders. The result of it was the social movements for reforms in those evils which were prevalent in the society. The reformist movements started in the 19th century. The leaders and the social reformers who were in the forefront of the struggle for women emancipation were Raja Ram Mohun Roy, Ishwar Chandra Vidhyasagar, Swami Dayanand Saraswati, Swami Vivekanand, Mahatma Gandhi, Jawaharlal Nehru and many others.

To Raja Ram Mohun Roy goes the credit of laying the foundations of all the principle reformist movements which subsequently became instruments for modernization of the country. He devoted whole of his life for raising the status and position of the women in India. He propagated his own democratic, rational and human conception of womanhood.

It is said that while Raja Ram Mohun Roy saved the widow from self-immolation or becoming Sati on the funeral pyre of her husband, Ishwar Chandra Vidyasagar released her from a living death, by helping to legalize the Widow Remarriage. He wrote a book on widow remarriage which was published in 1853. It was through his efforts that the widow remarriage Act of 1856 was passed which permitted the legitimacy of the issues born of such marriages. He also gave much importance to the education of the girls which was considered essential for the development of their personality. Swami Dayanand Saraswati felt that the woman's status must be raised. He sought to create equal status for the women in the field of Sacred Thread Ceremony. He considered that education must aim at making women capable of performing her duties in home as well as outside the home. He founded Arya Samaj in 1875 at Bombay. It started Gurukuls for widows, rescue homes for destitutes, etc.

Another social reformer was Swami Vivekanand. He was greatly pained at the miserable condition of women in India. He, therefore, recommended that women should be supported and educated as men. He said, "It is only in the hands of educated and pious mothers the great men are born. The ideal woman in India is that mother, the mother first and the mother last." He suggested that the women should be made ambitious through a sound system of education. For him the ideal of womanhood was not only Sita or Savitri but that of an ideal mother. He said, "Motherhood is the beginning. Motherhood is the end of Indian womanhood."

Mahatma Gandhi considered that if a husband is a God, the wife is a Goddess. Wife is not a slave but a friend and companian with equal rights. Gandhi held the view that women have a right to education. But he was of this view that men and women are not identical but complementary to one another. Education for them should be such that it makes of them capable of performing their duties. Gandhiji's efforts led to the elevation of the woman's status an involved her in the struggle for social progress and political independence. The women were able to develop their latent powers. Women like Sarojini Naidu, Kasturba Gandhi, Kamla Nehru, Aruna Asaf Ali participated in the political arena with all their might and potentials. Indeed India witnessed the rise of many great women.

India gained freedom in 1947. Her Constitution was adopted on 26th January, 1950. The Constitution gave full and equal rights to women as compared to men. Thereafter we arc witnessing a strong, persistent and unrelenting struggle for the emancipation, empowerment and dignity led by women activists, enlightened political leaders, educationists and social reformers.

The western countries being mostly Christianity dominated gave the status and the position to the women as indicated by their religion. Hence in most of them till quite recently women were given a very low status in comparison to men. The Christians considered the women as temptations of the world of flesh and of the devil. The fathers of the church believed in the myth that Eve led Adam into sin.

Earlier, before the advent of Christianity, the women of Greece enjoyed much better status and position than later Christian women. Plato, the Greek philosopher made no distinction of the sexes in his ideal 'Republic'. He, no doubt, admits that women are generally inferior to men but in his view they have similar, if lower, capacities and power. He emphasized that there is no occupation or art for which they may not be fitted by nature and education. He, therefore, wants them to share in government and war as well as in the various mechanical trades. Still the Greek opinion was that women are best suited for household chores. Aristotle had unshakable faith in the value of household and the family and considered man as its natural ruler.

The Romans held women in greatest honour as the words of Cato the Censor show: "All men, rule over women, we Romans rule over all men, and our wives rule over us."

In law, however, the women had an inferior status in that they did not have freedom. They were always put under the control of some male member of the family. Before marriage she was entirely under the control of father, on her marriage she passed into a similar position towards her husband, and if she remained unmarried, she was under the control of her nearest male relative. In spite of this legal position, the position of the women in their family was an honoured one. Roman girls did not, as a rule, go to school. They were taught all that they were to know of book learning at home by their mothers.

When Christianity came a new set of virtues began to be propagated in place of the vices which had engulfed the later Roman social order. It is to be noted that the Roman society, in the beginning of the Christian era, had become a completely debunked society in which ethical and moral values were completely eroded. Christianity combined and harmonized an ideal of personal morality, sincerity, honesty, chastity, love, loyalty, kindness and unselfishness. Womanhood was elevated and given a new dignity. Before the establishment of Christianity, divorce became frequent, infanticide, child exposure, cruel and bloody gladiatorial shows licentiousness in private life were the evils which had deformed the society. Christianity fought against these evils and created a better and just order. Women, even though remained under the subjection of male members, yet were given an honoured place in home.

In the early middle ages, from the sixth to the tenth centuries, the creeds and dogmas established by the church were accepted without any doubts or questions. But after tenth century, particularly, during the eleventh and twelfth centuries, Christian scholars started questioning the dogmas spread by the church. They adopted logical methods of discussion and analysed the various beliefs and faiths on the anvil of rationality. This period is, therefore, known as the period of Scholasticism. "The aim of Scholasticism was to support the doctrines of the Church by rational argument, to show essential harmony between reason and faith." The thirteenth century was the Golden Age of Scholasticism. In this age, Scholasticism projected two high peaks. One was that of the doctrine of St. Thomas, who along with Albert built Aristotelianism into a Christian system of thought. The other was that of St. Bonaventure. At this peak, the Augustinian thought of the middle ages reached its highest development , St. Thomas and St. Bonaventure were two sages who led to the construction of Scholastic synthesis middle ages.

We find in general in the doctrines of the church of the middle ages that woman was represented as the source of all evils in the world. St. Franciscan Bonaventure wrote.

> "Woman is an embarrassment to man, a beast in his quarters, a continual worry, a never ending trouble, a daily annoyance, the destruction of the household, a hinderance to solitude, the undoing of a virtuous man, an oppressive burden, an insatiable bee, man's property and possession ."

The view of St. Thomas Aquinas (1225-1274) about women were almost similar in that he also considered women inferior to men. He might be greatly influenced by the opinion of the age. In his opinion man represents in himself perfection, while woman stands for the imperfect. He also depreciates the functions of the woman. Woman is dependent on man for procreation and for guidance throughout her life whereas man needs woman only for procreation. Man is thus master and woman a mere helper. The woman has weaker body, the smaller growth and weaker intellect and lesser will-power.

During Scholastic period it was not compulsory for girls to go to the school. To them domestic education was given in their homes. The University rules did not allow the admission of women in the Universities.

Martin Luther (1483-1546) criticised and protested against certain practices of the established church of his times. He tried to combine the best ideals of the past with religious morality and a new idealistic approach to Christian religion developed in Protestantism. The Protestants advocated an honourable and equal status for women like men. According to them the man is the embodiment of the strength, power and greatness while woman is the embodiment of the smooth, gentle, softness and beauty. Man and woman are complements of each other. Their relationship is not that of a master and a slave. The Protestant reformers also advocated universal compulsory and free education for all classes and for both men and women.

The Protestant revolt was accompanied and followed by the humanists who initiated the period known as Renaissance. These humanists rejoiced the theological dialectic of Scholasticism. In this period the emphasis was laid on the popular and universal education for both men and women. The woman was now not given an inferior status but was recognized as an active partner of man in bringing progress and Prosperity to the society. Comenius demanded education for all children rich and poor, boys and girls, in all cities and towns, villages and hamlets. John Locke and Hobbes recognized that familial authority belonged to the mother as well as to the father.

The Protestant revolt did not put equal influence in all the countries of Europe. However, in France, the State, church and the government achieved a considerable degree of independence from Rome. At this time Jean Jacques Rousseau introduced the philosophy of Naturalism in education. However, his philosophy of education did not follow the principle of equality in the education of men and women. For him the procreative role of the woman makes her unlike man. Functionally the women are determined by their reproductive role. He also implied in his attitude towards women education that they are the source of evil. Modesty is the only virtue of a woman and man has the absolute right over his wife.

He gave a long list of women characteristics like shame, stupidity, weakness and ignorance. He was of the view that intellectual pursuits are not for the women. Nature intended women for domestic functions mainly. For him the woman was only required to please man. So woman has to learn singing, dancing, embroidery and designing. She may receive an early education in morals and religion so that she can provide a good home for her family.

The psychological developmentalists like Pestalozzi and Herbert and Froebal were however of a different view that the woman is neither physically weak nor morally inferior to man. She is the active sharer of sorrows and sufferings of life with man. Pestalozzi believed that it was possible to improve the status and position of woman only through education. Herbert emphasized that the aim of the education of the woman should be to analyse her interests, to discover which are best for her and for society and apply these interests in the various situations in life. His emphasis was that education of woman should develop the will to be good and the desire to make good moral choices resulting in a high degree of personal character and social morality. According to Froebel, "Education must be controlled development by which both man and woman come into realization of the life of the all encompassing, unity of which both of them are a part a development by which their lives broaden until it has related itself to nature until it enters sympathetically into all the activities of the society, until it enters into the achievements of the race and the aspirations of humanity". Thus it may be concluded that the developmentalists consider woman having equal position like that of man. They are the active members of the society who help to make a better home and society.

Jeremy Bentham was a covert feminist. He wanted to put untapped brains and energies of women to use. He believed that the sensibility of women is greater than men. The woman is more fit for a family life and man for outside life. But Bentham did not want to exclude women altogether from public life.

James Stuart Mill emphasized that the emancipation of women has a two way effect: "they themselves be happy, they will add to the happiness of society". Hence he laid stress on the women education as the surest way to cultivate them and to free them from the bonds of domesticity by opening up careers for them. Mill criticized the theory of inner inferiority of women as supported by Aristotle and Rouseau. But Mill did not question the traditional family system and its demands on women.

Among the socialists Marx and Engels are predominant. They were the forerunners of the doctrine of communism. According to this doctrine they preached that through the institution of family, the children became private heirs which meant the women's reproductive labour like their productive work underwent a transformation from social to private. And this led to the subordination of women in terms of the emergence of the private property.

The description given above about the status, position and education of the women both in India and western countries indicate that women, by and large, were given much inferior status and position in most of the periods of history and by most of the thinkers with a few exceptions. The great philosophers like Plato, Aristotle, St. Thomas Aquinas, Rousseau and others talked much of equality and goodness of mankind but did not acknowledge the same goodness and equality to women. John Stuart Mill may be taken as an exception. The social theorists considered that institution of private property was the root cause of relegating women to a secondary position.

The situation so far presented started to change in the later part of the nineteenth century and the beginning of twentieth century. The women education began to spread. The Industrial Revolution, American Independence and the world wars awakened the western women. Further the political upheavals and revolutions in USSR, France, India and China made the women aware of their enslavement by the male members of the society. The women began to demand equal rights with men.

The Industrial Revolution in Europe ushered a new era in the emergence of women from their homes to engage various other vocations. It inspired the women's movement for bringing change in their status and position. The First World War brought dramatic alteration in the image of woman. At the end of it the opportunities of women's employment increased many-fold. The women also asserted in their freedom of dress and in smoking and drinking in public.

The Second World War brought almost four million new women workers. There was an upsurge in the demand of women's equal rights with men. The women education spread rapidly. The women now entered in all types of professions along with the right to speak in public, to vote for and hold office. There was a revolt against the double standards of morality and against puritanism. As twentieth century advanced the women adopted swim suits, short skirts, started taking part in sports, driving cars, etc. The women got greater leisure by the introduction of mechanized kitchens. By the middle of the twentieth century women's liberation movements became more vigorous and involved more and more women's organizations, in Europe, in general and in America, in particular. The women now presented the cult of new feminism. It demanded full social equality for women. The women fought for more independence and discarded the traditional triangular roles for themselves that of children, kitchen and the church. The women's organizations rejected the 'Barbi-doll' stereotypical model of woman. The middle class educated women were in the forefront of the struggle for women's rights and for presenting a new image of feminism. They protest against a passive, conforming, dependent female stereotyped roles and a future which ties them down to the home and family.

The women's movements have achieved much. Still, even in the west the women have not yet attained that position and status which they consider is equivalent to men. They are still fighting for equal pay, status, position and security like that of men. They have become intolerant to any discrimination in their service conditions because of their sex. The battle is going on.

Movement for Empowerment

We have traced very briefly the history of women movements for empowerment, equality and recognition and worthy members of the society in the west. Let us now peep into the situation as it exists with respect to Indian women.

The Indian women have fallen from the high position and status held by them in Vedic times to a very degrading position in the medieval period and in the earlier decades of the modern period. It was for the enlightened Indians educated in the western tradition and culture that brought a change in the outlook of the Indian males and females regarding their mutual relationship. In Indian situation the movement for female emancipation was led in the beginning by the male members of the society. These Indian males who fought for a higher status and the position of women were those who were impressed by the regards and considerations which western women enjoyed but they made the case of women emancipation on the basis of the reinterpretation of Indian religious texts and exposing the gimmicks of the half literate clergy which advocated sati system and approved the ill treatment of widows, parda, system, confining of the women to homes, child marriages and calling any women as Kulta or corrupt if she deviated slightly from the norms of conduct laid by them for women. For the ill-treatment of women they were drawing support from a perverted interpretation of the religious texts and religious precepts. The enlightened Indians exposed their misinterpretation and based their argument for women liberation on their own very well studied and expressed interpretation.

The movement for women emancipation was also undertaken by enlightened women like Pandita Rama Bai and others. They set the trend which was followed by hundreds of women. The freedom movement launched by Gandhiji drew women into the central field of struggle. Women fought for the freedom of the country as well, as for their own emancipation. According to *Manusmriti* Hindu women were given a right to Stridhan properties but not to the joint family property on which she had only the right to maintenance. She was given an inferior position in the law of adoption. The status of the woman was determined according to the nature of relationship she had with a man. She was a "Sarvainini" as a wanton woman, "Veshya" as a prostitute, "Kishkashirii" as a woman discarded by her paramour or a "base" as a woman kept exclusively by the man.

According to Justice Bhandare "It was only later that during the time of Vijanesvera that the archaic Smriti law was freed from religious fetters and changed for the benefit of women". But it took a long time and centuries of oppression that women got some legal rights over their property. It was only in 1937 that the concept of widow's estate was developed in respect of property inherited by her from her husband.

The freedom struggle created an urge in the Indian male and female to ameliorate the conditions of the downtrodden and neglected sections of the society. The women, Scheduled Castes and Scheduled Tribes were some such sections. Hence when the constitution for an independent India was drawn, the emphasis was put on the development of an egalitarian society. For the elimination of discriminatory and derogatory practices against women Articles 14, 150, 16, 39(e) and 51 were introduced. These guarantee equality and special protection for women.

The Article 14 provided for equality of all before the law. Article 15 emphasized that the "State shall not discriminate against any citizen on grounds only of religion, race, caste, sex, place of birth or any of them." Article 15(3) stated that "Nothing in this article shall prevent the state from making any special provision for women and children." Article 16 mentioned that (1) there shall be equality of opportunity for all citizens in matters relating to employment or appointment to any office under State. (2) No citizen shall, on grounds only of religion, race, caste, sex, descent, place of birth, residence or any of them be ineligible for, or discriminated against in respect of any employment or office under the State.

Article 39 States: The State shall, in particular, direct its policy towards securing: (1)that the citizens, men and women equally, have the right to an adequate means of livelihood (2) that there is equal pay for equal work for both men and women (3) that the health and strength of workers, men and women and the tender age of children are not abused and that the citizens are not forced by economic necessity to enter avocations unsuited to their age or strength."

Article 51 A States: "It shall be the duty of every citizen of India to promote harmony and the spirit of common brotherhood amongst all the people of India transcending linguistic, logistic and regional or sectional diversities, to renounce practices derogatory to the dignity of women."

When the Universal Declaration of Human Rights was adopted on 10th December. 1948 its Article I provided that "all human beings are born free and equal in dignity and rights". Article 2 provided for equality of sexes. It states that "everyone is entitled to all the rights and freedoms without distinction of sex."

The International covenant on Civil and Political Rights, 1966 urges every covenant State to respect and ensure to all individuals within its territory the rights recognized by that covenant without distinction of sex. Article 3 of this document emphasize that covenant States should undertake to ensure equal rights of men and women in 1979 the convention on the Elimination of All Forms of Discrimination Against Women reiterated "that discrimination against women violates the principles of equality of rights and respect for women's dignity and is an obstacle to the participation of women on equal terms with men in the political, social, economic and cultural life of their countries, hampers the growth of prosperity of society and the family and makes more difficult the full development of the potentialities of women in the service of their countries and of humanity and urges that change in the traditional role of women as well as role of women in society and in the family is needed to achieve full equality between men and women".

Justice Bhandare writes "In spite of the enshrinement of these provisions, equality between men and women continue to be an elusive goal, not only in our country but all over the world. A wide gap exists between the ideal and the practical in our country, partly due to historical reasons. However, the main reason why such discrimination continues in our country is the attitude, of inferiority and bondage-towards women and an atmosphere in which women are deprived of all basic freedoms, starting with that of education, and are thereby exposed to easy exploitation".

This book concentrates on women's education and its impact on male-female discrimination and on the female psyche. In almost all the chapters, the book highlights the importance of education to the girl child as well as to the grown up woman.

Justice Bhandare raises some questions regarding disparity between man and woman and says that several of those questions do not have an adequate and satisfactory answer. An attempt is made to seek answers to these and similar questions by focussing our attention on the triad of sociological, psychological and educational aspects of female development in our country. The questions raised by Justice Bhandare are: (a)How is it that in public life-professions, business and services-women are not adequately represented? (b)How is it that women put in longer hours of work compared to men and yet do not enjoy equal status or opportunities? (c)Why is it that property owned by women constitutes a very small fraction of the property owned by men? (d)Why is it that maternity is not recognized as an essential social function? (e)Why is the rate of suicide so high among women? (f)Why is it that fairness vanishes when it comes to giving a fair deal to the 'fair' sex.

The struggle for the emancipation of western women had its impact on the emancipation movements in India. But in India the feminist movement did not take the aggressive and militant form which it took in some European countries. In India the feminist movements were not vehemently or violently opposed by the male members, or clergy or politicians. Rather they were supported by enlightened political and religious thinkers. The agitations for female liberation in India began in the later part of the nineteenth century and were carried on with zeal till the Constitution of India in 1950 gave them equality in terms of their lawful existence. Those agitations were largely spearheaded by women reformists and male thinkers who had the best of western education. These movements emphasized on the need of the small middle class educated and privileged women. The real breakthrough in the recognition of male-female equalities was made only when the Constitution of the Indian Republic was adapted in 1950.

Before that in 1949 the University Education Commission which was set up under the Chairmanship of Dr. S. Radhakrishnan has observed:

> 'There cannot be educated people without educated women. If general education had to be limited to men or to women, the opportunity should be given to women, for then it would more surely be passed on to the next generation".

The secondary education commission (1952-53) emphasized that:

"Every type of education open to men should also be open to women". Thus this commission did not make any distinction between the education of men and women and so the era of equality of educational opportunities to women began.

The Report of the National Committee on Women's Education (1958-59) made a strong case for the education .of women. Its important recommendation was:

> "The education of women should be regarded as a major and a special problem in education for a good many years to come and a bold and determined effort should be made to face its difficulties and magnitude and to close the existing gap between the education of men and women in as short a time as possible".

As has been specified earlier the movements for women emancipation in India were largely initiated by the Government on the insistence of the educated and reform-oriented women leaders. These leaders by and large did not lead independent movements but were more dependent on the government help, funding and the initiatives in framing laws and rules for women's upliftment. The National Council for Women's Education played an important role in spearheading the movements for women education and their upliftment. The Council set up a committee to examine comprehensively the problem of curricula for girls at all stages of education. This committee was set up on November 1 1961 under the chairmanship of Smt. Hansa Mehta.

The committee after carefully examining all the evidences produced before it came to the following conclusions:

> "Our enquiry has not imbued with any conviction that there are clear and ascertained differences between the two sexes on which an educational policy may readily be based. We have encountered a number of facile generalizations about the mental differences between boys and girls; we have found few, if any, which we are able to accept. Men and women have existed for centuries; but either sex is still a problem to the other and indeed to itself, nor is there any third sex to discriminate dispassionately between the two. In the mean time it is the part of wisdom neither to assume difference nor to postulate identity, but to leave the field free to both to show themselves".

The above mentioned conclusions show the confusion in the thinking of the women leaders who failed to arrive at definite conclusions regarding the differences between two sexes. We have endeavoured to point out, that, such conclusions have left the field wide open for discrimination particularly in education. The last words 'but to leave the field free to both to show themselves', sound quite traditional which emphasizes that woman's field is home and the man's work. The committee's observation may lead to the conclusion that both males and females should work freely in their own fields. However, the committee tries to refute traditional view by emphasizing that "the traditional view assumes that there are two different personalities-masculine and feminine, with widely different and complementary traits and that they owe their origin to sex. This view also has however been proved to be incorrect. Recent scientific studies have shown that the differences in the psychological traits of men and women are due, not to innate sex differences but to social conditioning".

The committee on the basis of such observations as above, recommend, for the education of girls and women that "Education is a great levelling force and one sure way to raising the status of women to real equality with men is to eliminate, or to reduce to a minimum, the existing wide gap in the education of girls and women."

The Education Commission (1964-66) endorsed the views of the National Committee on Women's Education and emphasized:

> "The education of women should be regarded as a major programme in education for some years to come and a bold and determined effort should be made to face difficulties involved and to close the existing gap between the education of men and women in as short a time as possible".

Thus we see that year after year various committees and commissions emphasized the education of the women for raising their social status. But besides some progress in the quantitative expansion of women education no significant developments took place in raising the status of rural, downtrodden, Schedule Castes and Schedule Tribes women. Hence the committee on the Status of Women (1971-74) concentrated on this anomaly.

It observes:

> "The deep foundations of the inequality of the sexes are built in the minds of men and women through a socialization process which continues to be extremely powerful. Right from their earliest years boys and girls are brought up to know that they are different from each other and this differentiation is strengthened in every way possible-through language forms, modes of behaviour of labour etc. They begin to learn very early what is proper or not proper for boys and girls and all attempts at deviation are noticed, discouraged and sometimes punished. The sissy and the tom boy are equal objects of

derision. There is nothing wrong in this if it were merely a question of distinction. But it soon gets inextricably tied up with the traditional concepts of the roles of men and women and their mutual relationships which are based on inequality. The process of indoctrination affects the development of individual personalities.

The only institution which can counteract the effect of the process is the educational system. If education is to promote equality for women, it must make a deliberate, planned and sustained effort so that the new value of equality of the sexes can replace the traditional value system of inequality".

The committee comes to the conclusion that the reasons for the variation of social attitudes and the consequent slow progress of women's education are both social and economic.

It found that a substantial number of girls are engaged in contributing to the family income by their own labour. The prevalence of child labour has been admitted as the greatest deterrent to the spread of education among children of the poor. The committee was appalled by the extent and degree of use of young girls of five to fourteen years in work for twelve hours a day.

The committee also found that large majority of girls by the time they reach the age of eight, are required at home to do various domestic chores, e.g., collecting fire wood, coal waste, cow dung, fetching water, at times from long distances, washing, cleaning, cooling, taking food and water to parents in their places of work, etc.

About the girls education in the rural areas it observed that:

"education in the rural areas often results in alienation of the girls from their habitat. While this criticism was voiced in many places, the most vocal opinion was expressed by

> women in the villages of Himachal Pradesh. Since the development of the state and the standard of living of its people depended on the continued efforts of women in agriculture, education in their opinion was becoming an adversary of progress. Girls who completed their formal education in the villages, did not want to continue living in villages or take part in agricultural activities. The problem became more acute when, owing to absence of secondary schools in the villages, they had to study outside, in urban or semi-urban areas. Many of them found village life with its hardships intolerable afterwards .... Most girls who complete secondary school develop a desire for white collared jobs, or urban life in some forms".

The National Policy on Education (1986) considered that "Education will be used as an agent of basic change in the status of women." It suggested that "the National Education System will play a possible, interventionist role in the empowerment of women. It will foster the development of new values through redesigned curriculum, text books, the training and orientation of teachers, decision-makers and administrators, and the active involvement of educational institutions. This will be an act of faith and social engineering".

National Commission on Self-Employed Women and Women in the Informal Sector (1987-88) has emphasized:

> "Education is both an important instrument for increasing and bettering the chances of women's employability and for empowering women as they learn to think for themselves, become confident and also develop the capability of recognising more acutely the areas of exploitation."

The National Commission for Women, a statutory body was set up under the National Commission Act, 1990 to safeguard the rights and interests of women. This commission reviews legislations, intervenes in specific individual complaints of atrocities and takes remedial action to safeguard the interests of women where appropriate and feasible.

In Indian situation the women's movement has not been in terms of radicalism or the violent assertion of the female rights. The reason for it seems to be the sensivity of both the males and female towards the necessity of the upliftment of the women from their miserable existence. The Government and NGOs all laid great emphasis on the empowerment of women for which they all recommended crash programmes for women education.

The feminist movement in India can be characterized by its sensible approach. In this movement almost all political parties except those who have leanings towards fundamentalism and orthodoxy in their outlook lend their support. By and large it is non-commercial and non-sectarian; But this movement has failed to break away, from the traditional approach of motherhood, housewife and kitchen queen. The movement has not yet reached a large section of rural and slum area women. It is the movement essentially spearheaded by urban, educated middle class. This class is in a typical paradoxical situation. It wants the best of both worlds. It wants to secure independence from male domination but is not willing to think in terms of a life pattern in which the male does not figure as a key person in the role of a father, brother or husband or in any other form.

In spite of the feminist movements, political support and increasing awareness of evil influences on national progress of the neglect of women, we find that Indian women's status and position has not undergone any revolutionary change. No doubt the urban middle class women have become more assertive, better educated and economically independent by involving themselves in all types of jobs, some of which were so far under the special male prerogatives like those in the army, police or as airline pilots. But the majority of the women of rural and poor classes are suffering from various types of disabilities. The main reason for such a situation seems to be the woefully low percentage of female literacy. According to Prof Moegiadi, UNESCO's representative in India "four South Asian countries – Bangladesh, India, Pakistan and Nepal account for the largest number of out of school girls and Illiterate women."

Addressing a national workshop on State Policieś on Incentive Schemes in Primary Schools and their Contribution to Girls Participation, jointly organised by NCERT and UNESCO, he said:

> "Though progress has been made, we are all aware that according to, the 1991 census of India we have 50.2 per cent literacy, and now according to the latest information we have 64 per cent literacy rate. It is estimated that in near future it can be 70-80 per cent" .

The number of females in the work force is also very limited. The 1991 census figures tell us that the working population was 317 million out of the total population of the country as being 846.3 (males 439.3 and females 407.0) million. The males were 226.4 (71.4 per cent) and females 90.6 (28.6 per cent) million who were working. The males in the organized sector were 23.0 million while women were, only 3.8 million. The respective percentages were 85.8 and 14.2. In the unorganized sector there were 290.2 million persons out of which 203.4 were males and 86.8 million women. The respective percentages were 70.0 and 30.0. Hence the women working in organised sector were very few as compared to men.

The National Commission on Self Employed Women and Women Engaged in Informal Sector observed that the women could be found to be largely confined to strenuous and monotonous work that might be irregular and seasonal and women workers could be rarely benefited from the introduction of mechanization and new technology. About eighty per cent of the total female work-force continues to work as agricultural labour. It may be said that one of the basic hurdles to the development of employment opportunities for the women has been lack of adequate training to women workers.

The percentage of Agricultural labourers according to 1991 census was 21.01 per cent for males and 44.83 per cent for females.

Indian women are also being increasingly victimized. Crimes against women are increasing. Crimes such as rape, bride burning, wife battering and ragging of girls are also on the increase. Emotional violence against females at work is a new phenomenon. The rape cases increased from 3,945 in 1982 to 9,752 in 1989. These figures are on the basis of the National Crime Records Bureau, Ministry of Home Affairs, Government of India. But the Marie Stopes Institute, Delhi thinks that these official figures are not correct. According to it on an average, two million women and girls are raped in India every year.

Thus we find that even now there is much discrimination against women and they are a neglected lot. Rajbala says that "A basic statistics paints a grim picture. Over 400 million women with 75 per cent illiteracy work 10-14 hours daily, undergo 4-6 pregnancies and run low income households".

In India, women have been surrounded in a web of myth and reality. She has been considered as a goddess as well as an evil incarnate. At one stage if she was put on a very high pedestal and at another stage she was thrown into the pits of filth and guilt. The casualty has been the reality of her existence. It is only recently that the emphasis has been put on the understanding of the women as she is, as also on the understanding of her relations with man in the light of the recognition of the fact that both are the equal parts of humanity. In this context her education is now considered as important and worthwhile as that of man.

Historically, in the Indian situation the rearing of the girl child and her education has always been taken with indifference. The only exception may be the Vedic period. The birth of a male child is celebrated with joy and happiness while the birth of a girl child is a matter of sorrow and gloom for whole of the family. This trend is changing in the enlightened households but by and large in majority of the families the situation has hardly changed.

The ambivalence with which the Indian women were viewed, has created a typical situation in the relationship between men and women. It was believed that since energy resided in women, they were objects of worship. The Devi cult assigned all the creative and protective powers to women. But at the same time the women were considered as the promoters of evil, seductress who destroyed men if given freedom and the power to exercise their free will. Thus the women's will power had to be controlled. The husbands were given their absolute rights over her body, soul and mind. The women accepted their subordinate status for centuries. It is only in the later half of the twentieth century that the Indian women started revolting against the stipulations that the women are inferior to men. The empowerment of the Indian women is the battle cry of the feminists of today. The enlightened men are offering their help in the emancipation of the women.

At the advent of the new millennium we find that the Indian women are joining the world of work in increasing numbers. In many cases it is creating stresses in the family life particularly in those homes in which the womens' role is confined to being housewives. The pressing economic demands make it obligatory for women to seek employment in various fields but the old conservative notions that the women's rightful place is in homes, create situations of stress, and conflict. Under the shadows of conflict and stress the education of the women is being planned, propagated and provided. This book highlights the conflicts and the stresses of the working as well as non-working women and also the influence of socio-psychological factors on women education.

In India, there is growing realization that the women education is of great importance to the healthy development of the social and national life. Efforts are being made to provide schools, for all the girls of school-going age and to give incentives to them to learn. Still the situation is far from satisfactory. The literacy percentage among Indian women is lawfully low. This may be due to the lower social status and the psychological make up of the women, particularly of the lower classes and castes.

The Dalit women and the women of the minority communities have by and large miserable existence. The Dalit women are exploited not only by the higher caste people but also by their own male relatives. Similar is the case with the women of the minority communities, especially in the case of lower class Muslim women. The reasons for their exploitation seem to lie in their ignorance. Most of them are Illiterate and so have neither the means nor the will to fight against their exploitation. Hence their education is a matter which has to be given top priority.

What will be the futuristic trends of women education? Whether women education should be of the same pattern as the education of men? If not then why and what type of education is required for them? Should women be trained for joining the world of work or only for the household work as the housewives? These are some of the questions which are being raised about women education. In the present book an attempt is being made to discuss these and some other vital issues concerning women education so that some appropriate measures may be taken for organizing it thus ushering in an era of equality, dignity, esteem, self-respect and self-confidence for the Indian women.

It may be emphasized that the issues in women education are not only confined to quantitative development. Equally important are qualitative aspects. In an article "The Burning of Roop Kanwar - Madhu Kishwar, who visited Deorala where bride burning of Roop Kanwar took place, reported that "the fascination with the sati cult has been attributed to the superstitious ignorance of illiterate village women, but it is noteworthy that the entire cult being created at Deorala is in the hands of educated men". When we think of women education we are concerned with the development of progressive outlook in them. We will not like to provide that type of education to our women which the menfolk of Deorala got, which led them to close their minds rather than broadening their vision. The leaders of the pro-sati campaign were urban, educated men in their twenties and thirties.

The main premise on which the argument throughout is based is that Indian women are by nature not docile, nor are they devoid of a mind of their own. It is due to four fold major factors that we find them in the state in which they are. These factors are: 1.Religious precepts from some eminent sages motivated by the desire to subordinate the assertive women. 2.The physical weakness perpetuated by multiple pregnancies and childhood marriages. 3.Women's own desire for showering motherly affection on their own men and for maintaining domestic peace at their own cost. 4.Lastly their complete economic dependence on malefolk which has a vested interest in keeping them ignorant and illiterate.

3

Societal Aspects

The Indian world is a male world with ambivalent attitude towards female. She is visualised as good and noble as well as bad and degenerative. Her reproductive functions are worshipped, but her sex is considered as a pull towards hell. She is respected as mother but hated as charmer. Still the Indian male wishes to enjoy her sex in every conceivable manner as is depicted in temple designs, architecture, erotic texts and in the pornographic material. Literature depicts his enjoyment; his keenness to impregnate her and to father many children even though they may be deprived of food and milk and live in abject poverty. The female submits herself to the male's demands because she believes she must serve him and raise the offspring she is destined to bear. She is absolutely dependent on male for her well-being. The willingness of the female for male domination, for letting him enjoy her body without her desire for it, for bearing children without having strength to endure pregnancy or money to feed them is explained by the fact that her life is woven into the myth of motherhood and service to man whom she has been conditioned to be economically dependent. Her weakness makes it obligatory for her to seek male protection and male in turn considers it as his birthright to hold the positions of power and authority over her.

The most vital questions which the modern psychologists and sociologists are concerned with are: Why are Indian women, even the educated ones, not prepared to emerge free from their mythical existence? Why are they submitting to the irrational male domination? Why are the Indian women still not prepared to lead a free and independent life? To seek answers to these questions we will have to peep into the psyche of the Indian women. To do so we will have to revert back to the women in ancient India.

There is no doubt in it that the ancient Aryan women were strong willed and dominating. The traces of domination can be found in the lives of the famous and respected women of ancient India. Hence it may be possible that the psyche of the Indian women is an offshoot of an urge to dominate. This may sound to be a view very much different from the prevailing opinion. But it has many elements of truth. We will present some arguments and facts in favour of this viewpoint.

Seeking Satisfaction

The powerful and strong women of ancient India, when controlled by scheming males contrived a way to seek satisfaction. Pardweshi, the wife of blind Rishi Drighatamas, threw him in the river when he proposed legislation that a woman should have only one husband in her life. She was not prepared to subordinate her sexuality to the whims of one male. Drighatamas saved himself by clinging to a raft and lived long enough to put through his proposals. Later women were bound by this law and were unable to physically revolt, because of weakness due to frequent pregnancies and domestication. These women learned to achieve supremacy not by trying to break the myths, but by strengthening them. They did not make demands, but submitted to the demands of men. As the men continued to assert themselves, the strands of the web increased and women internalised their domination and externalised their subordination until their external life became miserable and their internal life gained expression through entirely different channels.

Indian woman serves her husband and rears her children and finds happiness in being half-clad and half-fed so that her husband and children get the best. Then her son marries and she demands a great price for rearing him up in the form of dowry. When the daughter-in-law enters the house, the mother-in-laws dominant attitude becomes explicit. Many stories depict the harshness with which the mother-in-law treats her son's wife. In some marriage customs, the mother of the son runs out of the house and sits on the edge of a well ready to jump in until the son and daughter-in-law offer their devotion and shower her with gifts. Thus the urge for domination which she has repressed when she entered the house as a young bride now finds as outlet, as she becomes the domineering mother-in-law.

Harsh Moral Codes

The strict supervision and harsh moral codes under which women rear their daughters may also be outlets of the dominant urge. The Indian woman judges other women's behaviour patterns under strict social norms. Any failing on the part of another woman is a delight because it establishes her own moral superiority. By scandalising other she obtains a sense of power. No wonder that women gossip has become such powerful instrument for the maintenance of the status quo. Any change in existing norm releases dormant energy for domination.

We have made an earlier reference to the predominance of an element of masochism in the Indian female. This element is her weapon for dominance. She stoops to conquer and often become successful. Consequently, her husband becomes more sadistic and tries to crush her further. She submits to his cruelty and thus shows superiority in endurance, thus, a vicious cycle ensues.

Women's desire for dominance is a secret hidden desire. It is not evident at the external level of her existence but an analysis of her behaviour pattern throughout her life reveals it. Woman learns from early life that she is liked if she is helpless and dependent. She gets her needs met from her father and brothers when she subordinates herself completely and serves them devotedly. She learns that her path to any type of fulfillment lies through them. She also notices that her prestige and way of life depend on her docility. She, therefore, represses her will for independent thinking. She becomes completely domesticated and all her desire for dominance finds an outlet in leading a subordinated home life.

Carstairs while carrying on her study of "village women of Rajasthan" was warned by the men of the village that their submissive women were really quite strong-minded and often get their own way. The women even employed witchcraft. Carstairs says: "At first, I found it almost inconceivable that these meek, seemingly unassertive women could be seen as powerful agents of the supernatural; but on 7th March, 1950, 1 witnessed a scene which revealed them in a rather different light". ' That night when all the men of the village, except Carstairs and an invalid old man, left the village for joining a wedding party the women came out of their houses and with gay abandon indulged in dancing, singing, abusing and rehearsing many of the sexual acts. They were unbridled, strong in their expressions; and as fully emancipated as women in any part of the world can be. The next day Carstairs found their behaviour dull and demure. Carstairs writes: "Next day the wedding party returned from Togi, and the women of Sujarupa resumed their normal demure behaviour, but I felt that I had been shown a glimpse of quite a different side of their nature, one rarely given free expression".

Art of Concealing

It must be noted that Indian women have developed the art of concealing the extrovert side of their nature. From their external behaviour it is difficult to fathom their psyche. One must patiently go deeper into the analysis of their behaviour pattern. It is firmly asserted that they are neither treacherous nor evil. There has, however, developed some complexity in their behaviour promoted by the sadistic attitudes of the men and suppressed feelings of the women for, the ages.

In all the normal human beings, both the attitudes of dominance and submission may be found. Both are necessary for survival. In women, submission is overt, while in the men, dominance is external. But covertly, neither the domination in women nor the submission in men is completely lost. Women learn to submit in order to dominate, and men learn to dominate in order to submit. Thus it may be wrong to contend that the Indian world is absolutely a male world. It is true that men have the economic power but this is what the women desire. Until they learn to desire overtly their own freedom and independence the situation regarding their status and position is not going to change. Here is then a challenge for those who plan for women education in our country. They have to plan, for a different cultural training than that which is prevalent today.

Domination and Submission

We may again repeat that domination and submission are a universal parts of nature. When one is confronted by physical danger, the instinct of self-preservation leads him to choose either to fight or flee. Some animals play possum" and pretend they are dead until their predator leaves. Others attack ferociously. Pardweshi made an attempt to fight. Women after her learned to be more careful and played possum. They took flight in the inner dorms of their psyche and wage a battle in which their unconscious played the part of warrior who fought not with weapons of destruction, but with the weapons of seduction and devotion. If the Indian women are satisfied with the situation as described above then why bother to change it? If she is dominant in her own way why consider her the weaker sex? To find satisfactory answers to these questions the following consequences of her above described behaviour pattern must be taken into consideration. The most important consequence is that the development of the psyche of the Indian woman takes place in the direction of creating a split personality. The person who is responsible to subdue her becomes her passion. She becomes too ritualistic, superstitious and superficial. She becomes too modest and looses all her initiative in taking decisions. Her life becomes one, of rigidity and ignorance. She curbs independent thinking not only in herself but also in her daughter and other female relatives. She develops intolerance to any deviant member of her own sex. She becomes ruthless with her dependent relatives, particularly towards those women who are either divorced or widows.

Indian men respect motherhood in their women folk while women seem to want to turn their husbands into little boys so that they can "mother" them. The women want their men to be completely dependent on them to fulfil their needs. This type of behaviour pattern may be at the root of Indians lapses in taking bold decisions in the hours of crises and in the development of the "killer instinct" in the competitive games and competitive enterprises. They very often lose control even in the win-win situations.

The subordination of the Indian women served the purpose of securing for them the protection they needed so that they might avoid hardships for themselves and their children. Aileen Ross writes:

> "The attitude of Hindu women to this subordinate position has not often been understood by Western observers, for they have seldom seen it in the context of the total family setting. Bachmann interprets the satisfaction, which the Hindu women did, in fact, derive from her seemingly 'low' position. He describes Kasturbai, Gandhi's wife: 'Whoever knows her is bound to believe that the self-surrender of the widow which led to the custom of self-immolation on the funeral pyre, must in certain cases have been quite voluntary".

The Indian women are considered downtrodden, but to a great extent they are exercising their own will to this effect. They must now understand through proper education and training that the subordination might have been prudent in the past and the tension relieving in the present, but it is no longer necessary for the Indian women to submit to it. They must reflect upon on to what they desire and develop enough strength to achieve their goals of life. They must purge out old orthodox traditions and adapt to the modern world. It is satisfying to note that quite a few modern educated women are taking initiative in achieving their economic independence and in the free exercise of their will power. They are showing their excellence in very diverse fields. There are at present almost all the avenues of work or activities in which they are competing with men and achieving success. No doubt there are still a large number of women who are living the life of drudgery and toil mostly because of lack of initiative on their part and due to their ignorance. Hence the educational system in this country is facing the gigantic task of emancipation and empowerment of such women.

Eleanor Maccoby and Carol Jacklin (1974) reviewed and integrated the extensive research literature on psychological sex differences, reading through some 2,000 books and articles in the process. Most of these studies were comparisons of male and female behaviour in infancy and childhood, rather than in adulthood. On the basis of their review, they concluded that many of the differences that are commonly believed to exist between males and females are in fact myths. For example, there is no good evidence that boys are more independent, ambitious or achievement oriented than girls or that girls are more nurturant, sociable or suggestible than boys are. On the whole Maccoby and Jacklin conclude that male and female are much more similar to one another than they are different, and they share the same fundamental needs, emotions and abilities.

If many of the stereotypical differences between the sexes are myths, then why are they perpetuated? The main reason for the perpetuation of the myths seems to be the different opportunities that society provides for men and women. In fact, as children grow up, boys undoubtedly become more politically and professionally ambitious than girls, and girls become more interested in taking care of children. The differences that we observe probably result from social values and opportunities, rather than from basic psychological differences.

Our expectations about what men and women should do and what they should like are called sex roles. Boys are encouraged to be ambitious and assertive and discouraged from expressing their weaknesses or their tender feelings. Girls on the other hand learn to play a more submissive and dependent role. They are taught to be well-behaved and co-operative and to act as if they have no aggressive impulses at all. Girls are also expected to be tender and nurturing. These expectations are effectively communicated to the sons and daughters. This communication is sometimes done directly by suggesting the desired behaviour to the child and by rewarding the child for performing it. In addition, once the child learns his or her sex which all children do by age three, the child invariably wants to demonstrate that he or she can behave like a member in good standing of that sex.

Scene to Change

As we are marching towards 21st century, the growing age of computer technology, the psychologists and sociologists are coming to the conclusion that traditional sex roles are in need of change. They have come to believe that by putting people in slots labelled 'male' and 'female' and shaping them to fit the slots we are limiting their full development as human beings. Instead they propose that each child should be treated as a total person; without regard for the traditional notions of what a boy or girl should be.

It may, however, also be noted that as the idea of breaking down traditional roles has gained force, there has also been a great deal of opposition to it. It is argued that sex roles are based on biological differences that have evolved over the course of millions of years and, therefore, should not be tempered with. In his book Sexual Suicide, George Gilder (1973) writes:

> "When reforming the roles of men and women, we must always be careful to avoid gibberish-patterns of activity that so violates the inner constitution of the species that they cannot be integrated with our irreducible human natures"

Gilder's warning 'may have some validity, but recent research findings reduce the force of his arguments. Maccoby and Jacklin emphasise that psychological differences between men and women are small, and they are based on only a slight degree of biological predispositions. Considerable change in sex roles could be accomplished by changing our values and expectations, without negation of our biological nature.

A second argument against sex-role changes is the notion that if boys and girls do not develop the pattern of traits that are appropriate for their sex, they may become confused about their sexual identity and thereby run the risk of serious maladjustment.

But recent research provides little cause for such alarm. Virtually all girls and boys learn without much trouble which sex they belong to and they do this by the time they are three years old. The extensive sex-role training that follows is not necessary to develop a stable sexual identity. In addition, highly 'masculine' males and highly 'feminine' females are not better adjusted or healthier than people who are less highly sex-typed.

Sandra Bern (1975) has called the ability to behave in ways, traditionally associated with both sexes Psychological androgyny. An androgynous person is one who combines 'masculine' and 'feminine' behaviours. Bern has, measured androgyny by asking students how often various adjectives are descriptive of themselves. Some of the adjectives were traditionally masculine, as for example, ambitious, self-reliant, and independent. Some were traditionally feminine like affectionate, gentle, sensitive. Subjects were categorised as androgynous if they indicated that they are about equally well-described by masculine and feminine traits. Bern found that androgynous students of both sexes behaved more effectively in a variety of laboratory situations than students who were highly masculine or highly feminine. The androgynous men and women could be independent and assertive when they needed to be men or women. They were also responsive in appropriate situations. They were able to behave in a more flexible and humane manner.

The above finding has very significant implications for schooling. Some schools keeping in mind the value of androgynous personality have started to provide work experiences for boys and girls in order to develop the dignity of labour in them and to accommodate reciprocal roles. Some co-educational institutions have introduced cooking, homecraft and embroidery for both boys and girls in their curriculum. They are providing the same type of curriculum for both boys and girls. It is desirable that almost all the schools should provide such a curriculum, which do not discriminate between the two sexes.

In spite of various measures, which have been taken for ameliorating the conditions of the Indian women there is still much scope for reforms. Unless such customs, traditions, rituals and values and attitudes which view and treat women as inferior beings and less desirable than men are discarded and changed, the status and position of the Indian women are not going to improve. This change can be brought about through equalitarian, formal and informal education. Education must prepare both the sexes for becoming all that they can be without any discrimination or prejudice.

Depressed Women

We have described the socio-psychological factors which are influencing the education of the Indian women. In considering Indian women we have kept in our frame of reference a Hindu middle class woman. But Indian society is a very stratified one. There are many castes, classes and religions. The women belonging to upper and lower castes, rich and poor classes and Hindus, Muslims and Christians have their own specific problems even though as women they suffer from all those limitations with which the average woman of Hindu middle class suffers. In the present and the next chapters we are paying special attention to the problems concerning education of Dalit women and the women of the minority communities specially the Muslim women.

We are using the term Dalit women for all those women who are either put in the category of Harijans or Schedule Castes. These women suffer from many types of social disadvantages. Some of them were considered, untouchable while in the case of most of them the food touched by them was considered as defiled by the caste Hindus. Many of these indignities have now been sought to be abolished by the legal measures, but still their lot is far from satisfaction. One of the important reasons for this state of affairs is the woeful neglect of their education. Their ignorance is the major threat to their existence. Why has their education suffered ? What were the factors are still existing which have pushed them into a miserable existence? What factors which are putting hindrances in their respectable right of living? The thesis of this book is that these factors have to be searched out in the socio-psychological make-up of the women, particularly in relation to their education.

The Dalits have been put at the lowest level in the caste hierarchy of the Hindus. They were required to serve the higher castes. We are not entering into any discussion here as how and why this happened. This has already been a subject of a large number of investigations and discussions. Our concern here is that how this has affected the psyche of Dalits as well as the upper castes.

The Dalits were constantly reminded that they were the objects of hatred and their salvation lied in the service of the upper castes. This was done sometimes by persuasion but most of the times by force by the Brahamanical order of the Hindu society.

They were told that they must have committed some heinous crimes or evil actions in their past life and hence they are born as "untouchables". This developed in them a feeling of inferiority complex and they began to consider themselves as the inferior specimen of the mankind. This feeling was much more aggravated among the females of the Dalits since they were considered inferior to their own men. The Dalit women accepted their lower status and position and started believing that it was fated that they involve themselves in doing menial tasks. Since these tasks required no education or training they developed a mentality that education is meant for the upper and richer castes and not for them. They thus never made an attempt to send their children to the schools. Also the higher castes did not allow Dalit children to sit with their own children in the schools and there were no schools exclusively set up for Dalit children.

The literacy rate in India according to the census of 1991 was 52.11 per cent. The percentage of male literacy was 63.86 while that of female was 39.42 only. According to the census report of 1981 the general female literacy percentage was 24.82. The literacy percentage of scheduled caste females was as low as 10.93 and of scheduled tribe females was 8.04 (Census was not conducted in Assam and no castes were scheduled by the President of India for Nagaland, A and N Islands and Laskhadweep and no tribes were scheduled in Haryana, Jammu and Kashmir, Punjab, Chandigarh, Delhi and Pondicherry). These figures show that the education of the Dalit women was totally neglected.

The Dalit women were mostly working in the unorganised sector. In the organised sector their percentage Was quite low. There were only two scheduled caste women in Indian Foreign Services in 1987 while the number of male scheduled castes was 65. The male scheduled tribes number was 30 while that of the females was 5 only. Similar was the case in most of the other Central services. In all the Central services while the total number of the women employed was 994 in the year 1987 only 31 were scheduled caste women and 31 scheduled tribe women.

The employment prospects for Dalit women in the organised sector are very few. These women neither have the educational, nor technical qualifications and nor have contacts or social connections. They have also to face discrimination from two directions. One is that they are women and the second that they belong to low strata of the society. Hence in spite of the reservations for schedule castes and backward classes the benefit do not reach up to them. Hence most of the Dalit women in the urban areas are self-employed in the areas like hawking, scrap collection, domestic help, petty trade, etc. The women have to undertake such employment for their survival and for supporting their families. The income from such jobs is very meagre and also has uncertainties. There is no security also in these types of activities. Some Dalit women are also employed in wage employment activities. These activities include construction labour, earthwork, petty manufacturing activities like beedi making or candle making etc. They are employed by some traders in these activities and are being paid very low wages. In the rural areas the Dalit women are engaged for labour in agriculture and agro-based industries.

From the brief account of the education and employment of the Dalit women it may be evident that in spite of more than 50 years of our independence they are in miserable plight. It is, therefore, necessary for the government as well as the general public that serious efforts are made towards their betterment. We can tackle this problem only when we make all out efforts for their education. One way to do it is to open more and more schools for them and give them incentives like free tuition, dress and mid-day meals. But this is a very simple solution. The women may still not go to attend the school. The majority of the Dalit households will not send their girls of school going age to the schools as this may mean the loss of income for the family as these girls might have been employed in some type of wage earning work or these girls might be busy in looking after their younger siblings, etc. when their parents have left for work. If we wish to educate them and provide help in their social and economic progress we must understand their psychology and the sociological problems which they face.

Socio-Psychological Determinants

The Dalit women suffer from extensive inferiority complex. The indignities that they have suffered in the past have left such a deep mark on their psyhe that they had started considering themselves as persons meant to lead a miserable life. This complex has not been altered till the present times. Hardly they take interest in raising their pattern of life. The Dalit leaders have recently made very powerful efforts to bring changes in their thinking. Mayawati and Phoolan Devi are the present day examples of such leaders. But still there is a long way to go before the mentality of Dalit women as the scum of the society is going to change. The efforts of social workers and political leaders are undermined from time to time by the atrocities being committed on them by the upper caste and affluent members of the society. The tradition bound society in India do not relish that the Dalit women should think themselves as equal to them. They are prepared to commit all sorts of acts of aggression on them if they express any desire to achieve equality with the higher caste women.

The daily newspapers are full of incidents describing rapes, murders, and beatings of both the Dalit males and females. These have two types of reactions. One is that the Dalit leaders raise Dalit Sena and try to retaliate by attacking the citadels of the upper castes and the seconds that they take it as a matter of their fate. Both are wrong approaches. The Second approach increases caste tensions without offering any solution. The other approach of it being their fate is the pessimistic outlook that throws them back to square one. A better approach is to educate them in terms of their importance. They should not feel marginalised. It is the duty of their leaders to educate them in terms of their importance in the present day social and political order.

One of the factors responsible for their poor economic condition is the large number of children, which they produce. They do not realise that more children mean more mouths to feed. Unfortunately the Dalit leadership has failed to develop among Dalit women the value of family planning. The syndrome of what is fated will happen need to be altered. We may call such a syndrome as "fatelinked proverty syndrome". Unless the Dalit women are prepared to discard this syndrome their plight will remain the same.

As we have already pointed out the Dalit women's low status and position is due to their poverty and involvement in menial tasks. To improve their lot it is necessary that they should get better education and training. Now no task may be taken as menial. The technology has created a situation in which even the most menial task can be performed with machines. The handling of machines is the task of the technologists. The technologists are those who have got training in the handling of the machines. Thus the women are to be trained in handling machines and in the use of gadgets. One example may be given to clarify the issue raised here. We all know that Barber or Nai caste was considered among the low castes. His job was hair cutting, etc. Today this role has been taken up by the so called beauticians or by the owners of "air conditioned hair cutting saloons." The hair grooming is no more considered as a low task. Similar is the case with cooking. Now Chef is an honourable member of the society. The change has been brought about by the introduction of the specialised training being associated with these professions.

The Dalit women's aspirations and the motivations have to be increased manifolds. For this the social workers have to strive hard. The politicians cannot perform this task because they only want to keep their leadership intact or to get Dalit votes in the election. They have a vested interest in keeping the electorate ignorant and keeping it in the state in which it is so that these leaders can always exploit it by arousing its emotions for caste or class struggle. The enlightened electorate may question their leadership and may ask them to be accountable to the electorate. Only the leaders gain by creating hatred among different castes and classes. We may say that all the leaders are not like this.

There are many selfless workers. It is to them that an appeal to bring a change in the psychology of the Dalits should be made.

The role of teachers in bringing attitudinal changes among the Dalit women cannot be ignored. Education does not mean simply learning the language or some other subjects. Real education is that which has a bearing on a better personal and social life of that individual who is getting education. It is, therefore, very important that those teachers are appointed in the schools where the Dalit children are studying who are dedicated to the task of freeing the Dalits from the syndrome of linked poverty.

Are women different from men because of their physiological development? This question is raised time and again. The men establish their superiority by pointing out the biology of the female sex. Whenever the question of the equality of sexes is put someone is sure to say: "But it's just a matter of biology. You know women are different from men-they are more intuitive, nurturing, emotional, but also weaker and subject to fits of weeping once a month." Women are born to be mothers. Men are stronger, both physically and psychologically and so are fit for work and to play role of dominant partners in the men-women relationships. It is because of such notions that the education of women is considered not of as much significance as the education of men. But is it the right conclusion? We will now try to focus our attention on this question.

Basic Biological Differences

There is much divergence in the opinions regarding the basic biological differences between sexes. One viewpoint is that sex differences are biologically determined while the other viewpoint emphasises that the only difference between the sexes is reproduction. Only men can impregnate women and only women can give birth and lactate. It is true that one is born either male or female (not talking into consideration a small percentage of those born with no explicit sex or as eunuch). But there are six determinants of gender: (1) Chromosomes, XX for females and XY for males, (2) Gonads, testes in males and ovaries in females, (3) Hormone level, more androgens in males and more oestrogens and progesterone in females, (4) Internal accessory organs, which are the uterus and the organ of menstruation in female and the prostrate gland and seminal vesicles involved in the secretion of seminal fluid in male, (5) External genital appearance. (6) Assigned sex and rearing, usually based solely on external genital appearance (Hampson and Hampson, 1961).

There is research evidence that indicates that after birth the brain regulates secretion of sex hormones. Puberty seems to be initiated by an interaction between the sex hormone and certain cells of the brain. In normal child, both male (androgen) and female (oestrogen) sex hormones are almost undetectable in the urine until the child is eight to ten years of age. At this point the male hormones sharply increase in both sexes, while the female hormones increase only in females. In girls the production of sex hormone becomes cyclic at about the eleventh year and is accompanied by the beginning of menstruation, the appearance of secondary sexual characteristics, and a growth spurt. Thus in terms of hormones there are no appreciable differences between males and females up to puberty. After puberty both adrogenic and oestrogenic hormones are present in both sexes but in different proportions. Males have high level of androgens and low level of oestrongens, while females have high level of oestrogens and moderate level of androgens.

Social Factors

A very relevant question that may be raised here is: Do hormones determine our personality and behaviour completely or in their determination social factors are also involved? The biological determinists consider that hormones give us energy and direct that energy into natural channel such as sex and fighting. Thus our moods and behaviour are related to our own body state and socialisation factor is irrelevant. But this view is open to controversy. Research has shown that even our private emotions and their interpretation are shaped by reaction of those around us. While visceral sensations such as heart palpitation, flushing and tremor tell us that we are emotionally aroused, we have to learn whether that arousal means that we are excited, angry or happy. All body chemical hormones produce a physiological state that must be translated into personality and behaviour through a specific social control. Thus sex role probably enters into the very way we perceive and interpret our own bodily sensation even those due to hormone. This is not to say that hormone levels are irrelevant to personality and behaviour. It merely suggests that even with such purely biological differences as hormones, we need to keep a sharp eye for ways in which social factors help to translate these biological factors into every day behaviour. We may say that the differences in personality and behaviour of male and female are not only because of hormones but also the process of socialisation of girls and boys creates such differential behaviour, which is known as typically male or female behaviour. We may give a few more research findings to establish our above-mentioned belief.

The hormone androgen is found in greater quantity in males than in females. This is then considered as a factor governing more assertive behaviour among males. But Moss (1967) found that mothers tend to comfort crying female babies more than they do crying male's. It may be that the male infant experiences visceral sensation, such as stomach contractions of hunger pains. He cries but mother's attention is not drawn. He then learns that crying is not enough. He has to assert himself physically to attract the mother's attention. When this situation persists for months or years the male child may then associate this visceral sensation with greater activity or aggression and he may show it in his emotion of anger. On the other hand the female infant when experiences the similar visceral sensation due to stomach contraction she may also cry but in her case the mother comforts her. Gradually the female may come to associate these visceral sensations with comforting which may lead her to the emotion of happiness. The mothers perhaps do not attend to the male infant's cries as quickly as that of female infants because they may feel that males ought to be tough and should not cry. The finding of Moss may be taken with a sense of skepticism, in the case of Indian male child. In this country because of too high aspirations for a male child more attention is given to him by the mother. But this might be leading the male child becoming too much attached to the mother and an entirely dependent individual to the parental wishes.

It cannot be said that hormone levels are irrelevant to personality and behaviour. It merely suggests that even in dealing with such purely biological differences as hormones, we need to keep a sharp eye for ways in which social factors help to translate these biological factors into day to day behaviour.

The controversy surrounding aggression is not about whether males act more aggressively than females but about the causes for these sex differences, for regardless of how aggression is defined and measured, males of all ages show a consistent tendency to be more aggressive than their female peers. The greater male aggression is expressed not only in a variety of behavioural modes but also in a variety of situation and culture. But how do female hormones affect aggression? Unfortunately we know little about the answer to this question. Most researchers have assumed that male hormones increase aggression while female ones decrease it. Bronson and Desjardins found that administering female hormones to newborn may decrease the aggressiveness of males but increase the aggressiveness of females. Thus in females the oestrogens may mimic the effect of androgens in males, when given to males, however, oestrogens may interfere with the action of the androgens.

Further more, male androgens administered shortly before or after birth seem to increase aggressive behaviour in females but not in males, while female hormones administered at that time also seem to increase aggressive behaviour in female while decreasing it in males. Thus XX hormones, whether androgens or oestrogens seem to increase aggressive behaviour in females more than in males. This conclusion then suggests that it is the absolute level of all hormones androgens and oestrogens together that underlies aggression in women, rather than a level of androgens relative to that of oestrogens. The basic argument is that both the sexes are actually equally aggressive in their underlying motivation but carry out desires to hurt others in different ways. This argument takes two basic forms. The first maintains that the two sexes are reinforced for different forms of aggression: Girls are allowed to show hostility only in subtle ways, while boys are encouraged to show it more directly by physical attack. The second form of argument maintains that aggression in general, is less acceptable and hence more discouraged for girls, leading to greater female anxiety and conflict over aggression.

It is now widely known that there are no sex differences in over all scores on intelligence tests. Some psychologists have, however, suggested that the sex hormones influence general intellectual capacity. The most popular view has been that male hormones enhance intellectual functioning and development in both sexes and, perhaps is based on the assumption that several social and physical behaviour levels of male hormones are related to aggressive or energetic intellect. There are also some psychologists who argue that female hormones may underlie intellectual ability.

The fact that males and females obtain similar overall scores on intelligence tests which does not mean that there are no sex differences in intellectual abilities. The pattern of intellectual abilities that make up the overall IQ score differs for the two sexes. In fact IQ tests are carefully constructed to weight the various portions on which men and women, typically score higher in such a way that their average overall scores will be equivalent. Females generally excel in verbal ability while males in visual-spatial and mathematical ability. The females superiority in verbal is found in both "lower level" measure (fluency) and "higher level" tasks (comprehension of different material and creative writing). The males' visual-spatial advantage is about equal in non-analytical tasks (matching similar shapes and completing routine numerical operation, perceiving and manipulating parts and performing complex numerical operations).

The idea of difference in male and female brains continue to have popular appeal and has been hotly debated and researched for many decades in spite of numerous contradictions in both theory and data. About the differences between the male and female brains the researchers are only able to find that the issue is extremely complicated and does not offer any conclusive evidence that biological sex differences exist in intellectual performance.

Capturing Wisdom

Can the sex difference in intellectual abilities be erased through altered social experience or specific training? If they can, these differences might be attributed to differences in the training that males and females receive in the usual course of growing up in our culture.

Our entire educational system is based on the premise that training is crucial, that without it children would not be able to reason clearly or to complete complex verbal and non-verbal tasks. Yet every teacher knows that there is limit to what the best instruction can accomplish with each child. There seem to be a basic intellectual capacity that sets the limit for the rate and perhaps for the total amount of learning. With no instruction only a few children will develop complex skills, yet with the best instruction no all children will become highly skilled. The issue is whether instruction helps a child use basic cognitive abilities he/she already possesses, or whether instruction can affect the development of these basic intellectual abilities themselves.

Research on the training effect has focussed on the Embedded Figures Test (EFT) and the Rod Frame Test (RFT) developed by Witkin, in 1950. These tests assess spatial decontextualisation, or the ability to extract key elements of a stimulus from a confusing background. They measure "fields dependence versus fields independence" that is one's ability to assess external or internal stimulation independently of the environment. It has been reported that women are more fields dependent than men are." In other words, women have lower spatial ability scores than men have. It was also reported that the field independence does not increase with training. But these findings and Interpretations have been challenged. Mazy Brown Parlee (1973-74) conducted a thorough review of all published studies and concluded that sex differences were not nearly so conclusive as usually reported. Parlee maintained that field independence scores tend to improve with practice or training.

Emotional Support

Cross-cultural research results lead to the conclusion that the greater field dependence in women is an indication both of basic female dependence on others for emotional support and social stimulation and of a general lack of psychological differentiation" or development of a clearly defined and separate self-identity. Kogan and Kogan (1970) conclude that not only child rearing practices are associated with spatial ability scores in the predicted fashion, but sex roles are also implicated, i.e. men tend to score higher in spatial ability in those cultures with marked differences between the social roles assigned to the two sexes. The assumption is that greater sex role differentiation is associated with greater encouragement of dependence in females, and this dependence in turn interferes with spatial ability as measured by field independence and other measures.

Theme of Dependence

The cross-cultural argument is organised around the theme of dependence and assumes that the trait of dependence interferes with the restructuring of external physical and social stimulation and hence inhibits abstract reasoning. When cultures begin to adopt a modern lifestyle, allow children more autonomy, or define the proper role of the sexes less strictly, they are increasing the independence of their population. This more independent population then scores higher on field independence and other spatial ability measures. But increased childhood autonomy, decreased sex-role differentiation, and increased technological innovation are all associated with higher levels of formal education for the population in general and for women in particular. Thus increase in visual-spatial ability scores may be reflecting increased formal education rather than a personality trait of independence.

Intellectual Differences

To conclude the argument regarding physiological differences influencing the intellectual differences between males and females we once again raise the question: Do biological sex differences underlie any possible differences? It seems unlikely. Owing to traditional sex roles females are discouraged from being assertive and independent and therefore, their intellectual development and performance are inhibited. It is very well known that the parents treat male and female newborns differently. They encourage gross motor behaviour in males while viewing females as littler, cuter, cuddlier, and generally more fragile. The cross cultural research echoes this social theme by demonstrating that most cultures encourage males to be independent and assertive while encouraging females to be dependent, nurturing and responsible.

In 1912 in his book, The Psychology of Education Walton wrote that the profound physiological differences which distinguish the sexes are the correlates of equally important mental differences. While man lives by reason, women's outlook is molded and determined by feeling. In his opinion the advocates and promoters of equal education to the sexes sadly ignore the mental and intellectual differences between the two sexes. He is against coeducation. He emphasised that, as the psychological differences between man and woman are so intimate, so deep that the other cannot give the real training in character and in outlook in life of the one sex. A man cannot be a really sympathetic guide to a girl, nor a woman to a, boy, simply because the man has never been neither a girl nor woman a boy. But Walton clarifies that it must never be supposed that woman is an imperfectly developed man. That woman differs from man in intellect does not mean that she is in any way intellectually inferior to him. He proposes a different type of education for woman as her functions differ from that of man. He proposes a system of education which lays stress on preparation for an efficient woman.

Prevailing Educational System

Howard in 1928 drew attention to the prevailing educational system in which the boys and girls studied very much the same things even when their schools were separate. He advocated a separate system of education for boys and girls. In his opinion girls are liable to fatigue more readily after puberty when the amount of haemoglobin in the blood becomes lessened. With their thinner blood with lowered content after puberty, they are nearer to the threshold of anaemia. These girls in general are not so strong physically as boys are. They are also highly-strung and liable to nervous strain, which possibly is associated with the fact that physiologically they are liable to heavier drains upon the circulating calcium of the blood. These considerations of the physiology of the girl, Howard advocates, must weigh when laying down a particular system of education for girls.

Many other psychologists have also pointed out the physiological differences between men and women and recommended a different type of education for women. Geddes and Thompson in their book Sex (1927) argue that though certain differences between men and women are undoubtedly modification and natural, that is to say, the individual results of disparities or peculiarities in their education, training and occupations, many of the differences are constitutional, inborn and not acquired. They say that "the tenacity of life, the longer life, the characteristic endurance, the greater resistance to disease, the smaller percentage to genius, insanity, idiocy, suicide, and so on, are all correlated with the distinctively female constitution which may be theoretically regarded as relatively more constructive in its protoplasmic metabolism".

Stanley Hall (1920) has stressed the psychological differentiation between man and woman. Woman, he points out, are more emotional, altruistic, intuitive, less judicial, and are less able to make disinterested and impersonal judgment. He is of the opinion that woman thinks more in terms of the concrete, is slower in logical thought and has less patience involved in science and invention.

The psychologists, physiologists and social reformers till quite recently were pointing out the different physiological make-up of women as a ground for giving them a different type of education than that was to be given to men. They were emphasising that the existing female education was incompatible with the nature and need of woman. It had entirely ignored her function and mission in life, namely motherhood. The educational curriculum for her was a complete imitation of that of the man, as if like him she was going to be in future an office bearer. With only a few exceptions most of the women were going to be married and the motherhood was a undoubted fact. Hence they needed an education which would prepare them for motherhood. These persons were quite critical of the modern feminists whom they considered were criminally ignoring this vital fact in their zest of following the standards of male pursuits. According to them the girls should be given education in domestic economy, nursing of children, hygiene of pregnancy, general household management, and in all such subjects which would be intimately personal to them.

Dr. Saleeby in the Report of the Proceedings of the English Speaking Conference on Infant Mortality has remarked: "Education of a girl must be to prepare her for womanhood and not to show that at a pinch she would be a boy".

Truby King in the same report has mentioned that: proper education should be given but above all there must be a development of love of human life, and interest in children, and a development of proper womanly qualities".

The ideas expressed above are considered redundant now. The technological and scientific advancement has refuted all the arguments put as above in view of the women's physiology. It is now being said that because of technology, tomorrow's most challenging and rewarding careers will require the powers of mind, not muscles. The most modern psychological and brain research have made it very clear, despite all of yesterday's cliches, that women have all the intellect and ambition needed to go after these jobs. Science is also relieving the women from the tyranny of the biological clock, allowing women the freedom to delay bearing children until late thirties or sixties.

The changes in work and reproductive choices are women's family lives, encouraging "Parallel" marriages in which husband and wife both share the work inside and outside the home.

The study of biological and other sex differences is being carried out on many fronts by the anthropologists and psychologists, who catalog human behaviour, neuroscientists, who probe the brain, and endocrinologists, who trace the action of hormones in the body. It is still a very young science. But this science has given us new dimension regarding the biological and psychological differences between man and woman.

Male and female brains are different although not in ways that would support most of the stereotypes of the past. The distinction is certainly not one of intelligence, for the average female brain is as smart as the average male brain by whatever test we use to measure it. The difference lies in question of values, interests, style and Motivation. Different does not mean superior or inferior. We should also not deny biology in order to shake off the myths that have accumulated regarding female nature. Howard Gardner in his book Frames of Mind (1983) argues that the human intellect is not a single entity. Multiple forms of Intelligence exist, including musical, linguistic, spatial, logical ..... mathematical, interpersonal and bodily and kinesthetic intelligences. All individuals have an intellectual mix intellectual mix that includes all these types in varying Proportions. The mix may be weighted differently in each sex too.

The genetic engineering has revealed a number of facts regarding the physiological development of male and female. Now the scientists recognise that the creation of a male from the arrival of the chromosome to the testosterone that floods the embryo, is a precarious business, the result at best, is a creature with a single survival advantage over females: greater muscular strength. At every stage of life, men pay dearly to gain this advantage; fall victim to every threat from genetic defects to heart disease. Women are biologically superior to men in every other category but muscles. Boys are more likely to suffer than girls from birth defects and genetic diseases. So called X-linked genetic diseases such as haemophilia and muscular dystrophy strike boys almost exclusively because they are carried on the X-chromosome to protect them. But Y provides no such back up to a boy with a defective X. Infant boys suffer more illness and infection and in the first month of life three of them die for every two-baby girl. At every age, women have lower death rates from heart disease and heart attacks than do men. Even women who have high blood pressure and high blood cholesterol do not die as readily as men do. Women are less likely to die of infectious diseases. The endocrinologist Estelle Ramey says: "So women are an extraordinarily viable sex, right from the moment of conception".

In the modern times medicine has reduced the perils of childbirth and the threat of infectious diseases. Women are simply better prepared mentally and physically, to meet the pace and challenges of life and work in a technologically advanced world.

Women of all ages have more responsive immune systems than men, giving them protection from bacteria and virus. Girls have higher levels of a protective blood protein called immunoglobulin M or IgM than males, and a gene on the X-chromosome seems to be responsible for the immune system. The X-chromosome also carries other genes that influence various parts of the defense system. And after puberty, oestrogens increase the efficiency of the immune responses.

Life Expectancies

It is becoming increasingly clear as the gap between men's and women's life expectancies grown ever wider that women have better ways of coping with stress, physically, socially. Some of the biggest risks to life today – heart disease, alcoholism, lung cancer, suicide- arise from the way we handle pressure and stress. Although the same stress response takes place in both men and women it is more extreme in men because they need a bigger head of steam to get their larger muscles fueled for action. It has been found that women are about fifteen years behind men in accumulating significant heart damage. Men on average, start to develop heart disease between age of thirty-five and forty, women between the ages of fifty and fifty-five. Men between thirty-five and fifty-five are twice as likely to die of heart disease as are women. Today's women are entering into competitive athletics with the same intensity as men and their performance is improving dramatically. No doubt that there are some biological differences between the sexes that cannot be ignored, although they are not nearly as great as the myths about the women have been propagating.

Precious Commodity

Knowledge is the most precious commodity in the information age. The doors are now wide open for women to push against the frontiers of ignorance and it is very heartening to note that women have begun to take their mental and intellectual capabilities seriously. Keeton and Basrin in their book Women of Tomorrow (1985) write that women are forging new ways to care, applying their concern along with their intellect to much larger human goals. These authors emphasise that women can be system analysts and computer programmers, they can be hardware as well as software engineers; women can enter into the fields of infertility and test-tube baby research, of molecular biology and genetic engineering, women should prefer to study Bionics, (a field that's already produced artificial hearts, artificial pancreases to secrete insulin to diabetics, the first rudimentary artificial ears and eyes connected directly to the human brain, etc.). It's never too late for a woman to start to find a place for herself in any of these frontier fields. The country needs scientists and engineers to improve life on earth and help expand in space.

It can be said with confidence on the basis of the findings of various physiologists and the biologists that the women are not physiologically weak, rather they are by nature superior and their superiority lies in the power to give birth. It is argued that woman and woman alone have the capacity to give birth. Despite all the evolution of socioeconomic conditions and progress of genetic manipulation of medical knowledge, the fact remains that it is the woman and none else that carries the work of reproduction. It is this biological feature gifted by nature to woman, which is at the root of the existence of necessary minimal sexual division of labour.

The modern physiologists reject biological explanation of the inferior status of woman. They argue that the biological view does explain why men have been excluded from the task of reproduction, but it fails to clarify why women have been excluded from some activities, which are not reproductive. This implies that the inferior position of the women is not due to any natural deficiency in them but it has resulted from changing historical circumstances, which have always been tied to the reproductive role. Needless to say in the modern society women have been doing the same work that was once considered exclusively to be of men. For instance, women have gone to space, joined modern guerrilla groups and fought on the battle fronts, headed the country's administration, participated in sports and games and the like. To the chagring of men, women even surpass men in many of the so-called men's activities. Hence It does not stand to reason to attribute women's inferiority in society to biological or physical factors.

In view of the above mentioned facts we may suggest that the education for women must be as liberal and deep as for men. A woman must know the course of history, the rise and fall of different political systems, the co-ordination and contact of different cultures, the fundamental issues that this evolution in history involves. She must also know where she stands, how is she related to society, how can she promote solidarity in social life without injuring the growth of the individual. She must also know how life began. She must have knowledge of Botany and Zoology. She must learn Geography and Literature, which are the fountains of culture and civilisation. In short she must learn all, the areas of liberal education so that she knows her relations to the society and may thus prepare herself for real citizenship.

Domestic Hygiene

The woman must also have training in domestic hygiene and economy. She must learn the art of nursing children and decoration of home. She may also learn fine arts, dancing and music. Her education thus must equip her for twin task of keeping the household and involving in the world of work. We consider that system of education an ideal one which aims at making of each versatile artisan-versatile for changing conditions, a good citizen consciously playing a part in a general scheme and a well-disposed, considerate person in full possessions of all his/her powers.

The education of the women should usher in an era of complete rationalism and equality. Equality between men and-women means equality in their dignity and worth as human beings as well as equality in their rights, opportunities and responsibilities.

4

Problems and Perspective

Issues involving women are closely related to supportive services. These refer to the gamut of services and amenities that make the women more functional and productive, while at the same time reduce the overburdening drudgery of the daily chores which she is expected to perform for the survival of her family. The major supportive services that require attention are fuel, fodder, water, creche and housing services. One of the major hurdles to women's development activities is the difficulty of providing economically viable means of releasing them from day to day drudgery and survival activities which are neither awarded an economic value nor are shared by men. Data indicate that women are unable to avail of tubectomy services in the absence of a substitute who can care for the children while the woman is away. Similarly, the education of girls is impeded because they are invariably required to help the mother to look after younger children. It is well known that besides adult women, children are also expected to fetch fodder, fuel and water. Cooking also accounts for a large chunk of the woman's time. The use of inefficient smoky chulhas affect their lungs, eyes and health in general. This also interferes with social interaction.

The factors affecting women's advancement are thus critically linked to the socio-cultural environment. In keeping, with her sex stereotyped role as a housewife and home maker, an Indian woman irrespective of clan, creed, region, religion, spends, most of her time on household chores. While the actual time distribution would vary from place to place, undoubtedly many women are subjected to the drudgery of a day to day subsistence working up to 16-18 hours per day. Unfortunately, such 'shadow work' brings her no monetary returns nor does it enhance her prestige in the family or society which is necessary for her to participate in decision making.

In addition, women are often left to fend for the household's basic needs and sanitation, especially in the rural context. The Seventh Plan notes that women play an important role in agriculture, animal husbandry and other related activities such as storage, marketing of produce, food processing, etc. About 54 per cent of rural women and 26 per cent urban women are engaged in marginal occupations in order to supplement family income by collection of fodder, firewood, cowdung, maintenance of kitchen gardens, tailoring, weaving, teaching, etc. It is not easy for a woman to take up employment, unless there are alternative ways to saving time at home and sufficient remuneration to justify her employment outside. Thus all programmes for women, be it education, health, family planning, nutrition, social welfare or legislation are necessarily interrelated support structures for reducing the household drudgery.

Since drinking water, fuel and fodder are the basic requirements especially in the rural areas, a major portion of women's time is spent on collecting these. Strategies which help overcome such problems by providing the necessary support services need to be carefully devised and effectively integrated in development strategies/ plans for women.

In the previous plan periods, the emphasis was mainly on issues concerning education, employment and social aspects, without giving commensurate attention to supportive services. For example, the section dealing with the 'Infrastructure for Women's Participation in a Modernizing Economy', the Report on the Status of Women, touched only upon childcare services. The National Plan of Action (1976) was also silent on the structuring of various supportive services. However, the Sixth Five-Year Plan recommended separate Science and Technology (S&T) inputs for women (Item 19.35) as a part of Science & Technology for Human Resource Development. The Plan suggested the setting up of special cells for promotion of Science and Technology for women under the aegis of different organizations such as the University Grants Commission (UGC, Council of Scientific and Industrial Research (CSIR), Indian Council for Medical Research (ICMR), Department of Adult Education (DAE), etc. Although it was proposed to apply Science and Technology for the improvement of the living conditions and status of women, support services were not specifically discussed. The Seventh Plan is more emphatic on women's development and has a separate section on 'Socio-Economic Programmes for Women'. It notes that in giving Science and Technology inputs for women, special efforts have to be made to reduce their drudgery.

The interlinkages between various sectoral and support services have to be fully understood so that an integrated purposeful view is taken of women development. The programmes have to be planned on the basis of a detailed analysis both at micro and macro levels. The analysis should identify critical factors including resource availability, appropriate technologies, skill constraints, public awareness and organizational, institutional and policy supports.

Typical Rural Problems

Fuel and fodder are best taken up together since they are bio-mass based and often the same plant provides both. This system also integrates with food which, in turn, is linked to fuel through cooking. Hence the discussion here also touches upon forestry and wasteland utilization for growing a variety of biomass in the broader perspective.

Women participate in fodder production as a part of their activities in agriculture and in cutting and fetching fodder for feeding the animals. Generally green fodder is raised as one of the crops or in grasslands and is gathered from the fields as and when required. Alternatively a variety of straws and other agricultural residues are collected and stored as fodder or converted into silage or hay. Often women also have to visit the nearby forests to cut fodder from trees and bushes. This is generally done along with fuel collection. The harder biomass like twigs and firewood are used as fuel and the palatable leaves, as fodder. As for fuels, as indicated by a number of studies, cowdung (gobar) and agricultural residues and firewood form the major fuel for cooking and are gathered and stored mainly by women. The act of making and storing cowdung cakes has developed into an art, with 'bitodas' (cowdung storage structures) prominently standing out in the rural landscape. Cowdung cakes are preferred for slow cooking on low fires or heating milk, while firewoods and agricultural residues serve to produce more intensive heat. Depending on resource availability, the utilization pattern varies with cowdung being more prominent in the northern regions. The major portion of total energy, consumed is through such 'non-conventional' sources which, in rural areas, accounts for 90 per cent of the domestic energy expenditure.

The three plans (Fifth, Sixth and Seventh) had generally discussed the fodder under 'Animal Husbandry', fuel under 'Energy', and biomass under 'Forestry'. The Fifth Plan observed that the 'forestry' development has assumed a significant dimension as a source of timber and fuel and for the maintenance of the natural ecological system. Special plantations have been given high priority. Under the section 'Energy' it has been proposed to adopt a multipronged approach to develop biogas technology and tap new sources such as solar energy, tidal and wing power. The Sixth Plan noted that feed and fodder constitute 60 to 70 per cent of the cost of production of various livestock products and that the area under fodder crops has remained more or less static during the last two decades. It also stated that emphasis will continue to be placed on the promotion of fodder production as an integral part of crop husbandry through a mixed farming system, particularly, on the small landholdings. Effective farmer-oriented extension programmes will be taken up by the Government for evolving and popularizing high yielding varieties of fodder crops, and introduction of leguminous fodders in existing crop rotations. Production and distribution of high quality fodder seeds will also receive priority attention. Accordingly, a Central Fodder Seed Production Farm and Centres for Forage Production and Demonstration were set up during this plan. The development of extensive grasslands and creation of grass reserves were taken up by the State Forest Departments. Under the social forestry programmes marginal and degraded forests were allocated for cultivation on fodder trees.

As for fuel, the Sixth Plan (item 9.248 under social forestry) proposed: (i) Mixed plantation of wasteland; (ii) Reforestation of degraded forests and raising of shelter belts. In the districts where shortage of fuel wood was particularly acute, new centrally sponsored schemes of social forestry including Rural Fuel Wood Plantation and Farm Forestry were introduced in selected areas. New thrusts in the form of Tree for Every Child Programme, Economic Development Force, Eco-development Camps and Agro Forestry programmes were devised during the Sixth Plan. The concept of organic recycling (Item 9.36) and the propagation of biogas technology (Item 9.40, 9.41) were also envisaged. Further, this plan dealt with the new and renewable energy sources and suggested that energy forestry, biogas and biomass conversion technologies have to be taken up along with solar and wind energy and a variety of other technologies. For example, item 15.95 on 'Energy Forestry' notes that firewood is the most important traditional fuel accounting for two-thirds of the total energy contribution from non-commercial sources and is becoming scarce. In view of the pressure on land, all available unutilized pockets of land could be used for energy plantations. Considering that rural communities will continue to depend heavily on such resources, it was proposed to decentralize energy production and distribution as a part of an Integrated Rural Energy System (Item 15.105) which considers all energy resources in a given area.

In the Seventh Plan also, emphasis has been given to social forestry, agro forestry and various renewable energy technologies and the necessity of creating awareness among people through mass media. The Plan notes that a proper implementation of some components of forestry programmes may be entrusted to local and voluntary bodies (NGOs). Concepts like 'social fencing' may be tested. Infact the revised 20-Point Programme (1986) has advocated a "New Strategy for Forestry" (Point No. 16).

In recognition of the importance of renewable resources, a Department of Non-conventional Energy Sources has been set up. Also a National Wasteland Development Board was created with the objective of bringing 5 million hectares of land every year under fuelwood and fodder plantation.

In many of the above programmes, the role of women in the production, collection and utilization of fuel and fodder and the related problems are not adequately emphasized. However, it is heartening to note that the Department of Science and Technology set up a cell on "Science & Technology for Women" in 1982. This cell divided the various technologies required for women into the following four areas: Technologies for Drudgery Reduction; Employment Generation Technologies; Health and Sanitation Technologies; and Technologies for Minimizing Occupational Hazards.

Under the first category, the problems of fuel, fodder and drinking water were perceived from the point of view of women. Besides a number of projects funded through individual institutions, an All India Coordinated Project was also undertaken on 'Fuel and Cooking Aspects' through Science and Technology Department. More than 20 institutions from all over the country participated, analysing the data based on micro level surveys. The local specific and general problems of women in dealing with fuels were identified and the viability of a variety of technologies were field tested. Similarly, some of the selected technologies like the improved chulha, biogas solar cooking biogas based technologies, etc., are being taken to the people through the

Department of Non-Conventional Energy Sources. Apart from various governmental institutions like Department of Science and Technology (DST), Indian Council of Agricultural Research (ICAR) Council for Scientific and Industrial Research (CSIR) and Department of Non-Conventional Energy Sources, a number of relevant State departments are also taking up the implementation of such projects. Some reports analysing the reasons for the success as well as failures of experiments undertaken are available.

It is encouraging to know that recently a number of NGOs have taken up programmes with funding support from the various Government bodies noted above. A Bio-energy Society of India has also been established with a view to promote research and development as well as public awareness. Bio-energy education dealing with the production, conversion and utilization of biomass with special emphasis on fuel aspects is being given prominence. People's participation is being promoted through social forestry and other programmes. However, the linking of women with these activities is still weak. A few movements like 'Chipko' stand out, emphasizing that much can be achieved by organizing women at the local levels.

The agricultural universities, dairy development institutions and forest institutes undertake research in fodder and fuel production and have a network of extension centres such as Krishi Vigyan Kendras for taking these technologies from the lab to land. While agriculture provides fodder crops, special attention is also paid to trees and plant species like 'subabool' which can cater to both fuel and fodder needs. Researchers on social forestry and agro-forestry all over the country now recognize the need for integrating the food, fodder, fuel, fertilizer, fibre and other biomass based production and utilization aspects.

The various technologies developed are being compiled into suitable directories for dissemination, e.g., the Science and Technology Women's Cell has listed a number of technologies for women. Council for Advancement of People's Action and Rural Technology (CAPART) has undertaken the publication of several volumes of *National Directory of Rural Technologies*, the first volume titles '*Post-Harvest Technologies*' has already been printed.

However, the scope exists for designing and developing more technologies appropriate to women taking into consideration the agronomy, ease of handling, economics, etc. A special mention must be made of Agricultural Tool Research Centre at Bardoli, which has tried to make efficient agricultural tools especially suited for women.

Although India is one of the wettest countries in the world with an average annual rainfall of 1170 mm, it still faces and is expected to face in future the threat of acute water shortage. Among the various usages of water in rural areas, drinking water followed by irrigation, sanitation and agriculture are of importance for the overall developmental process.

Water resources are generally dealt with as a part of irrigation in agriculture. In addition to this, the Sixth Plan laid special stress on rural water supply as a part of the 'Minimum Needs Programme'. As in the Sixth Plan, the Seventh Plan also highlights the importance of drinking water. The supply of drinking water to all problem villages features at Point 7 of the Twenty-Point Programme (1986). A 'Technology Mission on Drinking water in Villages and Related Water Management' was established in 1986-87 under the Department of Rural Development, Ministry of Agriculture, Government of India. The collaborating agencies identified were Council of Scientific and Industrial Research, Ministry of Science and Technology, Department of Environment and Forests, Department of Defence Research and Development, Ministry of Health and Family Welfare, Ministry of Water Resources and State Governments. The 'problem' villages were identified as those with: (i) No source of water; (ii) Water sources more than 1.6 km. distance, 15 km depth and 100 metres elevation difference; (iii) Biological contamination (guinea worm, cholera, typhoid); and (iv) Chemical contamination (fluoride, brackishness, iron). The number of such problem villages amounts to 39 per cent of the total villages (2.27 lakh out of 5.57 lakh).

Apart from these, the strategy has focused on 50 project areas (Mini missions) to evolve new, cost effective science and technology techniques, to apply and replicate these techniques in the rest of the problem villages and to implement an integrated approach to water conservation.

A booklet outlining the project objectives, background, strategy, management structure, targets, methodology, milestones, accomplishment, resources and policy needs, has been brought out by the Ministry of Agriculture. Already this mission has started working with the State Departments concerned. In addition, universities, research institutions and voluntary organizations are also being involved. A first Regional Seminar to focus on these issues for Southern States and Union Territories was held at Gandhigram in Tamil Nadu in July 1987.

Most of the above efforts, however, are not directly addressed to women. Although in the Sixth Plan, special mention has been made about assuring the weaker sections of their due share of water, only a few organizations like the Science and Technology Women's Cell have looked at this problem from the women's development angle. In addition to sanctioning some institutional level projects on various aspects of potable water, an "All India Coordinated Project on Drinking Water" has also been proposed by this department.

Ideally, as in the case of urban services, the Government should be in a position to supply potable water to all households through pipelines and taps right at the doorsteps. However, considering the current constraints of finance and non-availability of suitable water sources, problem terrains, etc., this may not be feasible in the near future. Hence constructing and maintaining smaller water sources like wells, water tanks, hand pumps, etc., are to be given due consideration.

As with the implementation of any project, there is always the problem of ensuring people's participation in both maintenance and the distribution systems. Merely installing different kinds of units and equipment does not lead to sustained water supply. Thus, organizing women to adopt different technologies is a key issue. In this context, a successful experiment by a voluntary agency in Rajasthan could be considered as a model for replication. In this case, the people were involved in identifying the locations for tube-wells. A few persons were then trained in their actual construction and maintenance. The system of giving due remuneration for subsequent management to these trained personnel was also evolved. This ensured sustained working of the pumps/tube-wells and equitable distribution of water. Other case-studies worthy of note are the "Water Harvesting Systems" employed at Banwasi Sewa Ashram and the "Water Sharing System" evolved at Sukhamajari.

Although a number of technologies are available, only a few have reached the villages. More research and development is needed on issues like devices for carrying water in hilly terrain, water purification techniques suitable for different problem areas, storage at home levels, and rapid methods of water testing.

A list of available technologies have been compiled in a volume brought out by the Cell on Science and Technology for Women. The CAPART has also brought out publications on drinking water and the third volume of its National Directory of Rural Technologies will be on Drinking Water. The Technology Mission on Drinking Water has brought out two publications entitled *Sub-Mission on Desalination of Water and Sub-Mission on Eradication of Guineaworm.*

Housing Problems

With the advent of industrialization and modernization, and with the gradual disappearance of the traditional joint family and with its in-built security system, the problem of working mothers has become increasingly serious. Although it is mainly an urban phenomenon, rural India is beginning to experience it too. With increasing economic pressures more and more women have to take out of home jobs. The situation is serious because the majority of women who need daycare for their children are from economically backward strata of society.

Working mothers of low-income groups need day care most as they cannot afford to hire or pay for labour-saving devices. Thus, in addition to the general need for child care for all working mother's, there is also a more specific and strong need for child care for those belonging to the poorest sections of the society.

Rural mothers struggle hard not only in the fields but also to collect fuel, fodder and water. Thus their time 'out of home' is much more and the majority of them are forced to either take their infants along or to leave them under the 'supervision' of elder children who stay at home, or even alone. This situation not only keeps older children away from the educational system, but endangers the health of infants and small children. The need for childcare services had already been accepted, but the legal provision exists only for women in the organized sector, which comprise approximately 10 per cent of the working women.

After the submission of the CSWI report (1974), and the International Women's Year, childcare has been recognized as an important and essential support service in women's development. The CSWI report has stated that despite the laws and ILO Convention, maternity and childcare benefits are available only to 3-5 per cent of Indian women workers in the organized sector. The other 3-5 per cent of the organized sector (mainly in services) do not get creche facilities because they are not covered by labour laws. To the 90 per cent of women workers who are in the informal sector, these facilities have so far never been provided as highlighted in the report of the National Commission on Self-Employed Women and Women in the Informal Sector.

In 1950, creches were run by four national level voluntary organizations - The Indian Council for Child Welfare, Bhartiya

Grameen Mahila Sangh, Bhartiya Adimjati Sevak Sangh and Harijan Sevak Sangh. The then Ministry of Social Welfare launched a scheme of creches/day care centres for children of working and ailing mothers in February 1975. The aim of the scheme was to promote healthy all round development of such children. The scheme caters to the basic needs of young children of poor working and ailing women in the unorganized sector. The services under the scheme include health care, supplementary nutrition, sleeping facilities, immunization, entertainment and nursery school facilities for children. Starting in 1974-75 with 247 creches to cover 6175 beneficiaries, the scheme has been considerably expanded since then. In the year 1987-88 there were 3,137 agencies running 10,210 creches in the country which included both permanent and mobile units. The Department of Women and Child Development which now deals with the scheme had on its plan that by the end of 1988-89, 12,000 creches would cover 2,82,800 children. The training of creche workers under this programme commenced from September, 1986. Grants-in-aid to certain all-India level institutions were released for conducting training courses. In the statutory sector, around 55,000 children are taken care of in creches/day care centres.

The Balwadi Nutrition Programme is another programme being implemented since 1970-71 which looks after the social and emotional development of children in the age group of 3-5 years, apart from providing supplementary nutrition to them. About 5,045 balwadi centres are functioning in the country covering about 2.29 lakh children.

The Integrated Child Development Services (ICDS) scheme launched by the government in 1975 is designed both as a preventive and developmental effort. It extends beyond the existing health and education systems to reach children below six years and their mothers in villages and slums and delivers to them an integrated package of services - non-formal pre-school education., immunization, health checkups, supplementary nutrition, medical referral services and nutrition and health education for women. As on 31 March, 1988 information received from 1,455 ICDS projects indicate that 1,46,693 Anganwadis were providing supplementary nutrition to 96.10 lakh children. In these Anganwadis, 18.40 lakh nursing mothers were receiving supplementary nutrition. Though focused on the all round development of the pre-school child, it is also the largest scheme providing part time creche facilities to children in rural and tribal areas and in slums. As an employment generation scheme for women, it employs nearly 2,00,000 women at the Anganwadi level.

The National Policy on Education' 1986 (NPE), for the first time took note of the growing awareness that the performance of household chores, specially care of younger siblings, is a major reason for the stagnation in enrolment of girls in schools. At two, places in the policy document, (vide para 5.2 in Early Childhood Care and Education (ECCE) and para 4.3 in Education for Women's Equality, reference is made to the need for child care, attached to or near primary schools, as a support service to encourage and allow girls to attend school.

The rapid rate of urbanization in India, coupled with large scale migration of people into the metropolitan cities, has created a tremendous pressure on the housing situation in the country. On the one hand, is the ever increasing shortage of housing which is estimated to be to the tune of 5.1 million dwelling units in urban areas alone (NBO 1981), and on the other, is the steep cost of housing and new construction which is unable to keep pace with the increasing demand and is beyond the reach of the urban dwellers.

In the successive Five-Year Plans, the Government of India has launched several social housing schemes for different income groups under which, loan/ subsidy is given to the low income and economically weaker section families. The implementation of these schemes on a countrywide basis has created great awareness of the desirability of improving the housing and environmental conditions among all sections of the populations including women.

Several other measures which have been taken include providing house building advance, housing finance at low rates of interest through financial institutions, fiscal incentives, bulk acquisition and development of land and ceiling on land, land use regulations, promotion of housing through cooperatives, setting up of Housing Boards and City Development Authorities and Slum Clearance Boards to augment the housing stock.

A Central Scheme of assistance for construction of hostel buildings for working women was initiated in 1972. The scope of the scheme was widened in 1980 by including a provision for daycare centres for children. Financial assistance is given to voluntary organizations for construction/expansion of hostel buildings for working women. Local bodies are also eligible for taking up these programmes. The total number of hostels sanctioned so far is 429 with a total capacity of 27,292 working women with day-care centre facilities for 2,920 children, since the inception of the scheme in 1972. It has been decided to reserve 5 per cent seats in the hostels for widows and other women in distress who are otherwise, eligible for hostel accommodation.

Under the Minimum Needs Programme to ameliorate housing and environment conditions, the Government of India has been implementing various schemes, viz., Slum Clearance Improvement Scheme, Scheme for Environmental Improvement in Slum Areas and the Schemes for Provision of House Sites to landless workers in rural areas and other social housing schemes for improving the living conditions of the urban and rural poor. The benefits of the schemes accrue to women also.

In the Twenty Point Programme (1986) high priority was accorded to provision of drinking water supply (Point No. 7), improvement of housing conditions for 14.6 million rural landless families (Point No. 14) and those living in slums and squatter settlements (Point No. 15).

Large-scale housing programmes were taken up in different states under the National Rural Employment Programme (NREP) and Rural Landless Employment Guarantee Programme (RLEGP). Housing schemes with employment as the main feature have also been taken up in many States. For implementing the Indira Gandhi Grih Nirman Awas Yojna, an allocation of Rs. 125 crore annually has been provided in the Seventh Five-Year Plan to build one million houses for Scheduled Castes and tribal families.

Improvement in the quality of life of people depends to a great extent on the quality of housing and related facilities which determine the physical environment. It is in recognition of this fact that the world conference of the International Women's Year adopted a World Plan of Action in 1975 which included aspects related to housing amongst its recommendations. The Plan suggested that settlement planning and policies should be formulated keeping in view the trend to recognize women's role in the development process and should prioritize investments in infrastructure therein according to the needs of women. Subsequently, following the declaration of 1987 by the United Nations as the International Year of Shelter for the Homeless, the Ministry of Urban Development of the Government of India formulated a Draft National Housing Policy (March, 1987) with a view to ensuring every family a shelter by the end of this century. Nowhere in its text, however, had the draft acknowledged that housing and women's needs required to be closely linked. Passing references to women were made only at page 12 para 13.4 of the draft wherein it stated that special efforts would be made to improve women's skills and working conditions in the housing sector.

For women, housing has a wider meaning. It implies their working and living environment to which they are confined for a greater portion of their lives, performing their multiple roles that of production which is often home based and therefore implies the use of the shelter and its environs as the working space; that of reproduction which is traditionally viewed as their primary role and includes child rearing activities linked to domestic chores; and that of management of resources and assets within the family unit which includes activities such as storage, managing domestic provisions, processing, etc.

Women's housing needs, arising from their multiple roles, have been listed as follows; as child bearers, they need access to sanitary facilities and a healthy living environment; as child rearers, they need space for childcare and recreation within or outside the house; as managers of households, they need water, fuel, waste and garbage disposal, proper light and ventilation and space to perform domestic chores; and as producers, they need a working space as well as space for storage of raw materials and finished products, besides space for processing of materials. In addition, women also need privacy and security as well as facilities for education, recreation, production and training within the housing space. Housing thus, implies space beyond the confines of the immediate shelter.

An effective public distribution system for essential commodities like rations and cloth is a necessary support for women, especially women workers in the unorganized sector. Poor women are denied ration cards which forces them to purchase basic necessities from the open market at exorbitant prices. Even women with ration cards are often denied rations due to understocking or diversion of stocks.

Each of the above roles indicates that women's efficiency and effectiveness in performing the productive and reproductive tasks are linked to the quality of housing. Since they are in effect the primary users of housing, women must have a role to play in decisions regarding housing as well as ensure that they have access to ownership of the same.

In planning for women's development, priority needs to be given to creating access to assets for single women and female headed households. An estimated 30-35 per cent of households in rural India are headed by women according to available micro studies. Women have hitherto had no rights to ownership or inheritance of property within the framework of customary law.

Recent legislative provisions have tried to remedy this situation but ancestral property still remains inaccessible to women. By and large, the patriarchal patterns of land ownership and transfer have implied that land is transferred to males. This pattern has been adopted by the planners in formulation of housing programmes so that men are recognized as heads of: households and land is distributed in their names. Although distribution of land deeds or pattas has been legally sanctioned for men and women jointly, in effect, women are not given land titles. Where women are able to gain access to land or assets, they are often required to have a man stand surety for the same, as also for loans and credit.

Within the patriarchal norm, women may not customarily claim ownership of the matrimonial home. This has often denied women access to shelter in times of crisis. In cases where women have been deserted and are destitute, they have not had any legal right to claim access to shelter, housing or any such assets. Only recently have policy makers and legislators realized that, it is imperative to accord priority to the provision of housing for single and women headed households.

Various strategies have been evolved to augment the housing stock in the country by urban planners and specialists especially for economically weaker sections. The target groups have however seldom been involved in planning for such housing. The norms applied to make such houses affordable for the identified target groups have ignored women's needs for space in the dwelling unit. It is necessary to scrutinize established standards and develop norms in housing especially for economically weaker sections, and to determine their adequacy for women. There must also be visible participation of women in the planning and execution of housing programmes in order to ensure that women's needs are adequately considered in the housing designs.

Women have had no traditional access to capital assets or to institutional finance and credit for housing. They have had to resort to borrowing from traditional credit sources at exorbitant rates of interest. Institutional sources of credit such as banks have not recognized women as credit-worthy individuals in their own right so that they may borrow through existing schemes at differential rates of interest. Various agencies have tried to play an intermediary role in creating access for women to institutional credit but their out reach has been limited. It is essential, therefore, that institutions such as HDFC and HUDCO recognize women in their individual capacities as beneficiaries for housing credit and finance.

The housing market also offers a vast potential for employment, especially in the rural areas. Expanding construction activity in housing would ensure that greater opportunities for employment are created, while also creating shelter for the rural populace.

Possible Solutions

Problems specific to women have to be highlighted in considering issues like fodder, fuel and drinking water. Since these directly concern women, their involvement in the programmes related to such issues must be given prominence. The interlinkages among fuel, fodder and drinking water with other aspects of the development of women such as education, employment, food and nutrition, health and sanitation must be recognized and integrated programmes worked out on a holistic basis for optimal utilization of personnel and financial inputs.

As had been stressed by the Seventh Plan, the government must ensure public participation and draw upon the resources of voluntary agencies, educational (especially Science and Technology) institutions, industries and financial organizations in implementing various programmes for the development of women. Various funding agencies may consider sponsoring All India or regional projects on a coordinated basis wherein, Science and Technology experts could collaborate with the NGOs and the people in designing and implementing programmes based on micro-level surveys.

Women must be specifically organized by involving the NGOs wherever necessary to participate in the implementation of social forestry programmes, water sharing projects and in the maintenance of various gadgets and devices. The necessary formal and non-formal education has to be appropriately matched with their time schedules, seasonal occupations and socio-cultural constraints.

In training programmes, in addition to NGOs, educational institutions could play an important role. Agricultural extension centres, home science colleges, and youth forums like NSS should be purposefully involved. Science and Technology institutions can take up the task of training and provide the technical back up in technology transfer as well as monitoring and evaluation.

A data bank may be set up with such resource centres, where information may be made available not only on technologies but also on manufacturing availability of training facilities, etc. These centres must have working models readily available for demonstrations, and requisite resource persons. Interaction among the centres will enable them to serve as a national network.

Research must be undertaken both in improving and developing hardware and software systems. All the necessary technologies on collection, processing, storage and utilization of fodder, fuel and drinking water may be carefully analysed and gaps identified. Many issues are regional and location specific and tackled best at the micro level. For example, carrying water is more problematic in hills than in plains and fuel problem is more acute in arid zones. The choice of fuel and fodder generating plants would depend on the agroclimate and terrains. The type of improved chulha required depends on the food and cooking practices. Perhaps an area based approach can be taken combining locations with similar type of problems into groups or clusters.

The necessary industrial support in the manufacturing of various small equipments should be created, e.g., manufacture of small water storage systems, forage harvesting system, etc. Women and small entrepreneurs should be involved in such ventures with suitable subsidies.

The decision makers both at the bureaucratic and political levels should be sensitized to the importance of programmes specifically targeted for women in the context of national development.

The socio-cultural and traditional practices must be suitably modified for conservation of various resources and more efficient utilization of time, energy and capital. For example, cooking recipes which require more fuel and time in cooking have to be pointed out and corrected. Where possible, community kitchens should be encouraged. Especially in the periphery of towns, the food prepared in neighbouring areas can be brought in packages. This would reduce the load on fuel, provide employment to women in the surrounding areas while benefiting many working women.

Many of the local hardware and software problems especially with respect to fuel and drinking water are not easily solved at the household level. The right level of scaling has to be planned, keeping in view both the economic viability and the consumer's convenience. For instance, in a biogas system, a 80m' community biogas plant is more economical than a 2m' household plant but the former calls for a more elaborate management system. Perhaps a subcommunity biogas plant of 15-20M3 for 15-20 families could be a solution. Thus for each problem, a suitable community or sub-community system has to be worked out.

Some of the above recommendations have been noted both in the 'Country Report of 1985' presented at Nairobi and "Forward Looking Strategies for the Year 2000". However, at the level of implementation, the programmes of various governmental departments tend to get superimposed. Hence it is important to identify one of the Ministeries as the 'Nodal Ministry' for coordination and keeping abreast of all programmes related to women. The Ministry of Human Resource Development could perhaps take this up so that a Master Table could be prepared of all action/projects having a bearing on women, noting the time schedules - for implementation, and the agencies involved in planning and action at the central, state, regional local levels. This "Nodal Ministry" for women may constitute sub-committee with members drawn not only from government but also from other participating agencies to discuss the various issues and evolve strategies.

Service Structure

Creche services must be universally provided to all women, especially in the poverty sector. This would enable some of them to augment their family income and, at the same time, ensure proper care of their children. The children's health, sanitation, nutrition and early stimulation would get attention. Increasing the number of creches would also generate more employment opportunities for women. In view of the above, it is recommended that in rural areas, wherever ICDS infrastructure already exists, creches should be opened and attached to the Anganwadis. These creches should make provision for babies below 3 years age. The timings of Anganwadis which provide pre-school services for children of 3-6 years, should be adjusted according to the working hours of rural women. These creches will help in containing morbidity and mortality rates and malnutrition of infants and small children. They will also relieve the children in the school going age group from child care responsibilities, and give an opportunity to them to utilize the ICDS pre-school services.

The existing law that stipulates provision of a creche for employment of thirty or more women should be changed to thirty persons (men and women). This would ensure that employers do not use loopholes in the law to their advantage and would extend creche facilities to children of men workers whose wives, if they are not in the organized sector do not otherwise have access to such facilities.

The Government of India, being an employer of a large number of women, must provide creche facilities in or near all workplaces.

Creche service must follow an integrated approach to childcare.

Creche workers should preferably be local women to whom appropriate skill-oriented, on the job training should be imparted.

Technical institutions and home-science colleges should be utilized to train creche workers and also provide inputs for systematic monitoring and supervision of the creche programmes.

Organizations running creches should be given flexibility to adopt timings suitable to the needs of the working mothers.

Local women's groups and mothers of the children attending creches must be given training in preparation of toys, play materials out of low cost/no cost indigenous material. Employment for women can be generated by employing local women to prepare the midday meals, etc.

Action research projects, such as, a study of the impact of day care services on the education of girls should be initiated.

Home Front

Traditionally, women have had a significant role in resource management including housing management. It is important to recognize this role and provide for women's participation in development programmes, and for incorporating their needs in schemes for improvement of housing and environmental conditions in the following manner:

Identify the needs of women in relation to housing and community facilities and build them in an integrated manner into housing development programmes.

Integrate environmental factors into development planning for women including their requirements in settlement planning.

Involve women at all levels of decision making and bring about their participation in programme implementation so as to ensure that the benefits of housing, essential services, and community facilities are directed to women in general and to the poor and vulnerable among them in particular.

The special needs of women should be identified and adequately catered to while formulating minimum housing standards.

Necessary facilities in homes should be provided to lessen the burden and drudgery of women in performing productive and reproductive roles.

Priority investment in infrastructure such as water supply, sanitation, energy, transportation, working women's hostels, public distribution of basic needs, etc., should take into consideration the needs of women.

Provision of housing for working and/or single women is recommended on priority basis. In addition, women in difficult circumstances such as widows, refugees, destitutes, victims of social oppression, seasonal migrant workers, victims of natural disasters, etc., must be provided shelter as part of an integrated rehabilitation programme.

The National Housing Policy which has been formulated, must pay adequate attention to the special needs and roles of women in the implementation of housing programme.

The social and economic constraints which come in the way of women's participation should be removed and their active involvement in housing should be promoted by:

- Allotting house-sites in the joint name of wife and husband;

- Mobilizing savings of women for housing;

- Organizing self-help in undertaking house construction work;

- Imparting training so that women could become skilled labour (including masons and other skilled labour); and

- Ensuring access for women to institutional credit at low rates interest without collateral.

In India, rural women constitute nearly 80 per cent of the female population. They contribute largely to the country's economy which is mainly agriculture based. Although distributive justice has been categorically underlined in all the development plans, the needs of women have not been adequately addressed. While laying emphasis, on enhanced agriculture production in which the involvement of women is high, the plans have fostered a target group and area oriented approach to reduce regional and ecological imbalances disregarding women's equality as embodied in the Constitution. Rural development programmes for women have only in recent decades recognized the crucial role of organization and mobilization as strategies for women's empowerment and development. Rural women's organizations are also mechanisms for restructuring and redistributing power and have been utilized pressure groups that influence and/or bargain on behalf of rural women.

Assessment of Conditions

The launching of the Community Development Programme in 1952 was a landmark in the history of India and ushered in an era of development with the participation of the people. The Community Development Programme adopted a systematic integrated approach to rural development with a hierarchy of village level workers and block level workers drawn from various fields to enrich rural life. Agriculture, animal husbandry, public health, women's development, rural industries, etc., found a special niche in the framework cast for this purpose. Five thousand National Extension Service Blocks were created under the Community Development Programmes by the end of the Second Five-Year Plan. During the Third Five-Year Plan the momentum was maintained through a series of developmental schemes though allocations under the NES programme tapered. This was succeeded by the Small Farmers Development Agencies followed by Marginal Farmers Development Agencies, Crash Schemes for Rural Employment, Food for Work Programme, Drought Prone Areas Programme and Desert Development Programme in the early seventies. The contents of all these programmes were to strengthen the rural base of the economy, specifically the primary sector comprising agriculture, animal husbandry, etc., and employment through labour intensive works that would create the infrastructure of roads and other community assets for the benefit of the rural people.

It was recognized that the skewed pattern of landholdings stood in the way of creating an egalitarian society and obstructed modernization and intensification of agriculture. Land reform measures for abolition of intermediary tenures, tenancy reforms, imposition of land ceiling on agricultural holdings, distribution of surplus land to the landless agricultural workers and consolidation of landholdings were introduced through a series of State Legislations under Central guidelines.

Certain areas of the country are characterized by soil-erosion, water stress and environmental degradation. The Drought Prone Areas Programme was started in 1973 aiming at an integrated area development for optimum utilization of land, water, livestock and human resources through a watershed management approach to mitigate the effects of drought. A few years later the Desert Development Programme, a wholly centrally funded scheme, specifically to cover extremely arid areas for controlling desertification and restoration of ecological balance, was also started.

The emphasis shifted to fulfilling minimum needs of the people during the Fifth Five-Year Plan.

A systematic analysis and examination of the status and role of women within the agriculture and rural development strategies in India started with the National Plan of Action (NPA) for women which followed the report of the Committee on the Status of Women in India (CSWI). Subsequently, efforts of women activists, social science institutions and researchers produced enough documentary support to persuade the Sixth Plan document to include a chapter on 'Women and Development' for the first time in the country's history of planned development.

A strategy of direct attack on poverty was adopted in the Sixth Plan as the theory of trickle down benefits of general development programmes had not proved as a successful strategy for the removal of poverty. Forty-eight per cent of the population were found to be living below the poverty line at the beginning of the Sixth Five-Year Plan.

One positive outcome of these developments has been the recognition that rural women are not a homogeneous group to justify a uniform development strategy. The development plans in the case of women must be based on the assessment of their actual role and participation in socio-economic activities.

Women's employment has been recognized as the 'critical entry point' for Women's integration in mainstream development. The low and deteriorating status of rural women is attributed to their declining economic participation and other factors like the modernization of the agricultural sector. The need for giving a better deal to the rural women is beginning to be widely recognized. It is now accepted that the participation of women themselves in the development activities is the most effective tool for the promotion of the access of women to the benefits of development. A working group set up by the Deptt. of Rural Development, Ministry of Agriculture and Rural Development in 1978 recommended that the major objectives of the development plan for rural women should be: (i) The improvement of their economic status, and (ii) The promotion of women's organization to have the collective strength to articulate their needs and promote their participation in the development process.

The Integrated Rural Development Programme initiated in 1978-79 and extended to all the development blocks in the country in 1980-81 was conceived as one of the instruments for a direct attack on poverty. It dealt with individual rural families below the poverty line. Credit from banking institutions and subsidy from the Government were given to the families for self-employment and income generation. Under IRDP, a special place was accorded for training rural unemployed youth for employment with the introduction of TRYSEM. An exclusive scheme for the social and economic uplift of women belonging to families below the poverty line, DWCRA (Development of Women and Children in Rural Areas) was launched in 1982 as a sub-component of IRDR.

The Sixth Plan accepted poor rural women to be targets of rural development strategies. The specific problems identified concerning rural poor women were:

(i) Marginality of attention and services to them in rural and agricultural development;

(ii) Special constraints that obstruct their access to available assistance and services such as, lack of training to develop their awareness and skills; lack of information and lack of bargaining power;

(iii) Low productivity and narrow occupational choices;

(iv) Low level of participation in decision making;

(v) Inadequate finance and expert guidance for promoting socio-economic activity of rural women and their participation;

(vi) Inadequate monitoring of women's participation in different sectors;

(vii) Wage discrimination;

(viii) Inadequate application of science and technology to remove drudgery; and

(ix) Low health and nutrition status.

The Sixth Plan document stated that one of the most important means of achieving improvements in the status of women would be to secure for them a fair share of employment opportunities, to earmark a percentage of allocation for women, and to fix for them a quota in all the poverty alleviation programmes. The Seventh Plan reiterated the strategies suggested in the Sixth Plan with a sharper focus on the increased coverage of women in various rural development programmes.

Simultaneously, the National Rural Employment Programme (NREP), assuring wage employment to the unemployed rural population was introduced in 1980. Subsequently, concentration on the rural landless was attempted by the introduction of the Rural Landless Employment Guarantee Programme (RLEGP) in 1983. The Indira Awas Yojana was added as an important component of the programme in the Seventh Plan for constructing houses for SC/STs and free bonded labourers. Social Forestry was added as another component of the RLEGP with national emphasis on greening fuel and fodder.

The establishment of the Technology Mission on Drinking Water and Related Water Management gave a new thrust to the Rural Water Supply Programme. Safe and adequate drinking water is to be provided to the entire rural population by the end of the Seventh Five-Year Plan.

The impact of the poverty alleviation programmes coupled with the development in various sectors reduced the rural population below the poverty line to 37 per cent by the beginning of the Seventh Plan. The target is to bring this down to 28 per cent by the end of the Seventh Plan Period.

Agriculture and allied fields provide the largest sector for women's employment. It largely determines the rural women's socio-economic status. This is the sector where women's role as unpaid labour in productive activities is most prominent and is responsible for conferring women a non-working status. In case of both agriculture and animal husbandry, development strategies have provided very little attention to women in comparison to their active involvement in both the sectors. Some training is imparted to women in agriculture and animal husbandry under the programmes for Farmer's Training and Krishi Vigyan Kendras. But the Farmers Training Programme has lost much of its importance after the introduction of the new extension system of Training and Visit (T&V). Though women constitute a major work force in agriculture which with regional variation is estimated to be around 60 per cent, they are invisible in the T&V system. Currently there is one major extension programme for women in Karnataka and 2-3 such programmes on the anvil in other states. There is an in-built resistance observed in them in viewing women within their home making role. Even the visual presentations (slides, filmstrips and films) which are used for the orientation of the functionaries, often depict the women in the field and the extension agent talking to the contact farmer on the same field, fail to project the full dimension of women's role.

While rural women have become marginally visible in the anti-poverty programmes, they have not been adequately recognized in agricultural development, land reform, or rural industrialization. Non-recognition of women in agriculture has many implications. Intensive agriculture and the green revolution have reduced women's participation in farm activities but the work load related to the home based farm activities has increased considerably. That has only reduced them from the 'working' to a 'non-working' status. Limited employment opportunities created by technology resulting in the means of production being concentrated in the hands of a few, and increased landlessness for the poor led to men replacing women in many of their traditional areas of employment. But women have had to work and survive. They are thus found to be gradually moving to the non-traditional sectors seeking employment for survival.

Following the Sixth and Seventh Plans, the Department of Rural Development issued directives to the State Governments to give priority to women headed households, enhance the share of women under the anti-poverty programme (IRDP), and the programme of Training for Self-Employment (TRYSEM). Guidelines for NREP and RLEGP envisage increasing participation of women in wage employment and creation of assets specific to the needs of women's groups. At present the share of employment generated under NREP for women is approximately 20 per cent. A special programme for women entitled DWCRA was also introduced in 1982, as a sub-component of IRDP to accelerate the process of integration of women in the rural development programmes. Up to 1987, there were 11,553 groups which were reported to have been organized in 106 districts under this scheme.

The Integrated Rural Development Programme meant for the poorest in the rural areas has been formulated for creating assets with a view to increasing the productivity and income generation abilities of the beneficiaries. Efforts have been made under this programme to select female headed households. The scheme of DWCRA could be strengthened and modified in order to ensure that the benefits reach more target groups. The National Rural Employment Programme (NREP) and Rural Landless Employment Guarantee Programme (RLEGP) would generate additional employment to women in the lean season. Under Training of Rural Youth in Self-Employment (TRYSEM), one-third of the beneficiaries were expected to be women and special attention was to be given to improve existing skills of women and imparting to them new skills under the programmes of farmers training, fodder production, post harvest technology, application of pesticide, budding and grafting, training in horticulture, fisheries, poultry, dairy and social forestry, etc. The training of women under TRYSEM exceeded the target to 44 per cent in January 1988. Out of a total of 37.23 lakh families which received benefits under the IRDP during 1986-87, the number of women headed families was 5.67 lakh which amounts to only 15.23 per cent as against the target of 30 per cent. On assessment of the programmes, it is observed that considerable efforts are required to elicit the participation of women in these activities. The training provided under TRYSEM and DWCRA is not always viable and there is a tendency to limit to a few traditional crafts, though the Department of Rural Development is laying greater stress on taking up innovative activities too. Therefore, a fresh look is needed to be given to identification of trades and activities which may gainfully be taken up by women. Many income generating programmes have not succeeded due to full thought not being given to the input availability, training and marketing of products.

Special development projects linked to certain ongoing activities need to be taken up on a project basis to improve the effectiveness of the programmes related to women. Specific projects such as sericulture for tribals in certain states like Bihar and Orissa, development of dairy units linked to Operation Flood areas, fruits and vegetables cultivation linked to marketing through Mother dairy, prawn farming and fishing in the coastal region were commended. Agro-based industry schemes, etc., are essential.

The scheme of Training of Rural Youth for Self-Employment (TRYSEM) should be revamped with a view to organizing training in trades with assured employment potential to women in rural areas, as well as for wage employment in peripheral metropolitan and urban areas. State Emporia, marketing channels of KVXIC, etc., should be tapped to ensure elimination of middlemen and better prices.

The Accelerated Rural Water Supply Programme (ARWSP) and the Minimum Needs Programme (MNP) are of special significance to rural women who are the victims of drudgery, such as fetching water from distant locations. The Technology Mission on Drinking Water and Related Water Management lays emphasis on purification of water to make it potable, training in the use of water and maintenance of water sources. Women are the target of the awareness creation programmes as well as agents for creating awareness in conservation of water and maintenance of water sources. The low cost sanitation programme is also of great importance to women, who are otherwise subjected to a lot of privation due to lack of appropriate sanitation facilities. Rural Technologies and innovation promoted by CAPART aim at relieving the drudgery to women in several areas of their households and economic activities. They include the improved varieties of stone grinder, wheel barrow, ball-bearing pulley, groundnut shelter and smokeless chulhas.

The limited performance of the programmes introduced to achieve the integration of women in the development process suggests that only policy directives do not achieve the desired objectives. Programmes do not get implemented due to the lack of comprehension of the relevance of women's contribution to national development. Although a concern for development of women is well articulated at the central policy making level, an ambivalence is observed at the implementation level. The policy directives issued by the Government of India for the increased share for women in the development programmes and the promotion of a participatory approach, do not provide for corresponding development in the infrastructure, extension, training information support and a strong monitoring system which is particularly lacking at the State level. The programmes for rural women still continue as a separate exercise within the sectoral programmes with marginal attention, resources and inadequate monitoring.

The major shortcomings noticed in the implementation of the programmes for women with development objectives are:

(i) Perpetuation of the concept that women need only welfare services;

(ii) That the developmental benefits will automatically accrue to the women as a result of economic development of the family;

(iii) Inadequate knowledge and skills for designing socioeconomic activities for women and in group organizations; and

(iv) Lack of supportive services such as credit, childcare, marketing, training and technology for reducing the drudgery.

Strategic Issues

The approaches used for integrating women in the mainstream of development have raised some methodological issues. These relate particularly to the organization of groups, involvement of the voluntary sector, and the household approach in development programmes for rural women.

The organization of women's groups is considered to be one of the most effective tools for integrating women in the development process. Yet it has raised several issues which are not fully resolved. Some of the questions which are being asked repeatedly are:

(i) Who will organize the groups (the role of intermediaries)?

(ii) What will be the size, structure and status of groups formal or informal?

(iii) Should the groups be organized first and the choice of activities to be undertaken by the groups come next?

(iv) Should women be assisted individually under the IRDP, etc. or be formed into groups.

Apart from these unresolved issues, there are problems in selecting and working out economically viable group projects. Women activists argue against giving individual projects to be carried out within the household as it would only perpetuate their subordination in the household hierarchy. They claim that assistance to the voluntary agencies, which was expected to provide grass-roots structural support in this regard, is either not forthcoming or has not been sought.

It is logical that the size of the group to be mobilized should be such as to enable close interaction amongst the members which is only possible when they come from the same background and from one cluster of villages. It is also evident that poor women acquire confidence when they get organized. The delivery system will respond positively even if they are informally grouped. But in the interest of economic viability, and to strengthen their earning capacity, it is desirable for the group to be formalized. It is however, impossible or advisable to suggest one organizational model for all situations. The experience by and large is that the organization based on personal interface and on localized issues is more effective, more flexible and functional than the highly structured and impersonal form of organization.

Some of the processes under IRDP, such as identification of beneficiaries/ productive activities, preparation of loan applications, sanction of the same and procurement of assets have not been given much attention in terms of proper planning, particularly of the linkage required after the asset is given, to make the same optimally productive. Such linkages include most critically the supply of raw materials and facilities for marketing. These processes and linkages are more effective when implemented through the group approach.

The crucial question in the field of land reforms is how rural poor women should get land and have access to land. Power structures in the villages are dominated by the relatively better off classes. Considering that implementation of land reforms measures leaves much to be desired, there is an urgent need for people's participation more specifically of the women, by promoting their groups organizations and through Panchayati Raj institutions. Each village should have a village plan which should include cultivable lands, *gochar* lands and forest lands with clearly demarcated boundaries.

The involvement of intermediaries in development programmes for rural women has been considered vital, particularly in demonstrating and promoting the participatory model and to provide support to the grass-root structure. Here too, there are basic issues which need to be carefully resolved. Among others, it is queried whether the role of the intermediary organizations has been understood by the Government, or whether it is feasible for the voluntary organizations to function in partnership with the government, given the differences in approach.

There is no uniform understanding and acceptance of the role of the voluntary agencies in the States. In some cases, there is a complete lack of rapport between the Government and voluntary agencies. In others, there is the tendency of associating the women's programmes entirely with voluntary action, showing a lack of initiative on the part of the, Government. There is little doubt that the voluntary agencies are committed to the cause of women and have expressed a real concern for the enhancement of women's status. They have also demonstrated skills for mobilizing women, and in trying innovative projects. In view of this, the association of the voluntary agencies with the programmes is bound to enrich the programmes as well as the delivery mechanisms. Yet, they cannot be a substitute for Governmental action. To end women's isolation from rural development, the Government must work in partnership with voluntary agencies.

Currently debated issues in the context of women in rural development and in the anti-poverty programmes, is the household versus group approach; some argue in favour of ensuring a share of developmental resources and benefits to women in all sectoral programmes, while others argue in favour of having separate investments for women.

In India, the family is hierarchical, traditional and the status in the family is determined by sex and age. In the patriarchal society, it is the man who holds the position of the head of the family and the bread-winner. Therefore, it is the man who gets attention in the investment of developmental resources, training, extension and other supports. Women's contribution to the family's earnings goes unrecognized. This bias, in fact, is responsible for the earlier programmes not taking note of women headed households whose number is currently estimated at 30-35 per cent of all rural households. With mounting pressure on the government to give priority to this group, it has been convincingly argued that an improvement in the income of the household does not necessarily mean development for women. The household approach instead of creating equitable conditions, perpetuates the subordination of women and limits their opportunities for self-growth and self-expansion.

Having a special component within sectoral plans can stimulate action for women provided the components are monitored separately. The introduction of the scheme of DWCRA within the programme of IRDP was aimed at stimulating the response of the State Governments to integrating women into anti-poverty programmes. Therefore, in case of women, it can be contended that a combined approach is desirable. This would allow women to be adopted as a target in all sectoral programmes, with earmarked resources along with special component plans aimed exclusively at women. Such dual approaches can be continued until women acquire sufficient power to articulate their needs and demands, and until such time as women's concerns get to be internalized in the planning and administrative structures.

Land Ownership

In the economic sphere and in particular in the rural sector, the empowerment of women relates mainly to their access to means of production and control over the fruits of their labour. The access to the means of production implies ownership of land, other productive assets, access to capital and access to technology and acquisition of various skills required to make labour power more productive.

The aspect of ownership of land relates to rights of inheritance which are governed by personal laws of different communities. These personal laws at present are discriminatory against women and have a bias in favour of the male heirs. The State Governments of Kerala and Andhra Pradesh have sought to remove some of these discriminations with a view to give daughters in the family, coparcenary ownership in the family property on the same level as the sons. But even these changes do not go far enough and still discriminate against a married daughter and a widow and do not apply equally to the separate properties of the father in the Hindu Customary Law. There is discrimination against women of different types in the personal laws of other communities also. In the customary law of certain tribes, only male agnates in the male line are recognized as valid heirs and an unmarried daughter is only entitled to usufructuary maintenance. It would be necessary to introduce correctives to overcome the discrimination, in order that the gap between the State's proclamation to achieve equality of the sexes and its laws which deny it, is bridged. Women's undiluted access to land, the most productive resource, would undoubtedly bestow on her necessary economic independence and power and would improve her social position in the family as well.

Regarding access of women to land, the land records do not incorporate the rights of women in the landed property shown in the name of the husband or the father. Only where a woman is a widow and happens to be the 'karta' of the family, her name may figure in the record of rights as the owner of property.

Co-ownership of property by women, should not merely be confined to land but also to other productive assets like house, family wealth, shops, factory or any other income generating establishment or asset. This would provide sufficient conditions for women to participate in and influence the decision concerning the use and disposal of such properties.

As regards access to capital, there is a general reluctance on the part of the public financial institutions to extend credit to women independently of the male head or guardian of the family.

The existing land ownership pattern in India is largely male oriented except in some areas of the North-east and a few other places where matrilineal system is in operation and inheritance of property passes through the institution of the mother. The land records, to the extent they reflect the ownership and other interests in land, only record the names of men. Similarly, where shareholders of such lands are recorded, it is usually the male shareholder who finds mention in the land records. The processes of preparation of land records, i.e., the survey and recording of rights also deal with such male holders of interests in land. The only exception would be in such cases where a widow with no other male person, manages the land. Her name is recorded as the owner and manager of land. Land reform measures have also not taken into cognizance interests of women as co-owners or cultivators of land, and to this extent land reform measures seem to have bypassed the women. The most prominent example where this inherent discrimination in land reforms has been noticed is the case of ceiling laws where most State laws have provided for a separate unit of ceiling for major sons in the family but not major daughters married or unmarried. Although from the point of view of implementation of such ceiling laws, addition of yet another unit in the name of major daughters would have further defeated its objectives, nonetheless, the discrimination cannot be denied. Further, in the matter of distribution and allotment of various lands, it is usually the male head of the family who gets the 'patta' in his name. Recently, of course instructions have been issued to give joint 'patta' on the name of both husband and wife while allotting land and house-sites. Similarly, in the matter of collection of minor forest produce and enjoyment of rights over common property resources, the rights of women are not focused, even though it is the women, who have to collect fuel-wood and fodder and minor forest produce from such lands.

Tribal social structures are more egalitarian and open and less stratified than social structures of larger and more advanced communities in India. The status and position enjoyed by tribal women in society is, therefore, in certain tribes, much better than their counterparts in other communities. This is on account of many reasons. Tribal society has a tradition of both men and women working on an equal footing whether in agriculture or in other vocations. Thus tribal women have access to income and are therefore, economically independent. There are also no restrictions on women going out for work independent of men, and not necessarily along with them. Usually tribal women go out for work in large groups. In social matters and family life also tribal women are far more emancipated. They have a much greater say in the decision making in family and community matters and are not subjected to the same degree of social control by male members of the family as women in other communities are.

Despite this, in matters of inheritance of father's/husband's property and in access to land, there is a certain built-in discrimination against women in some tribal communities. The customary law of some tribal communities excludes women from inheritance rights, such inheritance rights being restricted to "male heirs in the male line". These customs are even enshrined in tenancy laws wherever enacted and applicable to these communities. This discrimination against women has a harmful effect on their lives, rendering them economically and socially powerless and driving large numbers of them into destitution. Infact, in certain tribal communities, for example, the Ho Tribe in Singhbhum district of Bihar, a large number of women remain unmarried so as to ensure to themselves usufructuary rights available to them as unmarried daughters. Many of them are harassed by their husband's and father's male agnates who wish to deprive them even of this usufructuary right. A number of women are forced to migrate in order to earn their livelihood, since their hold over the family land is so insecure and dependent on the attitude of their male relatives even though these women do the bulk of agricultural work. Sometimes, the women are declared witches, the concealed motive being to drive them out of the village or even to kill them in order to usurp the family property.

The married women also enjoy limited usufructuary rights in the deceased husband's property. Even these usufructuary rights cannot be freely exercised by them since the husband's male agnates often harass them and try to get rid of them in the hope of asserting their inheritance claims to the land. If the married woman has a son, he inherits the land from his father, and she has no legal claim to it. If the husband has one or two or more wives, the sons of other wives have inheritance rights to the land, and she is dependent on them for maintenance. In case, the marriage breaks up, or a man remarries or deserts his first wife, the woman is absolutely without land rights, since she has, by marriage, lost the usufructuary rights in her father's house, and she is also deprived of rights in her matrimonial home. Since tribal communities have their customary laws, the Hindu Succession Act, the Indian Succession Act, or any other succession Act do not apply to them.

The discrimination against women in the customary law of tribal communities, historically speaking, may have evolved with a view to preserve the integrity of the tribe and to prevent land passing from the tribal to persons outside the tribe which would have the effect of disintegrating the tribal society. While, it is necessary to preserve the integrity of the tribe and to protect the interest of the tribals in land against any encroachment by non-tribals, it is also necessary to protect the interest of tribal women in land by giving them rights to inheritance in father's and husband's property. But safeguards will have to be provided in the event of marriages outside the tribe.

Therefore, provision in law and customary practices which discriminate against women in matters of inheritance of property and restrict such inheritance to male agnates in male line should be changed, while at the same time preserving alienation of tribal land to non-tribals.

Women, especially tribals, migrate in search of work. They are employed in large numbers in the unorganized sector like brick-kiln, road construction, irrigation works, agricultural operations, forestry operations, stonecutting, domestic labour, etc. They are subjected to brutal exploitation at places of work by contractors and the middlemen, who recruit them. The exploitation is not merely confined to payment of low wages, long hours of arduous work and other dismal working conditions. They are also subjected to sexual exploitation. It is necessary, that for each category of employment in the unorganized sector, specific institutional mechanism be built-in to protect women's interests.

New Schemes and Programmes

Poverty alleviation in the rural sector remain central. It is targeted to bring down the percentage of rural poor below 10 per cent by 2000 A.D. The Department of Rural Development has already suggested that in case of women, poverty alleviation goals for the new millennium should be to:

(i) Bring all women-headed households (estimated to be 30-35 per cent) above the poverty line; and

(ii) Attain the target of having women constitute 30 per cent of all beneficiaries to be assisted under IRDR.

In addition, the endeavour should be to bring in the women's development dimension into the sectors particularly, agriculture and allied sectors which have hitherto not responded adequately to women's needs. Women's access to productive resources must also be ensured.

Political power and access to positions of decision making and authority are critical prerequisites for women's equality in the processes of nation building. Hence it is crucial that the representation of women in local bodies up to the district level be ensured.

Care for Health

Women's health status is basic to their advance in all fields of endeavour. Any serious attempt to improve the health of women must deal firstly with biased social customs and cultural traditions that have an impact on their health status. Though the health problems of women have been identified for priority attention and efforts made for maternal and child services since the beginning of planned development in India, much remains to be done to improve health care for women both in qualitative and quantitative terms. However, in subsequent plan periods it has been observed that resource allocations for health have been decreasing. There is need for a more comprehensive integrated approach to health issues if there is to be a significant impact on the present conditions of Indian women.

The cultural norms that specially affect women's health are the attitudes to marriage, age of marriage, the value attached to fertility and sex of the child, the pattern of family organizations and the ideal role demanded of women by social conventions. They determine her place within the family, the degree of her access to medical care, education, nutrition and other accessories of health. Improvements in female health status are, therefore, critically dependent on a number of non-health development components such as education, opportunities for skill-building, income generation and decision making and the availability of basic support services to carry out women's multiple roles. Thus it is essential to address the causes of women's ill-health. Measures to improve the social and health situation would have to form an integral part of a multi-sectoral package operationalized simultaneously, in complementary thrusts. Earlier analysis have emphasized this aspect. But gaps have existed in preceding plans and even more in the implementation of strategies.

The demographic trends are important indicators of women's health status. The sex ratio which illumines the survival scene for women versus men was 933 females per 1000 males in 1981. Not only is this ratio unfavourable, but its steady decline from 972 in 1902 to 930 in 1971 is a cause for great concern. Marginal improvement has taken place in the last decade, but even today fourteen States and Union Territories have less females per 1000 males then the national average and in eleven States and Union Territories, the ratio has further declined.

Life expectancy has increased over the decade from 44.7 years in 1971 to 54.7 in 1980 for women. It was estimated to be slightly higher in 1980 for women than men: 54.7 and 54.1 years at birth respectively. A general reduction in female mortality, as well as the greater differentials in death rate was observed over 1970-82 in both rural and urban areas. However age specific death rates indicate higher mortality for female children and women for every five-year period till 35 years of age. This higher mortality experience of female children and younger adult women during the prime reproductive years is largely preventable through appropriate health and other interventions, and points to the continuing neglect of female health.

Women face high risk of malnutrition, retardation in growth and development, disease, disability and even death at three critical stages in their lives, viz., infancy, early childhood and adolescence and the reproductive phase. In old age, they face threats of cancer, breast cancer and uterus cancer and menopause related problems.

Care for Children

Discrimination starts even before birth in the form of sex determination tests misusing the high technology of amniocentisis, resulting in a new kind of femicide, i.e., abortion of female foetuses. A survey carried out in Bombay during 1984 revealed that out of 8,000 abortions 7,999 were of female foetuses. Considering that this test facility has spread to even small towns and people from rural as well as urban areas are utilizing it, the magnitude of the problem can be imagined.

Micro studies have shed light on the fact that sex is the main determinant of infant nutrition, irrespective of economic development. It is worse in a situation of poverty. Studies indicate that while both boys and girls get less than recommended daily dietary allowances, girls are more deficient and suffer more from related disorders and illnesses. However, more girls go without treatment when ill, than boys.

Boys are breast-fed longer, given more of weaning foods, and get a bigger share of whatever food is available. Consequently, although the female children are biologically stronger when born, their morbidity and mortality rates are worse than that of male children. Age specific death rates are higher for female children, as noted earlier. Whereas, no male/female break-up is available for immunization rates, the total figures themselves are low. By 1982, only 25 per cent of all children below 3 years were given DPT, 5 per cent of infants were immunized against Polio, and 65 per cent were given BCG.

The shadow of the girl child's deprivation looms throughout her later life, but most particularly increases her vulnerability to the risks of child bearing, which in turn create risks for the child to be born. Thus is set into motion the vicious cycle of deprivation, debilitation, disease and disability. Leading to greater deprivation and debilitation and often death. That is the depressing lot of a significant numbers of mothers and children today.

Care for Boys and Girls

As girls attain puberty, they go through a second spurt of growth when their bodies grow much more rapidly to prepare them for child-bearing. But unfortunately, in addition to the poor economic conditions, their gender denies them proper nutrition. Even in situations where food is available, girls are taught to eat less so that they remain slim to rate better in the marriage market. Nutritional deprivation at all growth stages gets compounded during the inset of puberty resulting in severe growth retardation in girl children.

The half grown, uneducated, adolescent girl is married early and becomes pregnant soon. Teenage pregnancy interrupts the physiological growth spurt which brings a girl to her genetically determined maximum stature. As of 1981, 7 per cent of girls in the age group 10-14 and 43 per cent in the age group 15-19 were already married. They enter into sexual life and child bearing with no knowledge about sex and the reproduction process. As estimated, 10-15 per cent of all the annual births (around 25 million) are attributed to these teenage mothers. With their malnourished status, small pelvis, under-nutrition, and overwork during pregnancy, these adolescent mothers run a high risk of life. Their babies are of low birth weight and suffer risk of mortality many times higher than those of fully grown, well nourished, educated mothers.

Girls who marry before the age 18 are twice as likely to end up with a large family than those who marry after completing 20 years, and therefore not only face much higher risks in pregnancy when they first conceive, but also compounded risks and related ill-health over their lifetimes.

The Indian woman on an average has 8-9 pregnancies, resulting in a little over six births, of which 4-5 survive. She is estimated to spend 80 per cent of her reproductive years in pregnancy and lactation.

Dietary surveys have shown that the intake of women in low income groups is deficient by 500 to 600 calories. The corresponding findings for pregnant and lactating women reveal daily deficiency of 1100 calories and 1000 calories respectively.

Deficits in nutrient intakes have been observed in various occupational groups, particularly in those without land and are labourers. Women belonging to the lower socio-economic groups gain around 3-5 kgs. during pregnancy as against 10 kgs. in the developed countries. Over 50 per cent of pregnant women have a haemoglobin level of less than 10 grams. Anaemia in pregnancy accounts directly for 15-20 per cent of all maternal deaths in India, and indirectly for a much larger proportion.

With the fairly high fertility levels during the reproductive span prevailing in India, maternal mortality accounts for the largest to near largest proportion of deaths among women in their prime years. Official estimates place maternal mortality at 400-500 per 100,000 live births but figures as high as 1000-1200 have been reported from certain rural areas. A woman in the subcontinent runs a lifetime risk of 1 in 18 of dying from a pregnancy related cause. Anaemia, haemorrhage, toxemia, sepsis, and abortion are the major causes of maternal deaths in India. It has been estimated that 70 per cent of these deaths can be prevented. Multiparity increases maternal illnesses and deaths which rise significantly with the fourth pregnancy and reach very high levels after the fifth. In India, 38.4 live births in rural areas and 33.0 live births in urban areas are of the fourth order and above.

Accurate assessments of maternal morbidity are unavailable but evidence from available studies point to an appallingly high incidence of pregnant women not in contact with health services.. Around 71.1 per cent of deliveries in rural areas and 29.2 per cent of deliveries in urban areas are conducted by untrained personnel outside the health system. In Rajasthan, one-third of pregnant women reported illnesses lasting on an average for over two weeks. The maternal mortality rate was 592 per 100,000 live births; for every maternal death some 60 episodes were related directly to pregnancy and childbirth and together represented both the leading cause and over a quarter of overall morbidity.

Abortion has been legalized in India as a health measure since 1972 by the Medical Termination of Pregnancy Act, 1971.

Even so, because of non-availability of MTP services within easy reach for most of the rural population and ignorance of the law, 'illegal' abortions continue to be performed by incompetent persons under unhygienic conditions. As a result, abortion-related mortality and morbidity remain major problems. Only 507,719 terminations were performed through the health services in 1986-87 which is around 9 per cent of the induced abortions that were likely to have been performed during the same period. Since the inception of the programme, 5.1 million abortions have been performed under the MTP programme, which is less than the total number of induced abortions likely to be performed in one year. Induced abortions indicate an unmet need of women for family planning, highlight a gap between the availability of services and their accessibility to those in need, and demonstrate women's inability to make use of the services they need acutely.

Respite from pregnancy, and rest and care during pregnancy emerge as major needs. Studies have clearly shown that women engaged in hard physical labour during pregnancy did not gain much weight, and delivered low-birth-weight babies, as compared with women doing less work but having the same food intake. One study on energy consumption and expenditure per household per day, found the energy expenditure to be 5.68 units for men, 9.69 for women and about 3 for children. The major part of domestic energy consumption was for survival-cooking, fetching water, firewood, etc. Technology for reduction of drudgery in women, and providing water, and fuel within the easy reach of all, could go a long way in energy conservation for women.

Hardly any information is available for the health hazards of women engaged in different occupations, in agriculture and industries, birth during pregnant and non-pregnant states. In agriculture, they are exposed to heat and rain and have to work in standing and bending postures for long hours, which are hazardous to health. They also work in large numbers in industries such as beedi, carpet, jute, coir weaving, slate, electronics, etc. Micro studies have indicated that workers of these industries suffer from several health hazards.

The health services for children and women, particularly during pregnancy, childbirth and after are inadequate. About 40 per cent of pregnant women receive tetanus toxoid. Although data are unavailable separately on the proportion of pregnant mothers receiving iron and folic acid, it is roughly estimated that around 25 per cent of pregnant and nursing mothers receive iron and folic acid. About 46 per cent of pregnant women are estimated to register for antenatal care. Facilities and basic equipment for mid-wives have been found to be grossly inadequate.

The situation regarding women's health may be summarized as:

(i) Major disparities in health care in population groups in rural and urban areas; remote, backward, hilly and desert areas; and in socio-economically deprived groups.

(ii) Social attitudes and prejudices inherent in our milieu which are unfavourable towards girls and women, effect their health and nutrition negatively.

(iii) Poor health of women due to the synergistic effects of high levels of infection, malnutrition and uncontrolled fertility extending over a prolonged span.

(iv) Inadequate basic health care facilities (including facilities for MCH, family planning, MTP and nutrition) for women and children, in terms of outreach, range of services, quality, availability, etc.

(v) Inefficient use of resources available for health care of women, resulting in a slower pace of health development for them.

(vi) Ignorance and lack of knowledge related to health nutrition and family planning, affecting self-help efforts in health; and resulting in underutilization of existing resources.

(vii) Absence or inadequacy of essential non-health facilities which affect health, such as potable water, sanitation; female education; food supply, etc.

Health care has been accepted as an important intervention for women's development since the First Five-Year Plan. It was recognized that the high infant and maternal mortality would have to be reduced through the provision of maternal and child health services and family planning. The basic strategy for providing health care to the general population as well as women, in the 1950's during the first and second plan periods included:

(i) Expansion of physical infrastructure for health (including opening MCH centres);

(ii) Initiating the family planning programme;

(iii) Communicable disease control (for malaria, filaria, tuberculosis, leprosy and venereal diseases); and

(iv) Establishing facilities for training (attention was given to training female health personnel including nurses, auxilliary nurse midwives, health visitors and dais) and having more manpower.

The need to link hospitals at different levels into an effective coordinated hospital system, and correlate their functions with those of "clinics, domiciliary care services and public health activities", was recognized. The maternity centres which were established during the first two plan periods, were to be linked up with district and referral hospitals. MCH services in urban areas were generally provided through maternity and child health centres, in isolation from the rest of the services. 4500 maternity centres had been established, one-third of which were in urban areas; and about 2800 health units were also established in rural areas. In rural areas, the "health units" in the block were expected to provide MCH services in addition to other health services. During the decade 1950-60, female health personnel were increasingly trained and employed, which resulted in availability of 27,000 nurses (from 5,000 in 1950); 19,900 auxiliary nurse midwives (from 8,000 in 1950); 1,500 lady health visitors (from 52 in 1950) and 11,500 nurse-dais and dais (from 1,800 in 1950). From the First Plan itself, family limitation and spacing of children were noticed to be "essential steps for securing better care in bringing up children, and therefore, as an important part of public health." Though initially, family planning services were provided primarily through specialized family planning clinics, the need to integrate it with the general health services was realized; and when the fourth plan was put forth, maternity and child health services were stated to be integrated with family planning.

The basic strategies for health care in terms of expansion of physical infrastructure, training more female health personnel, communicable disease control and family planning were continued during the Third and Fourth Plan periods. Specific prophylaxis programmes were initiated to prevent anaemia in pregnant women, and vitamin deficiency in children 1-5 years of age during this period. Also, programmes were started to control smallpox were also formulated, which included a component for instruction of school teachers.

The primary objective of the Fifth Five-Year Plan was to provide minimum public health facilities integrated with family planning and nutrition for vulnerable groups - children, pregnant women and lactating mothers. The accent during this period was similar to previous plan periods - increasing the accessibility of health services to rural areas; correcting regional imbalances; development of referral systems for health care; and communicable disease control. The need for qualitative improvement in the education and training of health personnel was also recognized. Several schemes were initiated during this period to give increased emphasis to the health of mothers. The Integrated Child Development Services Scheme was accepted for countrywide application in 1977. Though primarily for child development, this scheme provides a package of health, nutrition and family planning services for pregnant women and nursing mothers who are socio-economically deprived. Since a large proportion of deliveries are conducted by traditional birth attendants (TBAs) particularly in rural areas, a scheme was initiated during this time to train them for safer mid-wifery practices; the target was to have atleast one TBA per 1000 population. In order to involve the community in health care, and to further promotive and preventive health care at village level, the health guides scheme was initiated. The norm of one health guide per 1000 population was suggested.

The guiding principles for the first two and a half decade of planned development in health in India included measures to:

(i) Make health services more accessible to the population;

(ii) Developing the needed human resources;

(iii) Provision of services for health, including maternal and child health, and family planning.

Over time, the need to interact more closely with people has been felt, and somewhat more emphasis was given to preventive and promotive aspects of health care.

Governmental Actions

The Committee on the status of women in India highlighted the impact of social attitudes on the health of women, which clearly revealed the poorer lot of women, from the time of birth. The demographic analysis brought into sharp focus the deterioration in the condition of the majority of women despite the advances in medical care and the general improvement in health services, pointing to the criticality of the social conditions.

On the health side, it was pointed out that more resources were being spent for curative than preventive and promotive services; and that major rural/urban and regional disparities existed in health care was noted to be an unfortunate distortion. The report further underlined that lack of security and mobility are major problems of female health personnel in rural areas.

However, their recommendations, while emphasizing the need for an integrated thrust for MCH, nutrition and family planning, were limited mainly to upgrading the posts of MCH officers at Central and State levels; the provision of a separate budget for MCH and separate units for MCH at primary health centres. Some modifications in the MTP Act were also recommended. However, while the legislative aspects were gone into detail, the main problems with medical termination of pregnancy, that is the wide availability of services and ignorance of the law, did not get sufficient attention. Altogether, while the analysis of problems was a powerful indictment of the existing situation, this was not matched by comprehensive suggestion to bring about the desired changes in women's health.

The National Plan of Action recognized that the health profile of women (and girls) in India was poor. While giving attention to the salient issues in the social and health areas, it did not however, develop the needed coordinated thrust for actions in each sector converging to achieve common goals. In fact, while emphasizing that the plans of action would have to cover a wide spectrum of programmes and needed to integrate with other strategies, it did not even attempt to provide any directions and made the action plans for health under six separate categories, namely: (1) Provision of Services; (2) Development of the needed human resources; (3) Mass Education Programmes; (4) Legislative Measures (5)Role of Voluntary Organizations; and (6)Areas of Research

Broadly, it stated that services for women, including mothers and female children, should be part of the general health system. It was recommended that the physical infrastructure be expanded and manpower for health care be augmented. However, their emphasis on the qualitative aspects of maternal care as well as training was inadequate. The necessary infrastructure strengthening at village, primary and secondary levels, linked by an affective referral system, did not receive much attention. Instead, they recommended the establishment of various types of clinics. The need to modify medical undergraduate curriculum, in order to cater to the needs of mothers and children in rural areas, was rightly stressed, so also, the need to orient doctors in services. The TBA was identified as one of the most important person, in the provision of maternity services, and steps to involve her were outlined. The Committee underlined the need to have mass education programmes for mother and child care. Several legislative measures were suggested.

They referred to the MTP Act, age of marriage, and provision of MCH services in municipalities and local bodies. However, the main issue remains operationalizing the law, ensuring that the necessary developments take place. This includes better services for MTP, specially in rural areas; more resources for MCH services through local bodies; and providing education as well as income generating opportunities to women to raise the age of marriage. Some legislative measures have been taken to ensure that advertisement of baby foods is curbed - this was also a recommendation. The committee suggested some areas, in which the voluntary organizations could be involved, such as school health services, MCH care in urban slums, training health workers and information dissemination. Though some efforts have been made to involve them, much more remains to be done on this aspect. Areas for research were suggested, on which only limited action has, followed.

During the Sixth and Seventh Plans, the major strategies for health care, including that for women, continued to be: (i)Expansion of physical infrastructure; (ii)Increasing the availability of trained health manpower; (iii)Strengthening services for communicable disease control, as well as other diseases; and (iv)Provision of family planning as well as MCH services.

During the Sixth Five-Year Plan period, in 1983, the National Health Policy was formulated and accepted for implementation. The policy for the first time, defined goals for women's health; reduction in maternal mortality, crude rate and crude birth rate; coverage with antenatal care and immunization of pregnant mothers, and the control of leprosy, tuberculosis and blindness (from which women also suffer), were specified. The levels to be achieved over time were also specified. The policy stated that:

"the highest priority" would have to be given to "efforts of launching special programmes" for the improvement of maternal and child health, with a special focus on the less privileged sections of the society. Such programmes would require to be decentralized to the maximum possible extent, their delivery being at the primary level, nearest to the doorsteps of the beneficiaries. While efforts should continue for providing refresher training and orientation to the traditional birth attendants, schemes and programmes should be launched to ensure that progressively all deliveries are conducted by competently trained persons, and that complicated cases receive timely and expert attention, within a comprehensive programme providing antenatal, intra-natal and postnatal care. Also, organized school health services, integrally linked with a general, preventive and curative services, would require to be established within time-limited programmes.

The Seventh Five-Year Plan clearly stated that primary health care will be the main sphere of action in health. It was stated that 'women would be organized around available economic activities to enable them to actively participate in the entire process of socioeconomic development, including health.' Care of pregnant and nursing mothers, young children and school-age children (both in and out of school) was stated to be a priority.

Major Issues

Some of the critical factors and issues related to women's health have evidently not received the necessary attention in the existing health programmes, Girls need adequate care so that they can enter motherhood without physical and social inadequacies. Optimal reproductive and child-bearing patterns (age of the mother at first childbirth - 20 years; interval between pregnancies at least 3 years; a small family; and no pregnancy after 35 years of age, which influence the health of mothers and their children) need to be advocated, and backed by policies that make them feasible for women. Measures to reduce the workload of women have to be promoted to conserve their energy. Adequate and appropriate information for decision-making, particularly during pregnancy and lactation, needs to be made available.

Recognizing that the renewal of the human race is the unique contribution that women make at considerable personal cost to the nation's existence and productivity, it must be taken as a national obligation to ensure that the fulfilment of this role occurs with minimum personal risk to women's lives and health. Control, over reproduction is a basic right for all women, as this right forms an important basis for the enjoyment of other rights. The enormous wastage of female life and well-being occurring at present has, however, been demonstrated to be containable within human capacity and existing resources.

Women are victims of possessive syndrome and many other kinds of neurosis. The majority of women face mental depressions due to family related problems which are the outcomes of the present social attitudes. Particularly, in the rural areas, such depressions are believed as "possessed by spirits". This encourages many cruel practices and treatment which often lead to physical harm to the women. The primary health centres are ill-equipped to deal with even simple mental disorders.

With rapid urbanization and commercialization, the nutritious foods produced in the villages like fruits, vegetables, milk and so forth are being exported to urban areas thereby denying them to the rural poor. Growing poverty in the countryside is also encouraging such exports. This results in a further drop of nutritional levels of the rural poor.

The Bhore Committee way back in 1946 recommended establishing one Primary Health Centre for each 30,000 population which has not yet been achieved.

Health for All goals and indicators have already accepted and accorded primacy to maternal and child health care inter alia including a halving of maternal mortality, hundred per cent coverage for ante-natal care and delivery by trained birth attendants by year 2000 A.D. The health services programmes are already committed to work towards the achievement of these goals. The Technological and Societal missions for eradication of illiteracy, immunization and safe water supply include certain critical indicators that will have impact on maternal and child care. However, as in the past, the present efforts lack in scale and systematic organization of the various components that together could radically alter the situation for women and children. Therefore, a comprehensive programme of health care of women needs to be developed with a special technological and societal mission to halve maternal mortality and morbidity and ensure optimum child bearing patterns by the year 2000. This mission, the details of which would have to be worked out by an expert working group, would need to, simultaneously gear the health services to reduce maternal, infant and child mortality and address the conditions that can assist women not to bear a child when this event will increase the risk to the health of the women and/ or the child to be born/already born. Inter alia, the observance of the small family norm through proper education of its impact on the health of women and children, will be an integral part of this mission.

It is unfortunate that the family planning policy is oriented towards fertility control and not concerned with providing a means for women and men to have control on their own bodies. A reflection of this policy is the encouragement of injectable contraceptives like Net-en which have been banned in most developed countries.

Though the family welfare and planning programmes have been a part of development planning since the First Five-Year Plan, actual achievements are below expectations. By March, 1987, the effective couple protection rate was only 34 per cent. From the beginning, emphasis has been placed on sterilizations rather than on temporary methods. Whereas in the early phases more vasectomies were performed, during the last decade, female sterilizations have been promoted at a very high rate. With the introduction of laproscopy, female sterilizations have reached high numbers amounting to almost 90 per cent of all sterilizations.

Research studies have shed light on the fact that the knowledge regarding family planning/methods is low despite the huge amounts of money spent on propaganda. The only method known to all is sterilization. The higher rates of abortions show the desire and need of the women for family planning and the failure of the family planning information and services to reach them in time. Laproscopic operations are being performed in several family planning camps without proper care and follow-up. Consequent problems tend to create apprehension among people. More intensive propagation of spacing methods together with innovative strategies for delivery of supplies has to be, taken up and spread of information about temporary methods accorded high priority.

The shift towards female sterilizations has to be reversed. Ironically, while that programme mainly provides female centred methods most of the women using these are not really happy due to the side effects. Hormonal reactions to oral pills, pain and heavy bleeding due to IUD, etc., are common complaints. In many areas women suffer from post-operative problems following tubectomy. The health personnel also concentrate most on' sterilization (female) as it helps them to realize their target and earn cash rewards.

Suggestions

1. Using amniocentesis for sex determination tests should be banned as in Maharashtra. Practitioners indulging in and abetting such acts should be punished severely and their medical licenses should be revoked.

2. Incentives should be considered to encourage parents to have female children. A couple who opts to limit their family to one female child may be given a regular monthly cash subsidy to attend to the girl child's needs. The amount must be given to the family over a period of time and not in a lump sum, as this might result in misuse of the female child as an instrument for getting easy money and later to neglect the child.

3. Infants and small children's growth and development should be monitored by recording their weights and heights at regular intervals. Proper corrective interventions should be made wherever necessary.

4. Universal immunization should be enforced to encompass all children.

5. Oral Rehydration Therapy (ORT) should be widely disseminated. ORT salts in packed form should be made available at a large scale in order to reduce the mortality from diarroheal diseases.

6. The ICDS should be strengthened and priority access should be provided to the girl child. Higher participation of women would also result from expansion of the programme.

7. Efforts should be made to bring a qualitative change in the attitudes against girl children. Media should be used for this purpose aiming to get the girl child to be accepted in the family and the society as an equal to the male child.

8. Focus is needed on the adolescent girl (12-18 years), so that she attains her maximum physical and mental capacities. It is necessary to provide alternative options to an early marriage. This can be ensured by a mix of education and employment opportunities and enforcement of the law on minimum age of marriage (18 years). The younger girl child needs to utilize health and education programmes more fully. It has been proposed that the ICDS will also address this issue in specific areas.

9. Adequate nutrition should be ensured for adolescent girls during the pre-puberty and pubertal growth phase to ensure 'catch up' on physical development by providing supplements to deprived groups.

10. Health and nutrition education should be promoted to ensure that preventive and promotive measures are adopted. The necessity of safe water, sanitation and personal hygiene also should be advocated.

11. Immunization against tetanus and rubella should be introduced for this age group.

12. Linkages with basic health care must be developed at the village level in the view of the special problems of mobility faced by young girls.

13. A massive communication campaign to create widespread awareness of the law prohibiting the marriage of the girl before 18 years and boys before 21 years and generate consciousness on the severe health implications in children and women of such early marriages must be launched.

14. The aim should be to implement the present legal minimum age of marriage effectively by creating a social consciousness for the desirability of marriage for girls only after 20 and for boys at 25. Preferential employment for unmarried males and females and priority in other developmental schemes for such youth, need to be seriously examined.

15. The comprehensive school health scheme which is being formulated, should be speedily implemented. Special efforts must be made for the health services to reach girls of the school-going age who are out of school. Each child should be examined and screened at least three times at primary school entry, before leaving primary school and at completion of high school. Similarly, a girl child out of school should be examined and screened three times - at around 6, 10 and 15 years of age. Screening kits and medicines should be made available. School teachers and non-formal education functionaries should be trained in the required areas of health care. The health programme for school and non-formal education systems should be integrally linked with the general health services.

16. It is necessary to impart information about reproductive processes, ways to prevent conception, need for spacing between children, optimum age of child bearing, necessary care for pregnant women and lactating mothers and small family norm, etc. This may be introduced as a part of the regular curriculum in school, colleges and universities.

For girls/boys who are not in school, Anganwadi workers/female CHWs may impart this knowledge.

17. To improve women's health status, there is no doubt that the general health services have to be made to respond to women's specific problems. A strategy for improving the health of women in the reproductive age group would be to reduce the risk of death and illness associated with pregnancy as well as to reduce the exposure to pregnancy itself. Comprehensive minimal care during pregnancy, childbirth and thereafter, steps to ameliorate malnutrition as well as decrease the workload of women, and improved access to health services, particularly family planning services, should be the salient instruments for improving the health of women.

18. Since women are severely restricted in their mobility, basic health care services must be made available to them as close as possible to their homes. Therefore, resources should be allocated as a priority to health services at the village, as well as at the first level of referral. The services would be provided by the female health workers, supported by the functionaries and the community from the village, as well as supervisory echelons within the health sector. Measures should be taken to reduce the incidence of low birth weight babies.

19. A minimum package of services should be available for pregnant women at village level. This should include at least:

    – Facilities for early detection of pregnancy, with low cost pregnancy detection kits;

    – Antenatal registration;

    – Minimum of three antenatal check-ups in the second and third trimester;

    – Screening of high-risk cases;

- Anaemia prophylaxis with iron and folic acid tablets; Tetanus toxoid coverage;

- Prophylaxis against malaria in high endemic areas; Advocacy of adequate rest;

- Health and nutrition education;

- Priority attention to locally endemic diseases affecting women; and

- Adequate safe drugs for her illness.

20. ANMs should be trained to assess pelvic proportions of pregnant women to identify the high risk cases and refer them to competent institutions. This will help in saving women from maternal deaths and also to reduce the incidence of still births.

21. The emphasis will have to be on providing better care to the pregnant woman in her home, as well as to ensure that adequate facilities are available at the first level of referral to deal with obstetric emergencies such as toximias, sepsis, obstructed labour and haemorrhage. In order to improve village level care during childbirth, the following are suggested:

    - Continuous training, supervision and support for better mid-wifery practices to the TBA and female health workers;

    - Provision for sterile delivery kits to the TBA, health workers and even to mothers;

    - Stocking adequate drugs and supplies with the health workers, and providing a restricted number to the TBA; and

    - Pre-arranged transport (or reimbursement of transport costs) for any emergency, when a woman has been registered for antenatal care.

22. Post-natal services should be available as close to the homes of mothers as possible. In rural areas in several, parts of India, women do not leave their homes for 40 days after delivery. Post-natal care should include:

    - A minimum of three contacts with the mother by the TBA and/or female health worker within the first 10 days after child birth;

    - One massive dose of vitamin A within one month after delivery to all mothers;

    - Iron and folic acid for 50 per cent of mothers;

    - Adequate drugs to deal with puerperal sepsis;

    - Education for the mother's nutrition and contraception as well as for infant feeding and health care, particularly immunization.

Women's Health Care

23. The health of women who are not pregnant or nursing, is an area which has received inadequate attention so far. Interventions thus made can cause a significant difference to women's health status not only between pregnancies, but also improve the outcome of future pregnancies. Moreover, the woman's right to health care as an individual must be promoted.

24. Women with chronic or serious illnesses, such as tuberculosis, leprosy, viral hepatitis, anaemia, sexually transmitted cases, etc., should be promptly treated and advised to postpone their pregnancy for a suitable safe period.,

25. High priority should be given to women for treatment/ control of all endemic diseases, specially those which have a harmful effect on the next generation (for example, goitre, sexually transmitted diseases, etc.)

26. Doctors of the Primary Health Centres be given in-service training to handle the cases of possessive syndrome and neurosis. Mass education programme be taken up to change the negative attitudes prevalent against mental illness.

27. Nutritious foods produced in the villages should be primarily utilized to cater to the nutrition needs of the rural poor. Only the surplus should be allowed for export to urban areas. A widespread public distribution system would be essential to make basic foods available at affordable costs.

28. Emphasis should be placed on Science and Technology research pertaining to sex linked diseases, occupational hazards, and indigenous methods of family planning as affecting women. Undergraduate level programmes should introduce courses relevant to women, i.e.

    (i) Work physiology (ergdonomics) as related to health, and occupational hazards.

    (ii) Basic tenets of genetics, related to family studies, genetic disorders and environmental effects.

    (iii) At the postgraduate level and above, research needs to be conducted in ergonomic abnormalities in women such as spinal strain after carrying loads. Also, work is needed on sex-linked, genetic disorders like muscular dystrophy and haemophilia, where women are the carriers.

29. More Primary Health Centres should be set up in the rural areas to achieve the target of having one Primary Health Centre for each 30,000 population as recommended by the Bhore Committee.

30. The timings of the dispensaries and hospitals should be fixed in a way which would be convenient to working women.

31. There should be a 24 hours creche facility for women patients with children in every hospital and PHC.

32. There is a need for a humane Drug Policy and check on the pharmaceuticals industry that at present operates on the profit principle like any other industry.

33. It is necessary to provide safety equipment including powerful exhausts to remove harmful dust from the work environment and, personal protective equipment like masks, feet protectors, eyeglasses, ear muffs and gloves and strong contraceptions for the safety of women workers.

34. There should be Refreshers /Orientation courses for the doctors on the subjects of women's work and health.

Family Welfare

35. Family planning policy should be such that it will help women have greater control over their bodies and enable them to make conscious choices on having or not having children and declining the number of children they want.

36. Injectible contraceptives as well as other contraceptives banned in developed countries should not be permitted in the country.

37. More research needs to be carried out to develop contraceptives that can be used by men and they should be propagated more widely.

38. Family Planning counselling needs to involve married and older women, selected from local surroundings for effective transmission of the concept and its urgency.

5

Social Justice

Significantly, the word 'gender' means much more than 'sex'. The gender of a man is masculine and that of a woman feminine. Neither a man nor a woman is sex alone or a biological species. So, the concept of gender may be said to be more inclusive than that of sex. But this distinction as such says nothing as to which of the two is inferior or superior. A bigger circle is only bigger than - not necessarily superior to — the smaller one, which it may include. In other words, the word gender in my view is a value-free concept. Differences of value arise only when we take genders in relation to their functions in society and, what is more important, when our way of looking at the matter is merely external. The point may be brought out as follows:

When female child becomes a wife, she acquires the functions of a mother, similarly a male child becomes a father. Now the functions of a mother are mostly confined to activities which quietly take place within the house. The father, on the other hand, earns a living by working in the outer world. What takes place in the open is noticed easily. What happens at home does not strike the public eye. So by the average man, whose way of looking is confined to the externals - that is, whose *drishti* is *bahirmukhi*-the male is taken to be superior to the female. Those who are careful enough to take a comprehensive view of the human life, attach as much value to the mother's activities of producing and nursing children and keeping a family together as to the bread winners outdoor activity of earning a living. It is really a defect in our ways of looking at things, and not the fact of gender as such, which is at the root of prevailing bias against women.

However, in the contemporary feminist literature, gender is not a value-free concept. It is a value-loaded term. It has acquired new dimensions and greater significance. It now refers to the social institutionalisation of sexual difference . It aims at exposing the present masculinist hegemony in the name of natural sexual differences, and also at uncovering the male connotations of the existing vocabulary of reason, morality, autonomy, justice and history. It, therefore, aims at suggesting an alternative epistemology and methodology, which can uncover the present gender bias, and may reflect more accurately the experiences and needs of all human beings. Feminists assert that any discrimination based on the basis of sexual differences is unjust; the body differences do not warrant such discriminatory differentiation; and, that they are only socially produced. Catharine A Mackinnon says:

> "Our issue is not the gender difference, but the difference gender makes, the social meaning imposed upon our bodies - what it means to be a woman or man is a social process and, as such, a subject to change. Feminists do not seek sameness with men. We more criticise what men have made of themselves and the world that we, too, inhabit. We do not seek dominance over men. To us, it is a male notion that power means someone must dominate. We seek a transformation in the terms and conditions of power itself."

The Traditions

It would be relevant here to discuss how political theorists in the past have neglected gender. John Locke defines political power as distinct from the power relations operating within the household. Rousseau and Hegel have clearly contrasted the two spheres and have justified this contrast in legitimising male rule in the domestic sphere. Locke has categorically mentioned that when "women hold the helm of government, the state is at once in jeopardy". Rousseau believes that women pose a permanent threat to political order. The natural morality of women fits them only for the 'natural society' of domestic life. He argues in Politics and the Arts, "even if it could be denied that a special sentiment of chasteness was natural to women, would it be less true that in society ... they ought to be raised in principles appropriate to it? If the timidity, chasteness and modesty, which are proper to them are social inventions, it is in society's interest that women acquire these qualities....."

Freud offers remarkably similar justification for women's confinement to domesticity. He writes, "for women the level of what is ethically normal is different from what it is in men. Their superego is never so inexorable, so impersonal, so independent of its emotional origins as we require it to be in men... They show less sense of justice than men, they are more often influenced in their judgements by feeling of affection of hostility..." Hence, Freud insists that the difference in moral capacity between the two sexes must be accepted.

Ironically, most contemporary political theorists continue the same neglect of gender by ignoring the family. Susan Moller Okin has rightly claimed, "the judgement that the family is 'non-political' is implicit in the very fact that it is not discussed in most works of political theory today". A number of examples can be cited.

However, there are a few exceptions. The works of Michael L Walzer, Philip Green, Allen Bloom and Michael J Sandel can be cited here.

Modern Theories

Contemporary feminist scholars have used the word 'gender' after two decades of intensive thought and research. To them gender is a social and political construct, related to and not determined by, biological sex difference.

In its most recent usage, gender seems to have first appeared among American feminists, who wanted to reject biological determinism implicated in the use of such terms as 'sex' or 'sexual difference'. Two major theories of gender are prevalent today-the psychologically focused theory of gender; and the historically and anthropologically focused explanation of gender.

Simone de Beauvoir, in her work *The Second Sex*, a quintessential example of modern feminist inquiry and critique, claims that "one is not born but rather becomes a woman". She claims that It is a whole process by which femininity is manufactured in society. To quote her, "she is defined and differentiated with reference to men and not he with reference to her; she is the incidental, the inessential as opposed to the essential. He is the subject, he is the Absolute - she is the Other".

Beauvoir argues that it is the child-bearing role of women which excluded them from the productive process, and prevented them from seeing themselves as subjects in their own right. Thus, an artificial idea of womanhood was created by society. She exhorts: "No biological, psychological or economic fate determines the figure that the human female presents in society; it is civilisation as a whole that produces this creation, intermediate between male and eunuch, who is described female."

Nancy Chodorow also subscribes to the above viewpoint and substantiates her argument from a psychoanalytical point of view. She argues that since women have always been assigned the responsibility of primary parenting and nurturing, they develop a psychology of being more suited to the task of nurturing and caring. Thus she chooses the role of a caregiver and confinement to the private. On the other hand, man from the very beginning is encouraged for more and more individuation and attaining status leading to personality traits impelling him to associate himself with the pubic.

Chodorow's use of the notion of gender identity presupposes three major premises: First, everyone has a deep sense of self, which is constituted in early childhood through one's interaction with his/her primary parent, and which remains relatively constant thereafter. The second premise is that this deep self differs significantly for men and women, but is roughly similar among women and among men both across cultures and within cultures across lines of class, race and ethnicity The third premise is that, this deep self colours everything one does.

The second theory of gender proclaims that in most societies across cultures, so far, gender has been a socially constructed category rather than biologically determined. However the proponents of this theory have also stressed that the nature of this social construction differs from one society to the other. So, there cannot be any unicausal, universalist and a historical explanation of it. Anthropologist Michelle A Rosaldo supports this theory on the basis of her cross-cultural research, which reveals that women are subjected to the authority due to the existing dichotomy between the public and the private.

Historian Linda J Nicholson also rejects the unicausal explanation of inequality of the sexes. She emphasises that it has been affected by various causal factors in different social contexts. She stresses the need to fight against the powerful tendency present in political theory to rectify the public-private distinction and to perceive it as rigid. She believes that one can comprehend this distinctly only through the study of history, for the gender structure of a particular time and place is less affected by other contemporary structures, such as political, economic, etc., more by the previous history of gender. Joan W Scott also stresses the centrality of history in analysing different aspects of the social construction of gender. She explains (a)how cultural myths and symbols reify the suppression of women: (b)how these symbols create the 'binary opposition of masculine and feminine male and female; (c)how social institutions like family, labour markets, educational institutions and polity reinforce this dichotomy; and, (d)how the subjective identity formation of individuals is psychologically determined. She, therefore, emphasises the need to expose the social construction of gender by deconstructing it. This calls for:

> "a refusal of the fixed and permanent quality of binary opposition, a genuine historicization and deconstruction of the terms of sexual difference... (we must) reversel and displace its hierarchical construction, rather than accepting it as real or self-evident or in the nature of things."

In fact, all of them are unequivocal in proclaiming that the public sphere till today, has been constructed under the assumption of male superiority and dominance. It has avoided a number of compelling questions such as that of incorporating the responsibilities of child-bearing and child rearing into the fabric of job-structure.

Dominant Paradigms

The above analysis of gender has helped feminists in rejecting many of the existing dominant paradigms. First, they reject the claim that separation of the public and the private follows inevitably from the natural characteristics of the sexes. They argue that a proper understanding of social life is possible only when it is accepted that the two spheres, the private and the public, are inextricably interrelated. Unless the separation of the two worlds is not destroyed, the public life would always be conceptualised as the sphere of men. Carole Pateman has aptly remarked:

> "In popular (and academic) consciousness the duality of female and male often serves to encapsulate or represent the series (or circle) of liberal separations and oppositions: female, or-nature, personal, emotional love, private intuition, morality, ascription, particular, subjection; male, or-culture, political, reason, justice, public, philosophy, power, achievement, universal, freedom."

The most fundamental and general of these opinions associate women with nature and men with culture. Nature is always seen in a lower order than culture. The feminists like Ortner argue that the opposition between women/nature and men/culture is itself a cultural construct and does not exist in nature. S.Firestone in her work *Dialectic of Sex*, argues against this separation of private and public. Women necessarily suffer from a fundamentally oppressive biological condition. It is their role as reproducers that has handicapped women over the centuries and made possible men's patriarchal power.

The consequences of this public-private dichotomy are disastrous. Due to this, women have been deprived of political power and effective participation. Citizenship for women is always seen as 'an elaboration of their private domestic tasks'. Thinkers like Ruskin could argue that "man's duty as a member of the commonwealth, is to assist the maintenance, in the advance and in the defence of the state. The women's duty, as a member of the commonwealth, is to assist in the ordering, in the comforting, and in the beautiful adornment of the state."

This has eventually led to the dichotomy between morality and poor. Women, in the name of being more moral, have been excluded from the public realm. Even the suffragists argued in favour of women's franchise by claiming women's superior morality as it would usher the state in a reign of peace. This is why J B Elshtain alleges that suffragists instead of challenging the separation of the public and private, merely "perpetuated the very mystifications and unexamined presumptions, which served to rig the system against them."

Against this background, one can understand the significance of the feminist slogan:

The feminists argue that public realm of politics can be so rational, noble and universal only because like the messy content of the human body, meeting its needs for production, care-taking and attending to birth and death, as too in politics are taken care of elsewhere.

So, a modern reflective political theory should recognise that the glory of the public is dialectically entwined with exploitation and repression of the private and the people restricted to that sphere so that they can take care of the people's needs. In view of this, the feminist political theory concludes that the 20th century politics requires a basic rethinking of this distinction and its meaning for politics.

Theory of Social Practice

The feminists are trying to develop a theory of social practice on the following premises. First, there should be no sexual division of labour at work place and in political organisations of all ideological persuasions; second, there should be a differentiated social order within which various dimensions are distinct but not separate or opposed, and which rests on social conception of individuality, which includes both women and men as biologically differentiated but not unequal creatures.

Third, there is a need to base and expand the conception of politics on the understanding that power relations between men and women are not confined to the 'public' world of law, the state and economics, but pervade all areas of life. This means that contrary to the assumptions of traditional political theory, the family, reproduction and sexuality must be included in political analysis.

The question arises how far this public/private dichotomy and its deconstruction is relevant to the women of the Third World? Can this empowerment epistomology rooted in white women's experiences, subjectivity and identity, fulfil the interest of the Third World women?

However, in the post colonial discourse, women of the North have understood the significance of the Third World women's realities, and they themselves have rejected the monolithic nature of the earlier feminist discourse on the grounds that it ignores difference, indigenous knowledge, and local expertise. For example, modernity is equated with westernisation, industrialisation and superiority, whereas non-modernity is equated with non-western countries, tradition and inferiority. In the 1970s, Eshter Boserup's pioneering work *Women's Role in Economic Development*, asserted that modernisation had marginalised women and their contributions in the Third World. Chandra Mohanty also questions the western approach, when she asks:

> "Is it possible to refer to the sexual division of labour when the content of this division changes radically from one environment to the next, from one historical juncture to another? At its most abstract level ... concepts such as the sexual division of labour can be useful only if they are generated through local, contextual analyses. If such concepts are assumed to be universally applicable, the resultant homogenisation of class, race, religion, and daily material practices of women in the Third World can create a false sense of the commonality of oppressions, interests, and struggles between and among women globally.

G Sen, and Crown too, are cautious against adopting a concept of gender that ignores differences and diversities. They believe that this diversity is built on gender oppression and hierarchy. He exclaims:

> "Feminism cannot be monolithic in its issues, goals and strategies, since it constitutes the political expression of the concerns of women from different regions, classes, nationalities, and ethnic backgrounds. There is and must be a diversity of feminism, responsive to the different needs and concerns of different women, and defined by them for themselves."

Positive Aspect

The most positive part of the whole discourse is that these concerns are reflected in practice also. Women involved in different social movements are fighting against injustice on their own cultural terms. Environmental activists like Vandana Shival are speaking of the need to decolonise northern assumptions such as the concept of sustainable development, and appeal to save environment through knowledge based on poor women's experience.

Thus, feminist scholarship has brought sweeping changes to social and political theory. It has cautioned us against constituting gender as a superordinate category of analysis. It should neither be an automatic starting point of analysis of adjustment, nor should it be ignored as a potential starting point. We must avoid approaches that are gender-blinded or gender-blind. Then only we can have true meaning of democracy and participation.

6

The Emancipation

As recognized in the Fifth Five-Year Plan, even with expanded employment opportunities, the poor will not be able, with their level of earnings, to buy for themselves all the essential goods and services which should figure in any reasonable concept of a minimum standard of living. The measures for providing larger employment and incomes to the poorer sections will, therefore, have to be supplemented up to at least certain minimum standard, by social consumption and investment in the form of education, health, nutrition, drinking water, housing, communications and electricity, and social welfare services. Social welfare services are intended to cater for the special needs of persons and groups, who by reason of some handicap-social, economic, physical or mental-are unable to avail of or are traditionally denied the amenities and services provided by the community. Women are handicapped by social customs and social values and therefore social welfare services have and should specially endeavour to rehabilitate them by inducing a change in the attitudes of society towards women, their role and contribution.

Main Issues

A statement of a plan of social welfare programmes relating to women, even if, it is within the purview of the overall social welfare programmes, will help in providing the correct emphasis on the problems and development needs of the weaker sections of women and provide voluntary organizations and voluntary effort "a certain" direction. The problems and consequently the developmental action required are, it appears, unlimited and the resources are limited. As such, priorities have necessarily to be assigned.

Among women, the following categories and some of the problems faced by them, call for special attention on a priority basis. The categories are:

(A) Working women. To include

  (i) The low-income women living in tribal and backward rural areas and urban slums.

  (ii) The migrant women.

  (iii) The divorced / separated.

(B) Physically and mentally handicapped women.

(C) Widows with or without children.

(D) Destitute women.

(E) Women who come into conflict with law.

(F) Exploited women and unmarried mothers.

The problems faced by each of the above categories are numerous and some of them are common to other categories. To decide on action plan priorities, the handicaps and/or the factors which impose constraints need to be understood.

Women Professionals

According to 1971 Census, women workers constitute nearly 12 per cent of the total women population and well over 90 per cent of the women workers are found employed in rural areas. It should be recognized here that the problems faced by women workers in rural areas are altogether different from those in the urban areas.

Rural areas including tribal and backward areas: Women workers in rural areas are largely landless agricultural labourers; members of households with uneconomic holdings; those engaged in traditional household industries like hand-spinning, hand-weaving, oil pressing, rice pounding, leather, tobacco processing, etc. These household industries-which are predominantly female labour intensive and which have been a major source of employment in villages appear to have declined in importance during the post-independence period. This is also evidenced by the distinctly declining trend in employment of women workers in the rural areas between the decennial Censuses 1961 and 1971. It has not been possible to reverse this trend because:

(i) Almost all the women workers in the rural areas are handicapped by illiteracy and lack of mobility.

(ii) In addition to this, incessant child bearing coupled with hard domestic work does not provide them any time to go through formal education/training to acquire new skills. Facilities for acquiring new skills are still sparse.

Urban Areas: Women workers in the urban areas fall into three distinct categories:

(i) The first category consists largely of migrants from villages and members of families whose economic position has deteriorated to near starvation. The women of this class work mainly as domestic servants and as unskilled labour in various unorganized industries.

This category of women workers, who are largely slum dwellers, are below subsistence level. Their problems are to find a job which is secure or provides them regular income at least to subsist, a place for comfortable living, as most of them are away from their homes located in villages; and rehabilitation facilities for their families, particularly children and preparing them for better livelihood, through better education and training; in that order.

(ii) The second category consists of women, who need employment either to keep their families away from starvation or to ensure better standard of living. Most of such women are found employed in industries, services and professions. Some are even self-employed. In the case of this second category of women workers in urban areas, their existence ranges from subsistence to security. Some of these women, particularly those residing away from their families, are likely to be exposed to the dangers of exploitation from undesirable and anti-social elements. Personal security is therefore a major problem for them.

(iii) The third category consists of women who are highly educated and work in higher ranks of services and professions for personal satisfaction and independence. Belonging as they do at least to the upper middle-class families, they do not as group face any serious problems requiring immediate attention here.

Divorced/separated women are part of each of these categories.

The Physically Challenged

There are several types of physical handicaps like blindness, deafness, orthopaedic handicap, leprosy, mental retardation, etc., which hinder two persons from even entertaining the hopes of equal participation in the overall social activity. These problems are common to both men and women.

Estimates of physically handicapped women are not separately available. To provide a basis for the formulation of Fifth Five-Year Plan, the working group on the Handicapped constituted for the purpose, estimated that "India may have well over 12 million blind, deaf and orthopaedically handicapped persons. In addition, an estimated 2 million suffer from moderate to severe retardation. The number of persons suffering from leprosy is believed to be around 2.5 million".

The basic problem concerning these physically handicapped persons is lack of adequate facilities for differential medical care, education, training and rehabilitation programmes and a lack of knowledge about these facilities by handicapped persons. Further, it is widely known that though the existing facilities are largely used by men, a majority of physically handicapped women are not coming forward to utilize the available facilities.

Women in Distress

The 1971 Census distribution of women according to marital status indicates that roughly about 9 per cent of the women are widows. Further, they are almost evenly distributed between the rural and urban areas.

Widowhood is a curse for most of the women in India for various reasons:

(i) It is almost invariably accompanied by economic disaster. This is because a large number of the families in India survive at below subsistence level and hence death of a male earning member pushes down the families concerned to near starvation. Also many of the females are voluntarily out of work force, and illiteracy remains the greatest barrier for the improvement of the economic position of widowed women, particularly in the rural areas.

(ii) Age-old traditions, social prejudices and cultural practices almost exclude widowed women from any socially productive work. Social acceptance of women is reduced with widowhood. In some communities/ regions. There is almost a sort of social boycott of widowed women.

Problems faced by Widows of Different Age Groups: The problems faced by widowed women are not all the same as between different age-groups; and as between rural and urban areas:

(a) For widows in the younger age group - particularly those belonging to 15-44 years of age - the problems are more - related to economic independence and rehabilitation in the society - preferably through remarriage.

(b) For widows in the age group 45 and above, the problem is more of social acceptance and security. Most of such women, if not previously employed, will be unfit for employment. Even in respect of employed women -widowed after 44 years of age - it is difficult to impart -of the needed training/skills for more remunerative jobs within the existing framework of education/ training facilities.

Problems of widowed women in the rural areas are even move severe than those in the urban areas. In addition to economic dependence and the social stigma attached to widowhood, there are no cpportunities for their emancipation. Many of them are possibly not even aware of the efforts being made by the government agencies through voluntary organizations to redress their miseries.

These destitute women can be classified into three age-groups as their problems are different:

Below 15 years: Persons in this group can be categorized as children. They are mostly orphans and are, therefore, deprived of the tender parental care. They are also subjected to malnutrition and the consequent diseases. This age group, viz., below 15 years of age constitutes the formative years in a person's life, as the process of development and learning are most rapid during these young years. During these formative years, the effects of environment greatly influence the personality development, mental attitudes, moral character, etc. Often, destitute persons in this age group fall a prey to the environmental disadvantages.

15-44 years: This second group of women are both in the productive and reproductive age group. Their main problems are those pertaining to economic independence, social acceptance and security.

45 years and above: In the case of third group of destitute women, their major problem is social security. They are mostly unfit to be employed. They cannot even be trained to earn their livelihood.

Women who fall under this category are: (i) juvenile delinquents, (ii) women in moral and social danger - particularly those who indulge in immoral traffic and (iii) women prisoners.

Juvenile Delinquents: are again a creation of the society and the environment in which they are brought up; the deprivation of proper nutrition and training/education which would enable them to earn a better livelihood, etc.

Prostitutes: Women subjected to severe economic distress and hardships often come into the clutches of persons who have vested interests in immoral traffic. Once they succumb, they do not receive proper health care - curative and preventive treatment for the diseases associated with immoral traffic; many of them are not aware of the existing health care facilities and added to it is the innate fear of being exposed to the general public and the resulting social reactions. The existing health facilities are also not adequate and are not perceived as being sympathetic towards their health problems.

Female Prisoners: Many of the problems faced by female prisoners are in common with male prisoners. However, some of the problems are peculiar to females alone. For example, women prisoners with children - particularly in case children are below five years - have problems in arranging for the care of their children. Also, problems in getting rehabilitated, after they are free, are more severe in the case of women prisoners than men prisoners.

Plight of Women

(i) Out-of-wedlock pregnancies are on the increase, judging from the number of abortions and live births among single women recorded at various institutions. Estimates of medical termination of pregnancies (MTP) in the case of single women alone range from 10 to 30 per cent of total MTP cases. In respect of live illegitimate births estimates based on hospital records range from 2 to 3 per cent of the total confinements. In reality many more clandestine live illegitimate births may be taking place which are not brought to public notice.

(ii) Premarital pregnancies, are as generally believed, no longer confined to the illiterate and depressed classes. According to some case-studies in this field, nearly 50 per cent of the pre-marital pregnancies were observed in the case of women who are at least matriculates. A few were graduates. Some of them were observed to be belonging to the privileged classes of the society. A more distressing feature, however, is that pre-marital pregnancies are being observed even in the case of school girls.

Among the reasons attributed to premarital pregnancies are: interactions between various social, psychological and economic forces like break down of joint families; overwhelming poverty, rapid urbanization bringing in its wake the social transformation which leads to increasing permissiveness, lack of communication between children and parents; emotional immaturity and craze for excitement among the youth; antipathy towards the introduction of basic sex education among school children, etc., are the most important reasons cited.

Permissiveness and promiscuity increase with rapid urbanization and measures to avoid such premarital pregnancies is a long drawn social education problem and cannot be expected to decline rapidly. However, the problems concomitant to premarital pregnancies can and should at least be tackled effectively.

The action plans should be directed primarily to solving the problems of these six target groups of women.

Plan for Action

There is considerable overlap both in terms of the causes and programmes and agencies concerned with eliminating the problems and building rehabilitation/development plans for these target groups. As such, the action plans are classified under broad groups of actions rather than in terms of categories of women discussed above:

I. Provision of Services/Infrastructure.

II. Education/Training Programmes for the Target Groups.

III. Promoting Voluntary Effort: The Role of Women.

IV. Development of Human Resources.

V. Administrative Set-up and Coordination.

VI. Legislative Measures.

VII. Areas of Research.

The Fifth Five-Year Plan has rightly emphasized the need for a shift in the approach towards social welfare, from a mere provision of curative and rehabilitative services - the kind of approach adopted during the past two decades of planning - to promoting the needed preventive and developmental aspects of social welfare. The action plans should necessarily have such a preventive and development orientation.

Provision of Services/Infrastructure

(i) Services for the care of girls below 15;

(ii) Facilities for women in the productive age group, i.e. 15-45 years;

(iii) Programmes for the care of aged and infirm women; and

(iv) General welfare programmes.

Services for the Care of Girls below 15: There are three categories of children who need particular attention, viz., children of working women, destitute children particularly female children and juvenile delinquents. The following action plans are suggested:

(1) The child population below 6 years of working mothers in urban and rural areas is estimated to be around 20 lakh and 166 lakh, respectively. With a view to helping the working mother discharge her duties - both as a mother and worker better family aid services like Anganwadis, Balwadis, creches and day care centres might be launched in a big way.

Both in the rural and in the urban areas efforts should be made to cover more than 40 per cent of the children of working mothers.

(2) There are about 11 lakh destitute children in the country. The girls among them need particular attention, because

they are likely to be exposed to social and moral dangers when they grow up. Efforts should be made to provide institutional facilities whether through the foster care programmes or otherwise for taking care of a majority of the destitute female children.

(3) It is impossible to discriminate between male and female juvenile delinquents, as the problems are common to both. However, the approach towards juvenile delinquency as such should be to provide the needed atmosphere for a child to develop personality, character and social conscience through setting up of clubs, play centres, juvenile guidance units, workshops, etc.

(4) Holiday homes schemes initiated earlier to provide organized and guided recreational facilities to children and be one of the measures to prevent juvenile delinquency. Such facilities should at least be extended to cover all the children residing in the slums of major cities.

Facilities for Women in the Productive Age Group: In some selected urban areas, hostel facilities are available for working women of the lower income groups earning Rs. 50 to Rs. 800 per month. However, the coverage of the programme in terms of the proportion of working women needs to be stepped up considerably. Similarly, district-wise investigation would be undertaken about the need for working women's hostels and appropriate facilities set up. The matching contribution for grants for construction/ addition/ alterations should be stepped up.

Socio-economic programmes were initiated in 1958 with the objective of providing full or part-time work to the needy/destitute women and the physically handicapped either through full wage or a wage sufficient to supplement the meagre income of their families. These programmes should be expanded considerably in both rural and urban areas, as they have the potential to provide the needed economic independence to women belonging to the weaker sections and thus act as a preventive measure to many of the social evils.

For effectively implementing these socio-economic programmes, active collaboration should be sought from agencies like Handicrafts Board, Handloom Board, Khadi and Village Industries Board, Small Industries Service Institutes, Small Industries Development Corporations at the State level and the nationalized banks.

To increase the employment potential for the following types of schemes additional steps should be undertaken within the purview of socio-economic programmes:

(i) Small-Scale industries.

(ii) Units as ancillary to large production of handicrafts.

(iii) Units for the procurement and production of handicrafts.

(iv) Handloom training-cum-production units.

(v) Agro-based industries like dairy, poultry farms, etc.

(vi) Traditional female labour intensive industries like rice pounding, oil-pressing, etc.

Attempts must be made to revitalize and activate the existing sick units falling under the purview of socio-economic programmes.

Ways to improve the working, efficiency and effectiveness of Mahila Mandals must be studied and necessary action taken. They should be reoriented to aim at increasing the earning power of women in the rural areas.

It is suggested that by the end of the Fifth Plan, about 10,000 Mahila Mandals, should be developed throughout the country to provide an effective media for organizing women welfare activities in the rural areas.

Scholarship programmes of the Central and State Governments for the handicapped should be expanded considerably and efforts should be made to encourage women to make use of the scholarships available.

Sheltered workshops should be organized.

Schemes for the welfare of destitute women between the ages 18-44 and 45-65 providing for basic amenities of food, shelter, clothing, basic education and training in crafts should be implemented through voluntary organizations who may be given grants to cover 75 per cent of the expenditure. It is suggested that this scheme should be revived and implemented in all the States.

Homes for the rehabilitation of rescued and released women prisoners should be started in all towns with a minimum of 5 lakh of population. Apart from providing shelter, food and clothing, the inmates should also be provided training in crafts like sewing, embroidery, knitting, etc. Efforts should, however, be made in the direction of making inmates self-sufficient and earn independent livelihood.

In some such protective homes, insane women are housed along with other women which is an unhealthy and undesirable practice and should be discontinued.

Programmes for the Care of Aged and Infirm Women: Women in the age group 65 years and over constitute roughly 85 lakh according to the 1971 Census. Many of the women lack absolutely any security They are mostly dependent on their children who often desert them. Thus, even women belonging to upper middle classes are sometimes reduced to the status of destitute. Efforts should therefore be made at least in a modest way to initiate social security measures through old age pension with the objective of providing economic independence to at least 25 per cent of women in the age group particularly in the rural areas.

For the women retired from active service and for those who are in need of some residential facilities, hostels should be started in all the major cities. If necessary, subsidies may also be extended under the grants-in-aid programmes.

General Welfare Programmes: Slum clearance programmes should be initiated in all the major cities and towns with a minimum of 5 lakh of population. People displaced should be provided alternative sites, with proper environmental sanitation, for building their homes.

Zila Parishads and youth in the districts should be entrusted with drinking water supply projects.

A vigorous campaign of education and action should be launched in favour of community sanitation and hygiene. Public utility services should be expanded. The practice of carrying night soil as headloads must be eradicated.

Education/Training Programmes for the Target Groups: Analysis of the problems faced by the target group of women indicated that illiteracy, inadequate education/training, lack of facilities for training in alternative skills and lack of knowledge about the existing facilities are some of the major problems that have hindered the progress of women in India. There is, therefore, the need for accelerating the efforts in this regard with renewed vigour. With this in view, the following action plans are recommended:

(1a) The Fourth Plan introduced a programme of functional literacy built round farmer's training in selected districts where high yielding varieties of crops were being cultivated. It is estimated that about 90,000 women received this training during the Fourth Plan and about 5 to 7 lakh of women are likely to be trained under this programmes during the Fifth Plan. This programme must be extended to all the rural areas.

(1b) Apart from imparting knowledge about farming, the curriculum for women should include courses of training, in occupational skills like kitchen gardening, food cultivation, poultry keeping, animal husbandry; household arts like cooking, nutritional values of foods locally available, sewing, knitting, etc.; and family planning.

(1c) Preference should be given to women belonging to Scheduled Castes, tribal women, widowed women and destitutes under this functional literacy programme.

(2a) For the non-student young girls without any education and school drop-outs - particularly for girls in the age group 11-14 years, the pre-vocational training programmes should be reviewed and strengthened by enlarging the scope of training and by increasing the number of trades.

(2b) In respect of girls in the age group 11-14 years, the objective of pre-vocational training should also be to train them to be self-sufficient in home management by organizing courses of training in sewing, cooking, nutrition, minor repairs of the house, motherhood, child care, etc.

(2c) Pre-vocational programmes should be extended to cover girls in this age group in the rural areas. In urban areas, preference should be given to girls in the slum areas and destitute girls.

(3) Condensed courses of education were started in 1958 with the twin objective of (a) opening new vistas of employment to a large number of deserving and needy women, and (b) creating a band of competent trained workers required to man the various projects in the rural areas in the shortest possible time. Under the scheme, women in the age group 18-30 who have studied up to classes IV and VI are trained for middle school/matriculation examinations

within a period of two years. The scheme was found very useful but the statistics reveal that the beneficiaries have been mostly women belonging to the middle-class families. Preference should be given to women belonging to backward classes, widowed women and destitute women.

(4) Special efforts should be made to cover women belonging to Scheduled Castes and Scheduled Tribes through condensed courses. An incentive of Rs.1,000 (as recommended by the Review Committee), be given to the institution for every successful Scheduled Caste/ Scheduled Tribe candidate trained.

(5a) The condensed courses should be organized in a big way and for smaller groups of say 5 to 7 with the help of high schools and colleges for girls. Efforts should be made to cover about 215 lakh women under the condensed course programmes, during the Fifth Plan period.

(5b) Apart from imparting general education, condensed courses should also aim at imparting job-oriented training with the active cooperation of existing vocational training institutions.

(5c) Under this programme of condensed courses, short-term courses should be organized to retain women who have been temporarily out of job-market to fulfil child bearing responsibilities.

(5d) For the failed candidates, short-term course of six months to one year should be organized.

(5e) Special efforts should be initiated to follow-up successful candidates with a view to helping them in securing jobs.

(6) Pre-examination training facilities should be offered to duly qualified poor women with the objective of equipping them to successfully compete in examinations for public

jobs. It is suggested that about 80 lakh girls in the age group 14-17 may be covered under this programme during the Fifth Plan period.

(7) The school curricula in various States in India should encourage the doing away of traditional prejudices of inequality of the sexes.

(8) Sex education should be introduced at the appropriate stage with the objective of also educating the young girls about the social and moral dangers they are likely to encounter.

(9) The value of physical training in the school curricula should be emphasized.

Promoting Voluntary Effort: The Role of Women: Voluntary welfare service organizations have been an integral part of the cultural and social traditions in India. Soon after independence, it was estimated that there were 10,000 voluntary organizations engaged in social welfare. In fact, all the schemes of Central Social Welfare Board are implemented only through voluntary organizations. The reorientation given to social welfare in the Fifth Plan calls for more effort on the part of both voluntary organizations and the State agencies involved. The following action plans are, therefore, warranted in this regard:

(a) Efforts should be made to promote a large number of voluntary organizations throughout the country. They have a critical role in mobilizing public opinion in favour of equality among men and women, and eradicating superstitions, social evils and waste. The motivational strategy for encouraging voluntary organizations needs to be well thought through and support facilities provided. Women should be promoted to take the initiative and responsibility for organizing voluntary effort, for not only can they bring to the tasks the necessary dedication commitment and empathy; but their very presence will provide their socially handicapped sisters a source of inspiration and set in a cycle of social rejuvenation. All voluntary organizations particularly those concerned with social welfare vis-a-vis women must be encouraged to have women members. Women Panchayats, Mahila Mandals, working women, etc., should be encouraged to spearhead such voluntary activities. Mahila Mandals should be promoted in every village so that they can function as field level agencies for social and economic transformation.

(b) Most of the voluntary organizations have been operating independently of each other. They have, therefore, not been able to fully benefit the community. The role of existing organizations should be determined and measures should be initiated to coordinate/supplement the efforts of various organizations at each district level.

(c) Many of the women's voluntary organizations are located in urban areas, while only a few organizations have endeavoured to work amongst rural women. Efforts should be made to promote a large number of voluntary women's organizations in the rural backward and tribal areas and urban slums to mobilize public support for different programmes and to implement them. This calls for liberation of the rules regarding the matching grant through voluntary contributions, simplification of the rules and procedures of obtaining the grant as well as administering the organizations, provision of trained staff, organization of leadership training programmes, etc.

Development of Human Resources: Administration of various social welfare programmes have become increasingly technical. During the past two decades of developmental planning, lack of technically competent workers has had an adverse impact on the quality and success of welfare programmes. With a view to provide the necessary support to various agencies, the following action plans are suggested:

(1) Training facilities for the workers attached to all the voluntary agencies, like Mahila Mandals should be initiated immediately. The training needs of workers, however, differ from organization to organization depending on the nature of tasks required to be performed.

(2) Through a proper investigation training requirements of workers in each district should be assessed and suitable training programmes designed.

(3) These training programmes should, as far as possible be organized at each district level.

(4) Trainees should preferably be local candidates.

(5) Effective implementation of the various socio-economic programmes require two cadres of workers: the grass-root workers and supervisory staff. The grass-root workers should be provided training in the latest techniques and methods of production with the active collaboration of well established industrial units and Industrial Training Institutes. The supervisory staff, on the other hand, should be trained in advanced techniques of production, business management, personnel management, etc.

(6) In the case of handicrafts units under the socio-economic programme, practising craftsmen should be trained as instructors and appointed.

(7) Short-term orientation should also be given to the members of the managing committees of the units - socio-economic programmes - about the general working of such units.

(8) Senior level officers in charge of the socio-economic programmes should also be exposed to short-term orientation courses in business management and allied fields through Small Industries Service Institutes, University departments of business management, etc.

Administrative Set-Up and Coordination: Administrative traditions in India have tended to attach least importance to departments dealing with social welfare. This is reflected even in the training imparted to administrators. Only recently it has been realized that administration must also be welfare oriented. The federal nature of our policy vests a large responsibility for implementing social policy and programmes with State and local authorities. There is, therefore, the need for reorganizing the administrative set-up with a view to effectively implementing the various welfare programmes. The following action plans may be taken up for consideration:

(1) Orientation/training programmes should be organized for social welfare personnel, particularly at decision making levels, to sensitize them to social welfare needs and adopt the extension approach of reaching out to the clients. The new developmental and preventive concept, of welfare also needs to be imparted.

(2) Every State Department of Social Welfare should have a Women's Welfare Division with responsibility for planning, programming and monitoring the implementation of schemes of women welfare.

(3) The Central Social Welfare Board is one of the most important agencies for the implementation of social welfare activities. It should be reorganized and strengthened, and vested with larger funds and responsibilities for promoting and developing voluntary effort particularly in rural, backward and tribal areas and among the weaker sections of the community.

(4) The Central Social Welfare Board should launch a massive campaign for enlisting and developing a cadre of voluntary social workers who should be provided some normal assistance to enable them to carry out this work.

(5) State Social Welfare (Advisory) Boards should also be reorganized and strengthened.

(6) The State Board should also be made to function as liaison among the State Government and the local agencies.

(7) Suitable infrastructure should be developed at each district level and block level for implementing and expanding the programmes of Central Social Welfare Board.

(8) Trained social welfare workers should be associated with all the committees to be set-up by the Central Social Welfare Board.

Legislative Measures

(1) International experience indicates that evolving a sound social security system takes a long period of time. However, suitable enactment can be initiated to provide public assistance to select groups like destitute women and people above 65 years but without any means of livelihood. Assistance here need not be in the form of cash. It should be in the form of medical, housing, feeding and recreational facilities, etc.

(2) It should be open to the States and Union Territories to go in for taxation or special levy to finance such public assistance schemes without prejudice to any assistance made available to States and Union Territories from the Central Government under plan schemes.

(3) No child should be tried in adult courts nor should any child be sent to a jail.

(4) State Governments should enact legislation for apprehension, institutional treatment and rehabilitation of beggars, particularly women.

(5) Machinery should be set up for speedy and effective adjudication in all cases concerning the family, including

the setting up of family welfare courts since the ordinary judicial procedure is not suited to handle such cases. Women, particularly in rural areas, should be protected against harassment.

(6) A vigorous campaign should be launched to educate women about their rights and the machinery through which they can seek their realization.

(7) Active public support should be mobilized by government agencies, voluntary organizations and public leaders against child marriage and dowry to support the legislative measures for the eradication of these undesirable practices. Ostentatious weddings and other wasteful social ceremonies should be banned.

Primary data available with sources such as the Census and National Sample Survey, are insufficient and are very scanty for social welfare planning, particularly on the needs and requirements of handicapped women, destitute women, women under the purview of the suppression of Immoral Traffic Act, etc.: In view of this, the following areas of research are suggested:

(i) Studies on 'Social profiles' with district as unit' wherein information on the prevailing conditions of social needs and requirements, etc., are investigated.

(ii) Studies on the requirements of physically handicapped children and women.

(iii) Studies on the requirements of destitute children and women.

(iv) Studies on the training requirements of workers in voluntary welfare organizations.

(v) Studies on the socio-economic and psychological factors behind the problem of premarital pregnancies.

(vi) Studies on the magnitude of problems facing prostitutes and their children such as problems of children of prostitutes, particularly female children.

Voluntary action in India has always been an integral part of the cultural and social traditions. A variety of social services were provided by voluntary agencies prior to independence and in the first few decades' of planned development in India. Traditionally, voluntary agencies undertook a wide variety of activities in the areas of social reform in the pre-independence period. Independence resulted in government policy and commitment to support and strengthen voluntary agencies. Voluntary agencies have currently opted for several alternative roles depending on their objectives, location (rural/urban) and resources available.

The role of voluntary agencies in national development has been considered vital due to their direct and first-hand experience and knowledge of local needs, problems and resources at the grass-roots. Further the commitment and zeal of the voluntary action movement is considered effective as it is not bound by rigid bureaucratic systems and is more responsive to people. The voluntary sector is observed to operate with great flexibility and bases its activities on felt needs. There is a process of continually learning from past experiences in programme planning and implementation, etc.

The essential strength of voluntary agencies derives from the fact that they are closer to the community and people. They represent in many cases the needs and aspirations of the people. Voluntary agencies often function more effectively than the government managed agencies in areas such as motivation, problem identification and analysis, project formulation, innovative methods of service delivery and involvement of the community, due to their spirit.

There are a number of lessons to be learned in such areas such as the demystification of technology; de-emphasizing formal educational qualification in favour of experience, capabilities, aptitude and ability to work with people; expansion of activities without adding on cumbersome bureaucracy; and reliance on community based and non-institutional approaches. The unique strength of the voluntary sector is its ability to pressurize the government without succumbing to it and losing its identity and lobbying on issues and ideas to make them acceptable to government and the people. The decentralized administration in the voluntary sector not only facilitates effective grass-roots, delivery mechanisms but also ensures the participation of the beneficiaries in the programmes.

Voluntary agencies in India have evolved as a result of a historical process that has brought them to their present status and role in the country's development. In the 1950s, most of the organizations provided either relief work or were involved in institutionalized programmes such as schools, destitute homes, hospitals as well as welfare activities. In the 1960s, many of these organizations realized that families with a weak economic base would be unable to procure the benefits of institutional welfare and relief services. It led them to the conclusion that services should enable beneficiaries to be productive and self-reliant through income generating programmes. In the 1970s, many of the voluntary organizations began to feel that economic inputs alone could not overcome poverty and a critical roadblock to development was the unequal social structure. A new type of education geared to raising the consciousness of weaker sections on their situation and rights so that they become active agents of their own development, and change was considered essential. Activist groups built around these considerations, subsequently came into existence in the voluntary sector.

The organization of women by voluntary organizations has acquired importance as the need has emerged for organizational structures to ensure women's participation in the development process. Many old established voluntary agencies have undertaken the task of setting up welfare development services for women in the country.

New Trends: From the mid 1970s onwards there was an emergence of many newly established organizations and activist groups. A large part of the activities of these groups have centered around combating atrocities and violence committed on women, dowry murder, brutal forms of maltreatment and exploitation. In many cases, women in distress have approached such groups for assistance in registering and follow up of cases, providing shelter, etc. These activist groups have identified themselves with oppressed, victimized, and harassed women and awakened new hopes, aspirations and consciousness among women on these issues. Recently many formal and informal groups have emerged throughout the country which have successfully mobilized women's awareness and have preferred to work directly with the women, relying less on material inputs from the outside and more on increasing the internal capabilities and resources-economic, social, cultural and political. These activist groups have also elicited the intervention of the State, especially of the judiciary and of the fourth estate, to project the rights of women and ameliorate their situations. At the same time, they have organized the women themselves for struggle.

Besides voluntary agencies and activist groups, there are many other functional groups such as Mahila Mandals, Youth Clubs, Nehru Yuvak Kendras, National Service Schemes, cooperatives and other people's institutions that have effectively taken up the issues of women in development with varying degrees of success.

Government's Stance on Voluntary Action: The Planning Commission has recognized the role of voluntary action in accelerating the process of social and economic development in most of its plans, particularly so in the Sixth and Seventh Five-Year Plans. Voluntary agencies at their best have played an important role in providing a basis for testing and devising innovative projects and new Models and approaches in programme implementation and in ensuring feedback, as well as in securing the participation of women living below the poverty line. They have developed competence in many non-traditional areas and played a vital role in supplementing governmental efforts so as to offer the rural poor choices and alternatives. They have often served as the eyes and ears of the people at the village level. By adopting simple, innovative, flexible and inexpensive means to suit their limited resources, they have tried to reach a larger number of beneficiaries with minimal overheads and with greater community participation. In the process they have successfully demonstrated how village and indigenous resources, rural skills and local knowledge are grossly underutilized at present, in a cost-effective manner. Voluntary agencies have also managed to mobilize and organize the poor to some extent and to generate in them the awareness to demand quality services and improve accountability of the local level functionaries. They have helped to train a cadre of grass root workers that believe in professionalizing voluntarism.

The increasing interest of the government in enhancing the role of voluntary agencies in the development of women is quite evident. Considering the magnitude of problems faced by women the government has rightly felt that it cannot assume the entire responsibility of service provision and development. It has sought to associate voluntary agencies in the various programmes aimed at women. The thrust of the current programmes is more towards development of women's potential and their productive participation in development rather than merely providing welfare services to them. A meaningful partnership with the voluntary sector has thus been an avowed goal and an essential variable in government's attempts to integrate women in development.

Women and the Voluntary Sector: Voluntary agencies have contributed immensely to the new directions and impetus provided to women's programmes during the decade for women. A number of innovative features in several government formulated schemes/ programmes are based on the experience of the projects run successfully by voluntary agencies.

The rationale for involvement of voluntary agencies in women's development is quite clear. Women in India suffer from multifarious constraints such as a low level of literacy, lack of access to resources and obstacles caused by the cultural and social customs and traditions that are discriminatory of women. In a situation such as this, the role of voluntary agencies in creating awareness among women of their rights and mobilizing women as well as developing in them appropriate motivation and leadership to realize those rights cannot be minimized.

The process of creating an environment conducive to the progress of women is dependent on a multitude of socio-economic factors, starting with a political will to enforce the development of women as a priority. The long-term objectives of the Seventh Plan spell out that raising the economic and social status of women is a critical goal of national development. The basic approach suggested is to inculcate confidence among women and bring about an awareness of their own potential for development. Within this framework, gainful employment to women is accorded the highest priority as an effective strategy. Various ministries and departments have formulated programmes for the development of women with an emphasis on the involvement of voluntary agencies as delivery mechanisms. The role of voluntary agencies in the mobilization of women in particular is seen as a critical factor for the development strategies of the future.

A higher involvement of voluntary agencies is thus envisaged in the implementation of such government programmes as the Integrated Rural Development Program (IRDP), Training of Rural Youth in Self-Employment (TRYSEM), Development of Women and Children in Rural Areas (DWCRA), Integrated Child Development Services Scheme (ICDS), and Adult Literacy programmes. Besides their involvement in these schemes, voluntary agencies can also assist in effective enforcement of minimum wages, supply of safe drinking water, afforestation, social forestry, consumer protection, promotion of science and technology, rural housing, legal education, etc. With the new focus on women, some funds should be earmarked for implementation of these programmes in the concerned ministries/ departments for voluntary agencies. Further through the Central Social Welfare Board (CSWB), Council for Advancement of People's Action and Rural Technology (CAPART) and the National Rural Development

Fund, the activities of and cooperation with voluntary agencies should be expanded and strengthened. To the extent that voluntary agencies are dependent on public funds, accountability has to be ensured but without cumbersome and rigid methods.

Voluntary Action in the Organization of Women: Empowerment of women cannot be ensured until they are enabled to organize themselves. Collective organizations spell strength. This is a prerequisite for initiating action, lobbying, pressurizing and bargaining. Grass roots organizations can greatly enhance the opportunities for poor women to participate in development programmes by providing an organizational base to operate from. By organizing, working together, sharing experiences and resources, building pressure groups and so forth, women can find independent access to opportunities for their betterment.

A large number of women are engaged in the unorganized sector working and living under precarious conditions and with no legal protection. The unorganized sector denies women all benefits of collective action. Dispersed and unorganized, they have no political power and no bargaining strength. As a result, it becomes much more difficult to implement protective labour laws relating to wages, conditions of work, insurance, provident fund, maternity leave, and creches, etc., and also to channelize economic inputs such as credit, technical training and marketing. In such a situation, the need for collective action becomes critical, and is dependent upon the organization of women in the unorganized sector. Many spontaneous and organized struggles have been launched by some voluntary organizations for the articulation of the needs of poor women, particularly the need to organize them for their interaction into the mainstream. For instance, the whole issue of women in the unorganized sector has been debated and seriously addressed through the awareness generated by certain organizations in different parts of the country.

Uncovered Territory: The issue of gender disparity at work is yet to be voiced effectively in the organized voluntary action movement. Of the vast masses in the category of the working poor, the unskilled ranks contain a larger proportion of females. These women are much less organized for any kind of market leverage or wage bargaining and even when organized, less inclined to redress gender inequalities at work sites. There is the need to replicate the success stories of voluntary action in organizing women in different parts of the country and to take up the issue to parity at work in a larger way.

The participation of women in development requires an all round transformation in the consciousness of both men and women as also in the socio-cultural norms, the mass media and pattern of education all of which at present tend to perpetuate a passive unequal role of women in social, economic and political affairs. There is a need for a strong voluntary action involvement in order to evolve a specific strategy based on the local situation, in this area, of women. Any voluntary agency that is serious about promoting women's participation would have to seriously consider the challenge of recruiting and training women catalysts, extension agents and functionaries for reaching and eliciting women's participation.

Voluntary Action for Legal Aid: The majority of women have no knowledge about their rights and very few have resources to obtain legal redressal. It is now being strongly felt that laws by themselves cannot bring about the desirable change in the status of women unless women become aware of their rights. At the same time, it is also felt that since most of the women cannot afford legal representation in courts due to high financial costs and lack of access to knowledge pertaining to the legal process, the countrywide network of voluntary agencies can play an effective role in providing legal aid and legal education to women. One of the priority areas for the legal aid movement in the country should be the mobilization of women through voluntary agencies. Voluntary organizations also have an important role in providing counselling, para-legal support and rehabilitation of women in distress. In fact, in the absence of such help, neither police nor courts can effectively help women. In many such cases, women are compelled to withdraw cases under the dowry prohibition act and compromise with unjust situations due to lack of alternatives. This situation could be remedied if women could be assisted through counselling support, employment training, and rehabilitation and development support by voluntary agencies.

The upsurge of interest in women's issues which characterized the decade, has left its mark on the legal scene. Voluntary organizations and activist groups are beginning to initiate action on various legal issues. It is felt that the Government should provide financial assistance to women's organizations for setting up legal aid cells. Evidently, there is a need for many more voluntary agencies to take up the issues of women and provide necessary legal aid to women.

Environment and Women: It is well recognized that the management of the environment requires the participation of people as they are closest to it and have a stake in its preservation. Active involvement of women and their organizations in environment protection is of paramount significance since women are most affected by the issue. There is a serious threat to the environment due to its degradation and pollution arising from various factors such as policies of government as well as the private sector, unplanned discharge of residual and waste, handling of toxic chemicals, indiscriminate construction of dams, large-scale deforestation, expansion of settlements and unplanned mining and quarrying work. Such conditions have pushed great number of women into marginal environment where floods, droughts, shortage of fuel, and excessive utilization of grazing land have deprived women of their livelihood.

Many voluntary agencies have taken up the issue of environment protection. Among these agencies are the Dasholi Gram Swarajya Mandal that has started the Chipko Movement in which women play a very important role. This movement has received international acclaim and was initiated by hill women. Women embraced (Chipko) trees to prevent them being felled and some women were killed while thus protecting these with their own bodies. Trees to these women and others are the source of life. The impact of environmental degradation and of soil erosion is first felt by women. Many grass root level women's organizations have begun to take up environmental issues in addition to their continuing concern for rural poverty due to the intrinsic link among environment, poverty and gender.

The responsibility for creating awareness, mobilizing public opinion and building a strong people's movement lies mainly with the voluntary agencies. The awareness generated by individual women pioneers/leaders and all types of women's organizations on environmental issues has focused on the fact that women and men have the capacity to manage their environment, and their access to productive resources should be sustained and enhanced. It is also recognized that the requisite knowledge and information can be disseminated by voluntary organizations to reinforce the self-help potential of women in conserving and improving the environment.

Demystification of Technology: A number of voluntary agencies are involved in commendable work in the, demystification of appropriate technology for the advancement of rural women. The programmes implemented by voluntary agencies in this area include, providing opportunities for gainful employment and self-employment for women, reducing the drudgery in their lives, ensuring adequate medical and nutritional facilities, improving sanitation and environmental conditions and protecting women from occupational hazards. However, there is a need for further voluntary action in this direction that can develop and disseminate appropriate technology for women. Since the technological marginalization of female work is endemic in both the agricultural and the nonagricultural informal sector, voluntary agencies should be involved in overcoming gender differentials in the application and generation of technology. There is a need to actively deploy technology to reduce the drudgery of the poorest working women in back breaking tasks such as gathering of fuel, fodder and water.

Training constitutes another important input, particularly for upgradation of skill and augmentation of earning capacities of women. There is a strong need for a diversification of training undertaking by voluntary organizations. Their role should be particularly geared to the sensitization of administrators functionaries and catalysts on the issues and needs of women in development and in the delivery of comprehensive training programmes that have a component of knowledge, attitudes and skills for women's development.

Guidelines

The increase in the number, expansion and diversification of activities of the voluntary agencies has not necessarily equalized the disparities between them. There are not only regional imbalances in the growth of the voluntary sector but within a particular state, the growth of this sector has not been even. It is also well known that a majority of voluntary agencies are urban based and that relatively few have taken up the issues of women. It is recommended that the focus of voluntary agencies move from urban to rural areas, as the situation of rural women warrants immediate support. There is also need for the government to encourage voluntary action for the development of women by provision of adequate financial and structural support.

There is an urgent need to improve the effectiveness of voluntary action. Improvement will have to be brought about both in the organizational structures as also in the quality of services offered. Voluntary workers need to be professionals, equipped with appropriate skills for managing women's projects and sensitivity towards women's issues. National and State level institutions and training organizations should provide adequate facilities for research and training relating to women's issues. They should take up activities guided by the felt needs of women and those that can make a qualitative difference to women's lives, rather than be confined to traditional areas of support and action. Their work should be related to contemporary issues and thinking on women. As a caution, they should resist the temptation of initiating more work than they can effectively manage.

Voluntary action should be directed particularly towards preventive rather than purely curative measures. Efforts of voluntary agencies should also be geared towards generating self-reliance rather than to create dependencies. To improve their capabilities in planning and implementation of programmes, voluntary agencies are in need of expertise and technical guidance as much as financial assistance. Unfortunately, in the existing system of grants-in-aid, financial assistance to them assumes overriding importance vis-a-vis other forms of assistance such as technical guidance in the area of programme planning, project formulation, financial planning, administration, monitoring and evaluation. The proposed Resource Centre at the national level could also facilitate in the training needs of functionaries and in providing necessary managerial and technical assistance to voluntary agencies.

The process of grant-seeking and receiving is considered by a number of voluntary agencies as a frustrating experience. There is an urgent need to review the working of the grants-in-aid system. Wherever needed, modifications should be introduced to ensure that rules are simplified, grants released on-time and the amount provided is commensurate and proportionate to the needs of a particular programme. While a system of accountability for government funds is unavoidable, it need not be painful. Further, it should be ensured that financial assistance from the government does not seriously affect the basic character of voluntarism, its flexibility and innovativeness.

A number of programmes implemented by conventional voluntary agencies have emphasized imparting skills to improve the efficiency of women as housewives and mothers, and to improve their earning capacities. Voluntary agencies tend to neglect the participative potential of women in the development process as well as conscientizing women on their rights and roles. There is the need for such efforts that could increase the awareness of women and improve their participation as equal citizens in national development. Further, voluntary agencies should play a surveillance role and observe, explore and analyse the extent to which social legislations implemented for women have actually benefited them. They should also act as pressure groups to better enforcement of laws for women.

At present, there is no proper mechanism of coordination among different voluntary agencies working for the development of women. An effective mechanism for coordination between the government and the voluntary agencies is also to be ensured. CAPART and CSWB are appropriately situated to make efforts for more effective coordination and implementation of various programmes for women through voluntary organizations. For them to perform this role effectively, there should be a proper representation of grass roots women's organizations in CAPART and CSWB, that can serve as pressure groups. There is also the need for a continuous flow of information from government to voluntary agencies and vice versa through such mechanisms as a clearing house for information.

A focal point is desirable in the rural areas to encourage women's voluntary activities. Mahila Mandals and women's groups at the village or community level should be organized or revived and encouraged to register and function as women's institutions for undertaking socio-economic programmes. These institutions should be effectively linked with the various development and service agencies, offering training facilities for income generations as well as enhanced awareness among women. This linkage will enable women to absorb institutional finance for the development of viable economic activities. Particular attention will need to be given to the training of the Mahila Mandal functionaries and women's group organizers and provide them an orientation to development perspective rather than purely welfare approaches.

The CSWB which has been the coordinating agency for voluntary action for women and children, must respond to the new thrust of government policy meant for women and recast its own programmes.

Greater coordination and cooperation among NGOs is called for to avoid duplication of services. Greater funding for networking among NGOs must be provided. This will ensure more efficient utilization of funds and greater coverage of programmes. Government support to voluntary agencies for providing assistance to women in distress, including the running of crisis centres and short stay homes must be expanded. Para legal training must be an integral part of such efforts.

Voluntary agencies must be increasingly involved in the provision of employment and supportive services for women.

The National Literacy Mission must involve women's organizations in a big way.

The voluntary sector should increasingly be involved to act as a catalyst/intermediary in organizing women for collective action.

There is the need to document success stories of major NGOs in India and learn from their success and failures. Further, it is necessary to analyse the cost-benefit of NGO Projects versus governmental projects, i.e., both economic and social costs. It would also be critical to total the overall number of women reached by NGOs in India. The areas of activities and fields of success would also highlight their strengths and limitations.

In order to ensure that the security and integrity of the nation are preserved, there is a need to adopt suitable policies to ensure that voluntary agencies abide by the rules governing the receipt and utilization of foreign grants and submit audited accounts, returns and reports periodically.

Identity cards should be issued to workers of voluntary agencies who are dealing with cases of atrocities against women, as is already being done in some districts.

In order to have sufficient infrastructure and facilities, there is need to mobilize more resources for voluntary agencies which are engaged in welfare and development of women.

There is a need to decentralize the planning process to stimulate local people's participation in planning, implementation, monitoring and evaluation of development projects. A suitable mechanism should be evolved to involve voluntary agencies and other people's institutions at various stages of developmental programmes / projects. Voluntary agencies should further ensure the participation of poor women in the development process.

In the preceding chapters recommendations have been made sectorally with a view to strengthening women's roles therein. Certain important issues, however, impinge on all spheres of women's lives and work. With a view to enhancing women's status and capacities to participate in the process of nation building, the following general recommendations are made:

The overall approach of this National Perspective Plan is to perceive women in a holistic manner. While the programmes for women will continue to be implemented by different ministries as part of their department plans, it is essential to have a strong inter-ministerial coordination and monitoring body along with its own supportive facilities service by the Department of Women and Child Development (Proposed infrastructure at Annexure 1).

All ministries must reflect the concern for the all round development of women. The concerned ministries must have women's cell which currently only exists in the Ministries of Labour, Small-Scale Industry, Science and Technology and Rural Development. It is essential that the new policy thrust for women's development should be reflected in the Planning Commission as well as the State Planning Boards. The National Commission on Self-Employed Women and Women in the Informal Sector, has also independently concluded that the Planning Commission and State Planning Boards need to focus their attention sharply on the realistic situation of (labouring) women.

An essential prerequisite for the implementation of these new policy directives would be a women's unit in the Planning Commission, to redefine categories of data collection for women, modify existing terminology and identify gaps in data collection relating to women and to give direction to plans and programmes for women's development. It is also essential to analyse the impact of the different macro policies on women while planning new endeavours.

Financial and fiscal resources should be apportioned and preferential allocations for women's employment in mainstream programmes and projects should be made. This would imply the rationalization on resource allocation within mainstream programmes so as to benefit women, rather than only seeking separate allocations for women. Critical emphasis must be placed on rate of investment in women preferred industries and occupations.

At the State level, the Departments/ Directorates of Women's Development should be initiated. Currently, there is no separate department of women in many States. Social welfare, handicapped, Scheduled Castes and Scheduled Tribes are subjects that are bracketed together with the development of women at the State level. This new department could also be the State level implementation body for the programmes/ policies of the Department of Women and Child Development of the Government of India.

In terms of programme implementation, the two major implementing bodies envisaged, are the Social Welfare Boards and the Women's Development Corporations. There can be a rationalization of service provision between these two bodies. The State Social Welfare Advisory Boards could eventually concentrate on implementing welfare/supportive programmes for women (homes for women in distress, working women's hostels, counselling centres for legal aid and paralegal training, condensed courses, etc.). Women Development Corporations would be responsible for the implementation of economic programmes through non-governmental and governmental agencies/ departments wherever necessary, concentrating on technical inputs like credit, marketing, design development, etc., and reaching out to women at the district and village levels.

Women should be entitled to a package of services at the block level created by the convergence of schemes such as Development of Women and Children in Rural Areas (DWCRA), Integrated Child Development Schemes (ICDS), Adult Education, Health Care, etc., at the grass roots administrative level. Every district should have a coordinator to assist in the integration of these programmes aimed at the development of women. The coordinator will also be responsible for motivating local planning of programmes and assist in their implementation and provide feedback for effective planning and evaluation. Since decentralization of planning monitoring and implementation of development programmes for women is suggested as also devolution of finance at district level, appointment of District coordinators for women's programmes would facilitate this process, and control over finance would empower them. The National Commission on Self-Employed Women and Women in the Informal Sector has also recommended the appointment of District Coordination Officers to be responsible for planning, monitoring, coordination and evaluation of the programmes affecting women. Rationalization of functionaries at the block and village levels to ensure coordination of programmes affecting women at the grass roots level also needs to be undertaken.

There are today sufficient number of programmes in the Government of India as well as innovative programmes in many States and sectors. What is needed is not merely larger resource allocation but technical inputs for greater effectiveness of these programmes, to guarantee better resource utilization. Emphasis has to be placed on more effective planning, monitoring and evaluation of existing programmes through a result oriented mechanism operating at different levels.

Recognizing that a critical input for women's development would be a new thrust to training and wider dissemination of information backed by research data and documentation. It is proposed to set up a National Resource Centre for Women. This resource centre would translate national developmental needs of women into a systematic grid of programmes and schemes for training at different levels in skills/ knowledge/ attitudes. The centre would identify and if necessary, strengthen existing governmental and non-governmental agencies including women's universities /women's centres and colleges through which the training, research/ dissemination could be carried out. The National Commission on Self-Employed Women and Women in Informal Sector has also recommended the need for a National Institute to cater to women's training as well as formulate guidelines and help the other constituent units at the State level, Divisional levels and district level to carry out training programmes.

Reorientation and sensitization of the administrative machinery at all levels in the Government of India, the States, as well as specialized technical agencies (both Government and Voluntary) to the issues of women in development is essential. Three levels of orientation are necessary, i.e., at the policy and planning levels, at the district or intermediary level, and at the block and village levels. The training of functionaries and their orientation to women's issues must also be in the right perspective, i.e., women should be perceived as producers and participants, not clients for welfare. The dynamic role of women's contribution to the national economy as partners and equal citizens must be reiterated and translated into programmes and projects. The National Resource Centre would be responsible for revamping the existing content/ methodology and monitoring of training at all levels.

A special division should be created in the Department of Women and Child Development for the enforcement of law for women. The officer in charge may be designated Commissioner for Women's Rights and must liaise with the various Special Cells for women created by the police, the CBI as well as with the Departments of Public Grievances at Centre and State levels as also the Women's Cell in the Home Ministry. This division will be concerned with the enforcement of law to ensure women's rights, to facilitate action oriented research in needs such as discrimination against women, protection at work, etc.

This Plan recommends that the Census in future must take into account women's unpaid work in the household and outside as well as the value added in performing her many survival tasks for the family. A greater conceptual clarity has to emerge on 'work' and 'non-work' as well as a distinction between work that produces economic value and other activities that are Consumption oriented. Data relating to women, especially in the unorganized sector should be reflected in the data of the National Sample Survey and the Central Statistical Organization.

7

Pressures and Constraints

A modern educated women suffers from various tensions. If she is a housewife she feels stressed because her education has not incurred her any relief from domestic chores. If she is working woman she is stressed because of lack of co-ordination between her home and office life. This chapter identifies stresses typical to the modern educated woman and offers some suggestions for dealing with them.

Role of Housewife

The ambivalence that women feel as they take on dual roles of housewife and worker is quite tension producing. Undoubtedly, many women are able to combine both roles with smooth adjustments, particularly if the husband and the family members are co-operative and supportive. However, in many families, the conflict between both the roles has created estrangement between either the husband or the wife or the wife and the other members of the family.

The psychology of the Indian women in terms of her desire for domination and her will for subordination. The large number of women who have traditional outlook are meeting with their tensions and stresses by overtly subordinating themselves to men and covertly trying to dominate them by their extreme devotion and sense of duty. The modern emancipated women are revolting against this duplicity. They are denying the superiority of the male and seeking an equality between the sexes overtly and covertly both. We have also advocated that through our educational system the women should learn to move towards equality of sexes without involving themselves in any duplicity in their behaviour pattern. But the danger in such a move is the enhancement of tensions and stresses in the individuals, in the families and also in the society.

Standard of Living

Ambitious men of lower income group want their wives and daughters to work and earn to help raise the family's standard of living. At the same time these men cannot tolerate the idea of independence such as that they themselves have on the job. They are unable to free themselves from the myths of Sita and Savitri. They become agitated when their women become assertive and begin to express their personal views and opinions and their likes and dislikes. They feel that women are transgressing their freedom, which they have so generously bestowed on them. Their ego is hurt if their wife's income exceeds their own Income. But the women when they go out for work cannot be bound in the chains of orthodoxy. Hence the modern woman's tensions enhance as she has to cope with the demands of her job and the dictates of her male relations.

In a study by Mukta Mittal on "Educated Women Power," it was found that the need for supplementing the family income was the chief motivating factor for encouraging the respondents belonging to "lowly educated" and "moderately educated" groups to become job seekers and get themselves registered at the Employment Exchange Bureaus. But in the case of "highly educated" respondents, the prime motivating factor behind encouraging them in their becoming registrants for job was "desire to be free from dependence on family members and relatives".

Many conflicts arise when both husband and wife are working. The husband desires that the wife should take up job but disapproves the complete involvement of the wife in the job. For him the job of the wife is only a secondary commitment. Her primary duty he feels is towards him and his family. He wants his wife to work and also to take up full time duties of looking after the household. When the wife is unable to cope with this situation the seeds of conflict and estrangement between the husband and wife begin to germinate. After returning from her work the wife is tired but she receives no sympathy or help from her husband or in-laws. When the tensions so created become unbearable the wife has no option but to resign from the job. But this is also not liked by the husband who resents the loss of income and blames the wife for not being able to reconcile between her job outside and her duties to her family.

The tension reduction in such cases is possible when all the family members recognise that the household work is to be shared and is a joint responsibility of all the members of the family. In those families in which the joint responsibility is recognised the tensions are suitably dealt with.

Till nearly three decades earlier the women were giving utmost importance to the role of the housewife. In a study by Cora Vreede Stuer in 1970 it was reported that quite a substantial number of girls "consider the role of the housewife as the most suitable." But when they were asked that if they had to go outside the home to work, most of them said they would prefer to teach or do social work. One girl in Cora's study remarked: "I would be willing to work in my field, but if my husband opposed it, I would submit to his wishes." Similar views were expressed by 18 of 15 educated women in Rama Mehta's study of the Western Educated Hindu women in 1970. One woman in her study expressed this view: 'Working was not important enough for me to go against my husband's wishes. After marriage, one cannot do as one wants, working is not an important enough issue to create tensions". It may be noted that till seventies or may be later also the working women, generally, perceived their main role as that of wife or mother. By such an attitude they were meeting with their tensions created by their becoming working women. But the situation at the end of the twentieth century is not as simple as that. The aspirations and the motivations of the women have increased manifolds and so also there is increase in their stresses and tensions.

Favourable Attitude

Society now has a more favourable attitude towards the employment of women in the middle income groups. It has become an economic need. Promilla Kapur in her study in seventies took a sample of 300 working women from three major occupations – teachers, office workers and doctors. She observed that because of society's change of attitude, as well as change in attitudes of the educated married women towards their own employment, their number has multiplied to the extent that they now constitute a class by themselves. This class is facing the greatest change and, challenge ever offered anywhere in the world to the feminine population.

The number of women seeking jobs has increased manifolds now from that of seventies. The challenges before them have also become quite serious. The educated women have first to face the spectre of unemployment. The job market is very tight. It is difficult for men to get the jobs and when women also compete with them the number of the job seekers becomes quite high. With the limited job opportunities the women also suffer from the various types of restrictions which are put on them by the society. They still search the jobs, which are considered feminine in nature like the teaching, or nursing or office work, etc. They also want a job in the town or place to which they belong. They do not opt for the jobs in the villages or remote areas. It is not only due to the intention of the women that they do not want to work at the distant places from their homes but also due to the living conditions. It is difficult for a single working woman to find a decent living place in most of the towns or big cities. The security environment in the country is also not such as the women may move very freely. The cases of eve teasing are on the increase and the single working woman becomes an easy prey of unscrupulous males.

The women's problems are three-fold with regard to getting employment. First of all, they have to compete in an overcrowded job market. Secondly, their families and society do not allow them to serve in those professions, which are branded as predominantly masculine in nature, even though there may be no restriction from the side of the employing authorities. Thirdly, they have the problem of finding suitable living accommodation if they get a job away from their homes or native place and added to this is the problem of security for a single working woman. All these problems are stress producing in the educated women. But it may be said that the stresses of the women can be reduced if they themselves and the society approach towards the solution of the problems with some dedication. There is no doubt in it that the number of jobs has to be increased. More efforts should be made to educate the women to generate self-employment. They may also be given vocational training. A change is to be brought in their own attitudes and the attitudes of the society and the family that it is a myth that the women are incapable of taking up some jobs which are masculine in nature. The women are capable of taking up all those jobs, which are considered masculine. In previous pages we have forcefully built the case of sexual equality on the basis of the physiology of the male and the female. Lastly, the government and the society must come forward to build "Working Women's Homes." In some towns they have been built. The need is to have a chain of such homes in each town and township.

Type of Conflict

There is another type of conflict with which the working women suffer. This is in relation to their work environment. The working women rightly demand that they should be accepted and respected as equally capable and efficient workers as males. The conflict occurs when they simultaneously demand special privileges and advantages because they are the women and the weaker sex. For example, they take up jobs that require night duties but after taking the job they may claim that since they are ladies they may be exempted from working in the night. They may press the employer to transfer them to some daytime job and transfer some male to this job. This becomes a conflict-producing situation. Some women also shirk work claiming that they are women and so entitled for light work. To avoid such conflicts the women need to develop professional attitude. There are many examples of successful women.

There is another side of the picture as well. The men resent the working women in their midst. In an office in which men and women both work the men do not feel as free with the women as with their men colleagues. If male becomes too intimate gossips are unleashed. If he ignores them he is branded as the chauvinistic male. There seems to be a need to develop a code of ethics for interpersonal relationships in those situations in which the males and females have to work in close co-ordination.

Serious Situation

A very serious situation is developing in some places of work where the boss is male and he tries to sexually exploit his female employees. The women organizations, the government and even the courts are seized with this problem. Some women take the courage to make complaints about this behaviour of their officers or male colleague but there are lots of women who silently suffer at the hands of office sharks. Sometimes men also become victims of women's manipulations. They make false complaints about their exploitation so that the persons concerned are defamed. It is because of this danger that the complaints of women regarding exploitation are being scrutinized cautiously. Such situations can be avoided in case men and women both are made to realise that there shall be no discrimination in the work situations on the basis of sex. Both men and women must view each other as equal partners in work performance and must expect that recognition shall depend on their efficiency and quality of work and not on their sex.

As has already been pointed out that greatest danger resulting from a woman being career oriented is disharmony within her family. In Kapur's study of much marital maladjustment, the husband expected the wife to work as well as serve him and the household. The husbands generally believed in absolute supremacy over their wives and desire complete surrender and devotion from them. Those women who asserted their individuality were severely punished and ruthlessly treated, In cases where women could not tolerate the brutalities, they were separated from their spouses.

If the husband demands that his wife quit work and she refuses, it creates much tension in the family. In those cases in which the husband is transferred and the wife refuses to quit her job and go with him, legal problems arise. The husband may sue his wife for the restoration of conjugal rights. In such cases the attitude of the Indian courts has not been very decisive. Kusum (1976) cited many cases in which the wife was asked to leave her job and join her husband. In one case (Gaya Prasad Vs. Smt. Bhagwati) in Madhya Pradesh, the wife worked as Gram Sevika due to financial circumstances. The husband petitioned for the restitution of conjugal rights. The observations of the court while delivering the judgement were: "Merely on the ground that the husband has a small income, and the wife if allowed to serve at a place away from the marital home, can substantially augment the family, cannot be held to be a sufficient reason to deny the wife's society to the husband".

The above judgement was given in the sixties. From seventies onwards the change in the attitudes of the courts is noticeable, as judgements have become much less traditional. The judges concede that in case of genuine economic necessity, the wife has a right to maintain her job. But the main problem here is not only the economic necessity but also a woman's freedom to take her own decisions. The woman's personal satisfaction, sense of confidence and security and her intellectual needs must be the guiding factors in making a decision about her quitting the job or remaining in service while living away from her husband or family. Whatever may be the decisions of the courts the stressful life between the husband or and wife will continue to be lived till there is the recognition that wife also has aspirations, ambitions and a will of her own. The idea that the women should work only to supplement their husbands income is to give them much inferior position in the family than that of husbands and of considering them as only the instruments for augmenting the family incomes. The women should not be viewed as the objects or instruments, but as entities unto themselves.

Concepts of In-laws

Narrow and conservative concepts of in-laws are also tension producing. The in-laws, in many cases want that their daughters-in-law take up jobs but at the same time are extremely critical if she is late in returning from her place of work or is not able to do the household work as efficiently as they expect her to do.

Some studies indicate that women seek work equal to the level of their husband's prestige. In case a wife is not equally educated or trained she may prefer to stay at home rather than accept work below her husband's level. In such a case if she is forced to undertake inferior status work, she remains tense and suffers from inferiority complex. The woman herself can take steps to come out of such situation by undertaking courses or training to improve her qualifications.

Perpetual Quarrels

There is another side of the picture also. If the wife is employed in a job which has higher prestige and emoluments than the husband's job, the husband feels jealous and threatened. In many cases the tension between the husband and wife becomes so intense that living under the same roof becomes a torture leading to divorce or separation or to perpetual quarrels between them. There can develop proper amity and understanding between them if the wife tries to understand the sentiments of the husband and the husband realises that his wife deserves what she is getting. Truly well adjusted couples are those who respect each others individuality. A husband and wife can achieve harmony through mutual support and self-esteem. When both work role differentiation should not exist. The husband should give full emotional support to the wife and the wife should be considerate to the needs of the husband, may they be either psychological, physical, sexual or economical.

The girls including those who are educated find it very difficult to get a husband who does not demand dowry. In fact now the eligible bachelors and their families are demanding that the girls be educated so that they can earn money and also a dowry to meet the initial expenses of setting the home. Dowry demands are increasing day by day with the rising ambitions for equipping the houses with the modern gadgets. The educated girls whose parents search bridegrooms who are well-employed and highly educated face demands of exorbitant amounts as dowries. Such demands many parents are not able to meet with. The sensitive girls feel themselves as the cause of their parent's woes and blame themselves for being born as girls. Sometimes their tensions increase so much that they even commit suicide.

The statistics relating to dowry are very grim. Sometime back it was announced in the Lok Sabha that as many as 878 cases of dowry murders and 1,479 cases of dowry suicides were registered in the country in 1990. The educated girls who resent their husband and in-laws demands of dowry are brutally killed or forced to commit suicide. In order to stop these great human tragedies and combat horrible social evils, it would be necessary to bring about radical transformation, in the old rigid social structure. The parents of the educated girls rear them up in such a rigid environment that they themselves are incapable of finding their own life partners. They have to depend on the traditional system of marriage. The educated girls may be saved from much stress if they are left free to make a choice of their own mates. The rigid social structure can be changed only when a brave new philosophy of life steeped in socio-economic and moral values of equality of all castes and both the sexes is evolved out and adopted. Such a philosohpy will enable the male as well as the female child to spontaneously internalise the principle of equality of man, woman of all castes and creeds.

Progress and Development

The Indian women are marching ahead in each and every field of work and activity. They are in the forefront of all the movements for progress and development. But unfortunately the area of social reforms, which touches them directly, is as yet a neglected area. The movement for women emancipation and empowerment are ridiculed and made fun of by the traditionally oriented males. The women have little say in the Parliament or state legislatures because their number is extremely limited in these bodies. The Bill for 30 per cent reservation of seats for women in the Parliament is opposed on one flimsy ground or another. Our Parliament and legislatures are responsible for the governance and the administration of the country. On them are needed such persons who are highly motivated towards efficient management, adequately educated, well-informed and possess a zeal for social service. The country at present has quite a substantial number of such women who can adorn the seats of the Parliament. There are, however, some leaders who want those women in the Parliament who are mere appendages of their husbands or male relatives. The ridiculous thing is that they want to do it in the name of social justice.

The stresses and the tensions of the modern educated Indian women can be minimised if they involve themselves in a strong movement of women emancipation and empowerment. In the Indian context it means the deliverance from the myths which have been woven around them and the false pedestal at which they have been put since long.

In 1963 Frieden wrote the Feminine Mystique which attempted to explode many myths about women. Her thesis is applicable to both East and West. She writes- 'the Victorian culture did not permit women to accept or gratify their basic sexual needs, our culture does not permit women to accept or gratify their basic need to grow and fulfill their potentialities as human beings, a need which is not solely defined by their sexual role". Just as the Indian women have been led to believe that their fulfillment lies in motherhood and wifely duties, so Friedan observes about American women: "In the feminine mystique, there is no other way she can even dream about herself, except as her children's mother, her husband's wife."

Simone de Beauvoir considers that the myth of feminine 'mystery' has several advantages for the male. He can dismiss inexplicable moods, behaviours, and feelings by saying:"Oh

Women! Who can understand them any way?" Rohrbaugh Joanna adds: "Since woman cannot be understood, man cannot be expected to build an authentic relationship with her. He is free to relate to her in terms of his own perceptions, fantasies and desires".

Williams referring to the myth of woman as mystery says "By defining her as mysterious other, man spares himself the necessity of analysing her behaviours and understanding it as a consequence of her position vis-a-vis him. To do that would require acknowledgement of her oppression, and a possible shift in their power relationship? The price would be very high".

In such a 'mystique' or lifestyle, a woman's intelligence has no meaning and her capability is negated. By following a monotonous daily routine, she loses all interest in the outside world, draws herself into a shell and spends her time in gossips. She is little more than an instrument, which keeps a constant supply of members through her powers of reproduction.

Friedan emphasises that one's individuality when becoming a wife and mother should not be given up, but strengthened. She says: "Maslow found that the individuality is strengthened, that the ego is in one sense merged with another, but yet in another sense remains separate, and strong as always. The two, tendencies, to transcend individuality and to sharpen and strengthen it, must be seen as partners and not as contradictory". Self-actualised educated women should serve their society and contribute their best to humanity, just as men have the opportunity to do so. The world has suffered enough because half of humanity has remained dependent on the other half.

Passive, Prudish and Fragile

Indian women are often viewed as passive, prudish and fragile. Many of them feel that a mere lustful glance or touch by a non-relative male leads to the loss of their chastity. The women's movements should actively try to alter such a nonsensical perception. It may be remembered that the women in general and the educated women in particular are in danger of becoming not only household slaves but also work place slaves if they do not learn to become individualistic and assertive.

An Indian woman with lustre with a brilliance of her won, with a dynamic attitude towards life and with the charm of a sturdy woman going about her business is always in danger of being branded as aggressive, too outgoing and, perhaps, flirtatious, This type of woman is incongruent with the image of the ideal that has been imprinted on the minds of the Indians for the centuries. The women's movements should be in the direction of relieving intelligent, modern women from the clutches of orthodoxy. The real women's movement which India need and towards which the Indian feminists seem to be fully conscious is that of removal of orthodoxy, blind faith, poverty, helplessness, dependence and complete subjugation of woman's will. The reformers should try to bring the changes in the attitudes of both male and female regarding marriage and the family. The must attack fanatical religious rites, ill conceived notions of virginity, wrong notions of chastity, custom of giving or taking dowry, wastage in the marriage ceremonies and similar other outdated customs and traditions.

We may agree with Carden when he says that : 'The new feminism is not about the elimination of differences between the sexes, nor even simply the achievement of equal opportunity; it concerns with the individual's right to find out the kind of person he or she is and to strive to become that person".

8

Effective Planning

The Perspective Plan for Women is an effort at a long term overall policy for Indian Women, guided by those constitutional principles and directives relevant to the development process. It is linked to the national targets determined for the end of the century in respect of certain basic indicators especially of health, education and employment. The Plan views women not as the weaker segment of society or as passive beneficiaries of the development process, but as a source of unique strength for reaching national goals.

The Plan aims at:

Economic development and integration of women into the mainstream of the economy.

Equity and social justice for all women.

These are critical goals for the all round development of women not merely as producers and providers, but also as individuals with a right to human dignity in a society where 'culture', 'caste' and 'class' tend to discriminate against gender.

The overall purpose of this plan is to find the highest common denominator for all national endeavour, running across the spectrum of class and religion; functions, sectors and disciplines; to harness the resource represented by the people-both the women as well as the men. This renewal of efforts, from the fifth decade of political independence, will have meaning only if the full potential of the silent half-comprising the 331 million women and girls of India, (about 150 million of them in material poverty and many more close to it) is harnessed. The direction and design, priorities and pace of national development, must have direct relevance to their lives and future. Every dimension of development-political, economic and cultural, not just social-has to assist and hasten their generation.

If the results and lessons of the past are any guide, a larger allocation of resources for women within the prevailing patterns and structures of development, does not promise a reversal of trends. A parallel sub-stream of women's development even if possible, will only perpetuate discrimination and subordination. An alternative strategy of national development which will provide not just some additional space for women, but create a democratic, egalitarian, secular, cooperative social structure has to be defined and tried. In such a scheme, it will be necessary to accelerate the women's component of composite programmes, to ensure the integrity of the enterprise as well as a measure of compensatory justice. The goals of holistic human development must not be at the expense of one another and the ascent to equality must be collective.

Assessment of Conditions

For outlining a development perspective, a review of the existing situation of the Indian woman is an essential prerequisite. Both, positive indicators as well as negative indices that are a growing cause of concern to policy makers, planners, administrators and activists are projected to present her overall status. A brief review of the Five-Year Plans and the programmes for women launched in the last few decades, is also included.

Among the positive developments affecting women are:

The expectation of life at birth has improved from 44.7 years in 1961-71 to 52.9 years in 1971-81.

The sex ratio has registered a slight rise-from 930 women per thousand men in 1971 to 933 per thousand men in 1981. The average age at marriage for girls has reached 18.3 years in 1981 as against 17.2 years in 1971, achieving for the first time an average higher than the minimum prescribed age for marriage.

The focus in the programmes for women has shifted from welfare to development. This shift can be perceived in the creation of a separate department for the development of women.

The Programme of Action of the National Policy on Education (1986) lays stress on women's equality and has identified for the first time three areas for special attention, viz. (i) review of school textbooks to remove sexist bias and developing approaches to promotion of the value of equality through school curricula; (ii) reorientation of teachers to promote gender equality through their teaching and (iii) increasing the coverage of women and women's issues in the research and teaching activities of higher education.

Women's Studies and Development Centres have been set up in constituent colleges of several universities with the objective of using students and teachers as resource groups for creating social awareness and bringing about attitudinal changes in society.

There is an effort to sensitize administration to the women's perspective in development programmes, through the introduction of a women's component in training programmes for senior administrators conducted by the Department of Personnel in the Government of India.

There is a special effort launched to involve women at all levels in the planning and implementation process of programmes for women.

There is an increasing emphasis on professionalizing women's programmes by providing technical expertise for their implementation.

For the first time since Independence the elected representation of women in Parliament has gone up to almost 10 per cent of its total membership.

The Prime Minister's office has now identified 27 beneficiary oriented schemes exclusively for women. These schemes though falling under various Ministers are monitored by the Department of Women and Child Development, Ministry of Human Resource Development.

A National Advisory Committee on Women has been set up with the Prime Minister as Chairman.

Several legislative enactments/amendments have come into force to protect the interests of women.

Overshadowing the positive indicators, there are certain distressing negative indices as follows:

Though a marginal improvement has been registered in the sex ratio, the projected ratio for 2000 AD is depressing with 500 million males to 480 million females.

Amniocentesis tests are being misused to determine the sex of the child in the womb, resulting in the female foetus being aborted.

Age specific death rates indicate higher rates for female children and women up to 35 years of age.

As per the 1981 Census, 75 per cent of women are illiterate. This is compounded by the high drop out rate for girls which is estimated at 55.5 per cent at the primary stage and 77.7 per cent at the middle school stage. Enrolment of girls in higher education has been almost static from 1975 to 1985. There are also substantial disparities in the enrolment of girls and boys at the university stage, and in technical and professional colleges.

The work participation rate for females declined in the census decades up to 1981. In 1981, it recorded a marginal improvement.

The fertility rates in 1981 showed only a very marginal decline-average number of children born to a woman during her lifetime being 4.6. There are in addition many incomplete pregnancies. Over 50 per cent of women suffer from anaemia in pregnancy, which accounts directly for 15-20 per cent of all maternal deaths.

Approximately 90 per cent of the women workers are engaged in the unorganized sector. Of these over 80 per cent are in agriculture and allied occupations. In the organized sector women constitute only 13.3 per cent of all employees. In the public sector, they account for 11 per cent of total employment and in the private sector for 17.8 per cent.

The number of female job seekers through employment exchanges increased from 11.2 lakh in 1975 to 51 lakh in 1986. After showing an increase between 1975 and 1982, the percentage of placements declined in the subsequent years, i.e., 1983-86.

Studies show that modernization and mechanization are tending to marginalize women in many sectors. They are either pushed down or out of the workforce. There are also indications that agricultural modernization/ industrial growth policies have tended to widen gender disparities.

Estimates of the average hours of unpaid work done by women outside their homes vary from 6.1 and 7.5 hours per day, with some women working up to 10 hours and more. Apart from their domestic duties, women are engaged in agricultural operations for an average of 12 hours a day. Despite this, their access to ownership of land, credit and other productive resources remains negligible.

Recent surveys indicate that, 30-35 per cent of rural households are headed by women due to male migration, neglect, abandonment.

Only 994 women hold senior management/administrative posts as against 15,993 men in similar jobs in the All India Services, constituting only 5.8 per cent. There are only 21 women officers in the Indian Police Service as against 2418 men (0.9 per cent). In the Indian Administrative Services, there are 339 women against 4209 men (7.5 per cent).

Women comprise only 7.5 per cent of the membership of registered trade unions and approximately one per cent of the office bearers and executive committee members.

Proportional representation of women in elected offices either remained stagnant or declined in the last decade. This is not withstanding their increased voting turnout in the general elections.

> Crimes against women continue unabated, there were 6668 reported victims of rape in 1987 and 1517 dowry deaths including by burning (provisional figures).

The *First Five-Year Plan* (1951-56) envisaged welfare measures for women. To spearhead welfare measures, the Central Social Welfare Board (CSWB) was established in 1953 which symbolized the welfare approach to women's problems. The CSWB was also reflective of the community development approach, which envisaged for the first time, the need for organizing women into Mahila Mandals or Women's Clubs. A number of studies have shown that the community development (CD) worker, perceived more as a harmonizer of interests rather than a stimulator of awareness, worked closely with the rural elite. Moreover, although rural women came within the purview of the CD programmes, they were not specifically catered to as a target population based on economic or other specific class related criteria. A large majority of poor rural women thus remained untouched.

The *Second Five-Year Plan* (1956-61) was closely linked with the overall approach of intensive agricultural development. The welfare approach to women's issues persisted. The plan recognized the need for the organization of women as workers. It also perceived the social prejudices/disabilities they suffered. The Plan stated that women should be protected against injurious work, should receive maternity benefits and creches for children. It also suggested speedy implementation of the principle of equal pay for equal work and provision for training to enable women to compete for higher jobs.

The *Third Five-Year Plan* (1961-66) pinpointed female education as a major welfare strategy. In social welfare, the largest share was provided for expanding rural welfare services and condensed courses of education. The health programme concentrated mainly on the provision of services for maternal and child welfare, health education, nutrition and family planning.

The *Fourth Five-Year Plan* (1969-74) continued the emphasis on women education. The basic policy was to promote women's welfare within the family as the base of operation. The outlay on Family Planning was stepped up to reduce the birth rate from 40 to 25 per thousand through mass education. High priority was accorded to immunization of pre-school children and supplementary feeding for children, expectant and nursing mothers.

The *Fifth Five-Year Plan* (1974-79) emphasized the need to train women in need of income and protection. It also recommended a programme of functional literacy to equip women with skills and knowledge to perform the functions of a housewife (including child care, nutrition, health care, home economics, etc.)

This Plan coincided with the International Women's Decade and the submission of the Report of the Committee on the Status of Women in India (CSWI). The overall task of the CSWI was to undertake a comprehensive examination of all the questions relating to the rights and status of women in the context of changing social and economic conditions in the country and problems relating to the advancement of women. The report stressed that the dynamics of social change and development had adversely affected a large section of women and had created new imbalances and disparities such as:

- The declining sex ratio;
- Lower expectancy of life;
- Higher infant and maternal mortality;
- Declining work participation;
- Illiteracy; and
- Rising migration.

The CSWI Report led to a debate in Parliament and the emergence of a new consciousness of women as critical inputs for national development rather than as targets for welfare policies. A second significant outcome was the recognition of women as a group adversely affected by the processes of economic transformation. It was realized that constitutional guarantees of equality would be meaningless and unrealistic unless women's right to economic independence is acknowledged and their training in skills as contributors to the family and the national economy is improved. A major outcome of the CSWI report was the National Plan of Action (1976) that provided the guidelines based on the UN's World Plan of Action for Women. The National Plan of Action (1976) identified areas of health, family planning, nutrition, education, employment, legislation and social welfare for formulating and implementing action programmes for women as called for planned interventions to improve the conditions of women in India.

An immediate outcome of the National Plan of Action was the setting up of the Women's Welfare and Development Bureau in 1976 under the Ministry of Social Welfare, to act as a nodal point within the Government of India to coordinate policies and programmes and initiate measures for women's development. The Women's Welfare and Development Bureau was charged with the nodal responsibility of:

(a) Co-ordinating and collaborating with multifarious programmes in other Central Government Ministries;

(b) Initiating necessary policies, programmes and measures;

(c) Collecting data to serve as a clearing house;

(d) Monitoring programmes for women's welfare,

(e) Servicing the National Committee on Women;

(f) Following up on the recommendations of the CSWI by formulating proposals and providing guidelines;

(g) Working out financial and physical targets;

(h) Liaising with multinational /UN agencies in the field of women's welfare;

(i) Legal issues and problems concerning women; and

(j) Implementing programmes and schemes.

In 1977-78 as an exercise for the Sixth Plan, the Government appointed the Working Group on Employment of women. Two other critical reports on village level organizations and participation of women in agriculture and rural development were prepared as part of the exercise. This plan was undoubtedly influenced by the CSWI Report of 1975. It devoted a whole chapter to Women and Development. For the first time a shift was perceived from welfare to development approaches for women. Influenced by the era that heralded concepts of social justice, the Sixth Plan recognized women's lack of access to resources as a critical factor impeding their development and, among others, the programme providing joint *pattas* (titles) to men and women was initiated. However, though the plan defined the magnitude of women's problems and suggested development strategies, the 'Family' rather than the 'women' remained the basic unit of development programming.

The *Seventh Five-Year Plan* operationalized the concern for equity and empowerment articulated by the International Decade for Women. For the first time, the emphasis was qualitative, focusing on inculcating confidence among women; generating awareness about their rights and privileges; and training them for economic activity and employment. In keeping with the spirit of the decade which aimed at integrating women into mainstream national development, the Plan emphasized the need to open new avenues of work for women and perceive them as a crucial resource for the development of the country.

The access of women to critical inputs and productive resources such as land (joint title on *patta* scheme initiated in the Sixth Plan period) were expanded in the Seventh Plan period to include support through credit (or small scale capital), marketing, training in skills/management and technology. At the same time, it was emphasized that technology that causes unemployment or displacement of women must be resisted. Another salient and crucial recognition was the need for organization of women workers and unionization that could:

(a) Make demands for improving legal services to safeguard rights; and

(b) Reduce occupational and health hazards.

The Plan acknowledged the long hours spent by women in activities within the household especially in the collection of fuel, fodder, water, etc., as well as their labour on the family farm or in family business. While the Seventh Plan did not call for the computation of women's work in these two areas as part of women's contribution to the GNP, the identification of these hitherto invisible areas was a significant beginning. Complementing the productive endeavour were the supportive services offered to women, especially maternal and child care facilities as part of the total package of services for women.

Schemes in Force

Currently, the Government of India has over twenty-seven schemes for women, some women specific and others both for the male and female population. These schemes are located in different departments and ministries of the Government of India such as

Rural Development, Labour, Education, Health Science & Technology, Welfare, Women and Child Development, etc. The total outlay on the women-specific schemes in the Seventh Plan is 2.4 per cent of the total while a gender break-up of beneficiaries or targets is unavailable for general schemes (RLEGP, NREP, etc.)

In 1985 the Government of India constituted a separate Department in the Ministry of Human Resource Development, for the development of women and children. This Department funds the Central Social Welfare Board that has developmental and welfare programmes for women. The Department also plans and executes programmes for women besides monitoring programmes for women in other Ministries /Departments. A number of these programmes were envisaged in the Sixth/ Seventh Plan period-viz., Women's Development Corporations, Support to Training and Employment Programme (STEP), Training-cum-Production Centres for Women, Awareness Generation Camps for Rural and Poor Women, Women's Training Centres or Institutes for Rehabilitation of Women in Distress, Short Stay Homes for Women and Girls, Voluntary Action Bureau and Family Counselling Centres, Free Legal Aid & Para Legal Training, Working Women's Hostels, etc.

Women specific programmes implemented by the Department of Women and Child Development include:

(i) Strengthening and improvement of women's work and employment in agriculture, small animal husbandry, dairying, fisheries, handlooms, handicrafts, khadi and village industries, and sericulture;

(ii) Economic rehabilitation of women from weaker sections of society in the form of training and employment on a sustained basis;

(iii) Better employment avenues for women to bring them into mainstream national development;

(iv) Providing Short Stay Homes for women and girls in moral danger together with counselling, medical care, psychiatric guidance and treatment and services, and development of skills; and

(v) Preventive and rehabilitative services to women and children who are victims of atrocities and exploitation.

The thrust of these various programmes is to provide five principal categories of services:

(a) Employment & Income Generation Services;

(b) Education & Training Services;

(c) Support Services;

(d) General Awareness Services; and

(e) Legal Support Services

New Perspective

Poverty is a consequence as well as a cause of several factors that limit life. The obstinacy of this self-perpetuating cycle needs to be broken before its grip can be loosened and overcome in the measurable future. The poverty-induced cycle affects all the people but impinges hardest on girls and women. Material poverty starts a chain of consequences, namely, infections, nutritional deficiencies, ill-health, growth retardation, slow learning, small body size, low productivity, repeated child bearing, excess of unpaid and unrecognized work, low earning capacity, unemployment and perpetuation of poverty. The strategic response need not tax the nation's resources and can yield decisive social benefits if it spans the spectrum of needs through the life cycle-the girl's education, food, security, safer environment in the home and neighbourhood, vocational training, support services to save time and energy, income and employment opportunity, safe motherhood, breast feeding and proper weaning, immunity against childhood diseases, management of common illnesses like diarrhoea and respiratory infection, growth promotion and early childhood stimulation as educational foundation leading to full and equal participation in socio-economic life. The process of inter generational (and now intragender,) improvement, which is what development planning is about, has to ascend these steps in an unbroken sequence.

These may not necessarily cover women in specially difficult circumstances such as refugees and migrants, prostitutes and victims of atrocities, the mentally and physically handicapped, etc., as these would require separate and detailed studies as has been done in the case of women in custody. However, for the majority of women, especially the rural poor, an integrated and decentralized approach to planning is envisaged. While the plan perceives main-streaming as long-term goal, it also realizes that some sector-specific measures will have to be undertaken to elicit higher participation of women in the development process during the interim period.

Recognizing the need for a holistic approach, the Perspective Plan offers sectoral reviews of the situation of women in rural development, employment, supportive services, education, health, legislation, political participation, media and communication and voluntary action, while suggesting inter-linked and converging strategies towards a holistic development of women in the new Millennium.

Women's development began mainly as a welfare oriented programme in the First Five-Year Plan (1951-56). The Central Social Welfare Board (CSWB), set up in 1953, undertook a number of welfare measures through the voluntary sector. The Second Five Year Plan (1956-61) organized women into Mahila Mandals to act as focal points at the grassroot levels for development of women. The Third, Fourth and other Interim Plans (1961-74) accorded high priority to education of women and introduced measures to improve maternal and child health services, including supplementary feeding for children and nursing mothers, etc.

The Fifth Plan (1974-78), saw a shift in the approach for women's development from 'welfare' to 'development' to cope up with several problems of the family and the role of women. The new approach aimed at an integration of welfare with development services.

The Sixth Five-Year Plan (1980-85), marked a landmark in the history of women's development by including a separate chapter and adopting a multidisciplinary approach with a three pronged thrust on health, education and employment.

In the Seventh Plan (1985-90), the development programmes for women continued with the major objective of raising their economic and social status to bring them into the mainstream of national development. A significant step in this direction was to identify/promote the 'beneficiary-oriented programmes' for women in different developmental sectors which extend direct benefits to women.

The Eighth Five-Year Plan (1992-97), which was launched in 1992, marked 'a shift from development to empowerment in approach to women development schemes. It promised to "ensure that the benefits of development from different sectors do not bypass women" and women must be enabled to function as equal partners and participants in the development process.

In the Approach Paper of Ninth Five-Year Plan (1997-2002), two major, steps towards gender justice have been taken for the first time in the history of planning. Their first is the listing of empowerment of women as a major plan objective. The other is to propose inclusion of a Women's Component Plan in the Plan of all Central Ministries/Departments and State Governments/Union Territory Administrations.

New Policies

In addition to the women-specific and women-related policies enunciated in various Plan documents, the government has been creating an enabling environment in which women's concern can be reflected, articulated and redressed by the governments, the voluntary sector and the corporate world. As part of this effort, many policy instruments have been brought forth over the years, leading to Action Plans and programmes in several spheres. Some of the important policy-guiding documents include The National Plan of Action for Women, adopted in 1976, which became a guiding document for development of women till 1988, when a National Perspective Plan for Women was formulated. The National Perspective Plan for Women (1988-2000) drafted by a core-group of experts is more or less a long-term policy document advocating a holistic approach for development of women. Shram Shakti - the Report of the National Commission on Self-employed Women and Women in Informal Sector (1988) examines the entire gamut of issues facing women in unorganized sector and makes a number of recommendations for the betterment of women in the informal sector relating to employment, occupational hazards, legislative protection, training and skill development, entrepreneurship development, marketing and credit, etc. The National Expert Committee on Women Prisoners (1986) examined the condition of women prisoners in the criminal correctional justice system and made a series of recommendations relating to necessary legislative reforms, prison reforms and reforms of other custodial institutions and rehabilitation of prisoners insofar as women prisoners are concerned. The National Policy for Children adopted in 1974 considers children as country's supreme assets. Therefore, the State accepts their nurture as its own responsibility. Further, it also recognizes child development as an important step in building up human resources which are pivotal to the economic and social progress of the country. The National Nutritional Policy articulates nutritional consideration in all important policy instruments of Government and identifies short-term and long term measures necessary to improve the nutritional status of women, children and the country as a whole. The National Plan of Action for the Girl Child (1991-2000) is an integrated multi-sectoral decadal Plan of Action for ensuring survival, protection and development of children with a special gender sensitivity built for girl children and adolescent girls. In addition to these women specific policies, there are many more women-related policies, like National Health Policy (1983), National Policy on Education (1986), National Population Policy (1993), which have been influencing the welfare and development of women and children in the country. The National Policy for the Empowerment of Women has been drafted after nationwide consultations to enhance the status of women in all walks of life on a par with men and to actualize the constitutional guarantee of equality without discrimination on grounds of sex.

The various developmental plans and programmes over four developmental decades (1951-1991) have brought about perceptible improvement in the socio-economic status of women in the country. Important achievements have been made in major thrust areas.

In the field of health, significant gains in respect of women's health status have been achieved. Expectancy of life for females at birth which was 31.6 years in 1951, was estimated to rise 59.7 years in 1989-93. The infant mortality rate for females declined from 131 in 1951 to 75 in 1993. Similarly, the sex differential, which was quite high in the 70s has now been bridged. However, the 0-4 age specific mortality rate, even though it has significantly declined from 55.1 in 1970 to 24.8 in 1993, continue to show higher female mortality. The maternal mortality rate in rural India still continues to be uncomfortably high at 324 per 1,00,000 live births although it showed a declining trend from 468 in 1980 to 324 in 1989 (Source: RG's Office, 1991).

Similarly, in the field of education, a number of steps were taken up for promoting women's education and equality in line with the National Policy of Education, 1986. The main strategy for education was a distinct orientation in favour of women's equality and empowerment. There is considerable improvement in female literacy as it came up to the present rate of 39.19 per cent from 8.9 per cent in 1951. The enrolment rate of girls in primary schools has also improved from 24.8 per cent in 1950-51 to 92.6 per cent in 1994-95. The drop-out rates amongst girls at primary level showed a continuous decline from 62.5 per cent in 1980-81 to 37.8 per cent in 1994-95. However, the higher decadal growth rate of female literacy (66 per cent) as compared to male literacy (43 per cent) provides some consolation.

In the field of employment, the female work participation (total workers) has grown from 19.7 per cent in 1981 to 22.3 per cent in 1991. This could be to some extent, due to the special efforts made by the nodal department of women and child development to capture women's work in the informal sector and, thus, remove their present invisibility. Similarly, number of women in the organized sector has also risen from 12.2 per cent (27.9 lakh) in 1981 to 15.4 per cent (42.3 lakh) in 1995, recording an increase of 51.6 per cent. Of the total 42.3 lakh women in the organized sector, public sector accounts for 61.5 per cent while the private sector accounts for 38.5 per cent.

Further, employment of women in the Central Government has also been rising steadily from year to year. Women's share has grown from 3.64 per cent in 1981 to 7.58 per cent in 1991 reflecting a change in women's participation in the government. At the senior and middle management levels, though limited at present, their participation has increased marginally from 875 in 1985 (based on the data related to 12 selected all India and their allied services) to 1,511 in 1995-96 (8.4 per cent). Women's participation in decision making in the government (taking the IAS, IPS and IFS services into account) has also increased from

379 in 1985 to 631 in 1996 showing an increase of 66 per cent over a period of 11 years.

Schemes for Empowerment

Creation of Separate Nodal Agency-Department of Women and Child Development: The first step initiated by the government to strengthen the national mechanism and focus on women's development was the setting up of an exclusive Department of Women and Child Development (DWCD) under the Ministry of Human Resource Development in 1985 and designating the same as the national machinery for the advancement of women in India. The support structures of the national mechanism, as instituted over a period of time include the Central Social Welfare Board (CSWB), a charitable company registered under Section 25 of the Indian Companies Act, 1956 assisting both in promoting voluntary action and implementing programmes fully funded by the Department; the National Institute of Public Cooperation and Child Development (NIPCCD), a society registered under the Societies Registration Act, 1860 extending both research and manpower development services to the Department; the National Commission for Women (NCW), a statutory body set up in 1992 for safeguarding the rights of women; the Rashtriya Mahila Kosh (RMK), set up in March 1993 to extend credit to poor and assetless women through the intermediation of NGOs; the National Children's Fund to support projects of NGOs for Child Development/Welfare and the National Creche Fund to extend assistance to NGOs to open new creches.

In March 1997, Joint Committee of Parliament on Empowerment of Women has been set up with the functions of examining measures for women's equality and considering the reports of NCW, among others.

The Department, in its nodal capacity, formulates policies and programmes, enacts/amends legislations affecting women and coordinates the efforts of both governmental and NGOs working to improve the lot of women in the country. The programmes of the Department, which are women specific, include - employment and income generation, welfare and support services and gender sensitization and awareness generation programmes. These programmes play the role of being both supplementary and complementary to the other women related development programmes in the sectors of health, education, labour and employment, rural and urban development, etc., being implemented by different sectors. Some of the important on-going interventions of the Government of India are detailed below.

Institutions for Welfare

In order to give the necessary thrust to development of women in the states, Women's Development Corporations (WDCs) were set up in 1986-87. The major objective of the scheme is to play the role of catalytic agents to create sustained income generating activities for women to provide better employment avenues for women so that they can become economically independent and self-reliant.

The functions of WDCs are to identify women entrepreneurs; to prepare a shelf of viable projects and provide technical consultancy services, to facilitate availability of credit through banks and other financial institutions (through the scheme of marginal money assistance); to promote and strengthen women's cooperatives and other organizations; and to arrange training of beneficiaries in concerned trades, project formulations, financial management, etc., through existing institutions, such as women's polytechnic and ITIs.

So far, such WDCs have been set up in Andhra Pradesh, Goa, Gujarat, Haryana, Himachal Pradesh, Jammu & Kashmir, Karnataka, Meghalaya, Orissa, Punjab, Tamil Nadu, Uttar Pradesh, West Bengal and Union Territory of Chandigarh. As per the decision of the National Development Council, in its meeting held in December 1991, the scheme stands transferred to the State sector in April 1992.

Rashtriya Mahila Kosh was set up as a registered society under the Registration of Societies Act, 1860 in March 1993 to meet credit needs of poor women, particularly in the informal sector, who have little or no access to formal credit institutions.

The policies and procedures for lending to women borrowers through the intermediation of NGOs and other women organizations like cooperative societies, WDCs, etc., for which suitable eligibility criteria, such as lending/credit management experience, sound financial management, etc., have been prescribed by the governing board of the RMK.

An amount of Rs 31 crore was released to the Kosh during 1992-93 as the corpus fund. Short-term loans and long-term loans per borrower are extended through the medium of NGOs, and other eligible organizations. Since inception, total sanctions of Rs 3,355-99 lakh have been issued to benefit 1,88,146 women through 154 agencies as on March 14,1997.

Special Schemes

In pursuance of government's policy to empower women by raising their socio-economic status, an innovative MSY was launched on October 2,1993. The scheme aims at promoting self-reliance and a measure of economic independence among rural women by encouraging thrift.

The DWCD implements the scheme through 1.32 lakh rural post offices working under the department of posts.

MSY has received a very enthusiastic response from both rural and tribal women, including those living in the remote areas of the country. Since inception of the scheme, 2.46 crore women have opened accounts with a total deposit of Rs 265.10 crore, till March 1997.

In order to coordinate programmes and facilitate their convergence to empower women IMY was launched as a strategy on August 20,1995. It proposes to bring out a mechanism by which there could be a systematic coordination and a meaningful integration of various programmes of different sectors to meet women's needs and to ensure that women's interests are taken care of and provided for under each scheme. This mechanism will be operated at the district level as a 'sub-plan' for women to percolate down to the village level appropriately through the Indira Mahila Kendras (IMKs) at village level and Indira Mahila Block Kendras (IMBKs) at Block level to be established as a registered society and supported by mechanisms at both State and Central levels. The ultimate objective of IMY is to empower women by ensuring their direct access to resources through a sustained process of mobilization and convergence of all the on going sectoral programmes. The IMY will be operated as a Centrally sponsored scheme.

The major objectives of IMY include: (1) to ensure convergence of sectoral service at the local, Block and district levels through active involvement of women and sectoral departments; (2) to optimise utilization of scarce resources in speeding up of process of mainstreaming of women in development; (3) to create awareness in women through provision of information on different developmental programmes and issues of specific concern to women; (4) to initiate a process of awareness generation/education to enable them to understand, and analyse their problems and find solutions through their collective interaction; and (5) to help women become self-reliant and independent by their economic empowerment through income generation activities and active participation in decision-making at various stages.

The IMY has three basic constituents, namely, convergence of inter-sectoral services; income generation activities; and sustained process of awareness generation/education. Under the proposed convergence of inter-sectoral services, IMY will provide the umbrella cover and all sectoral programmes aimed at women's welfare, including non-formal education, training, formal primary education, skill development, health, family welfare programmes and other minimum needs programmes like drinking water, sanitation, housing, roads, electrification, etc., would converge at the village level as per the needs, demands and requirements articulated by the IMK. Income generation activities include creation of employment opportunities through group dynamics and participation in a broad range of economic activities suited to the local requirements and use of thrift and credit services to expand the income-generating activities. Under a sustained process of awareness generation/education, IMY seeks to create a general awareness among women through ensuring information specific to equality of social status, legal rights, like those to property and inheritance, constitutional safeguards and on different development, programmes/ issues of concern to women.

In addition to amount of Rs 5,000 given by the Government of India to the corpus fund of the IMK, each member of the IMK shall contribute Rs five as membership fee and will continue to contribute Re one per month to the Kendra. Such nominal contribution by each member will create a corpus of fund and ensure their effective and continuous participation in the group activities. The corpus so formed will be used as a revolving fund for small credit requirements of the individual members and send money wherever necessary, and for expenditure on holding of awareness generation camps and any other activity resulting in furtherance of the cause of IMY.

The IMY has been taken up in 200 Blocks of the country, on a pilot basis and will be extended in the subsequent years. Selection of these Blocks will be decided by the States keeping in mind the need to ensure maximum convergence of services; care will be taken to ensure that the Blocks are compact and not dispersed over, a number of districts. The IMY will initially be sanctioned for a period of seven years starting from 1995-96. The number of IMBs registered is 113 and the functional Indira Mahila Group (IMG) is 13,717, till March, 1997.

In line with the Eighth Plan strategy, the nodal DWCD has reset its priorities to accord special emphasis on employment and income-generation activities for women. The ultimate objective in all these efforts is to make women economically empowered and self-reliant. For this purpose, the Department implements some programmes directly through voluntary organizations and interacts with other departments/ministries to ensure flow of benefits to women through their programmes.

The STEP scheme launched in 1987, aims to upgrade the skills of poor and assetless women, mobilize, conscientize, provide training, and subsequently employment on a sustainable basis in the traditional sectors of agriculture, animal husbandry, fisheries, handlooms, handicrafts, sericulture, social forestry, wasteland development, etc., in addition to the training and employment support, the programme advocates gender sensitization, women in development (WID) inputs and provision of support services.

Since inception of the programme 61 projects benefiting 3.32 lakh women, have been launched in various states. Dairying, handlooms, handicrafts and sericulture have been some important areas, since inception of the scheme till March 1997, it has provided employment opportunities for 3.32 lakh women with a total expenditure of Rs 94.13 crore. In 1996-97, 12 projects to benefit 76,875 women were sanctioned with a total expenditure of Rs.17.00 crore.

The second major programme of Training and Employment, which is commonly known as 'NORAD assisted Training Programme for Women', extends financial assistance to public sector undertakings/corporations/autonomous bodies/voluntary organizations to train women in non-traditional trades, like electronics, electricals, watch assembly and manufacturing, computer programming, printing and binding, handlooms, garment making, weaving and spinning, hotel management, fashion technology and beauty culture, tourism, bakeries/ confectionery and office management, etc.

During the Eighth Plan, an expenditure of Rs 38.28 crore has been incurred benefiting 79,797 women. Since inception in 1983, 1,10,002 women benefited with training for employment. In 1996-97, 275 projects to benefit 50,000 women/girls were sanctioned with a total expenditure of Rs 19 crore.

In the recent past, there was a progressive shift and increased attention on the most upcoming modern trades, like computer operation, electrical appliances, bakery and confectioneries, fashion technology, beauty culture, ANM training, canteen and hotel management, tourism, etc. This programme not only plays a preventive role in keeping the young and adolescent girls away from early marriages but also keeps them gainfully engaged with economic independence and self-reliance.

Courses for Welfare

The CCE&VT scheme, in operation since 1968, has been revised from time to time to provide educational qualifications and relevant skills to needy women so that they become eligible for identifiable remunerative work opportunities.

Under these programmes, voluntary organizations are given grants to conduct courses of two to three years duration for women of the age-group of 15 and above for passing primary/middle/ matric and secondary level examinations. Under the Vocational Training Programme, grants are given to impart training to needy women of 15 years age-group in different vocations leading to wage/self-employment. Under these programmes, 5823 courses have been sanctioned during the Eighth Five-Year. Plan and a sum of Rs, 39.07 crore was sanctioned to benefit about one lakh women. In 1996-97, 598 courses were sanctioned with the total expenditure of Rs five crore.

Programmes for Welfare

The Central Social Welfare Board had started the socio-economic programme (SEP) in 1958. Under this programme, financial assistance is extended to voluntary organizations to undertake a wide variety of income-generating activities providing opportunities of 'Work and Wage' to needy women, like widows, destitutes, disabled, etc., particularly those coming from economically backward and underdeveloped areas for setting up industrial units, handlooms and handicraft units, dairy units, and other allied economic activities like piggery, sheep and goat rearing, poultry, etc.

During the Eighth Five-Year Plan (1992-97), an amount of Rs 30.33 crore has been released to 2,457 units to benefit about 20,100 women in 1996-97, 13 units have been sanctioned with the total expenditure of Rs six crore.

The national machinery has spread a wide network for women and large number of welfare and support services for women and children belonging to lower economic strata through voluntary organizations. These support services represent an important plank for empowerment of women as they reduce the burden of child care and employment related problems, as detailed below.

Hostels for Working Women: In order to promote greater mobility for women in the employment market, the Department launched a scheme of hostels for working women in 1973 to provide 'safe and cheap' accommodation to single working women who come to the cities/towns for the sake of employment. Under this scheme, financial assistance is provided to the extent of 50 per cent of the cost of land and 75 per cent of the cost of construction of the hostel building to voluntary organizations. Assistance is also extended towards purchase of ready-built buildings. Besides, voluntary organizations, public trusts, local bodies, women development corporations, universities, schools/ colleges of social work also are eligible for financial assistance programme. Working women, whose consolidated income does not exceed Rs 5,000 per month, are eligible for accommodation. A resident is allowed to stay in the hostel for a maximum period of five years. Till now 805 hostels with attached day-care centres have been sanctioned to be constructed all over the country to benefit about 56,195 working women and their dependent children numbering about 7,558. In 1996-97, 28 hostels were sanctioned to benefit 3,122 women/girls with the expenditure of Rs 8.25 crore.

Creches for Working/Ailing Mother's Children: The Central Scheme of creches for working/ailing mother's children is under implementation since 1975-76. The scheme is implemented through voluntary organizations. The scheme envisages day-care services for children of the age group of 0-5 years. Service includes health care, supplementary nutrition, sleeping facilities, immunization and play and recreation for the children. The creche workers are employed to look after the children. The scheme of running of creches is being implemented by the Central Social Welfare Board through voluntary social welfare organizations and by two other national level voluntary organizations, viz., Indian Council for Child Welfare and Bhartiya Adimjati Sevak Sangh, all over the country. There are 12,470 creches in action all over the country benefiting 3.12 lakh children. Because of paucity of funds, the scheme has not been expanding and is stagnating at this number since 1988-89. In 1996-97, a total amount of Rs.19.75 crore has been sanctioned. In view of the increasing number of working women even in small towns and rural areas, there is a need for mobilizing the community to provide services of creches on a self-sustaining basis without financial burden on governments, etc.

Short Stay Homes for Women and Girls (SSH): The SSH scheme for women and girls, launched in 1969, extends temporary shelter and rehabilitation to those women and girls who are in social and moral danger due to family problems, mental strains, social ostracism, exploitation or other causes. The services extended in these homes include medical care, psychiatric treatment, case-work services, occupational therapy, educational-cum-vocational training, recreational facilities, etc. Under the scheme, grants are given to voluntary organizations to run short stay homes in various parts of the country. As per the approved schematic budget, each SSH receives an annual grant of Re 1,87,300 towards recurring expenses and Rs 25,000 as one time grant to meet the non-recurring expenditure.

National Creche Fund (NCF): The NCF was set up on March 21,1994 with a corpus fund of Rs 19.90 crore made available out of the Social Safety Net Adjustment Credit of World Bank to meet the growing requirement of opening more creche centres. The scheme envisages that 75 per cent of the centres to be assisted by the Creche Fund would be general creches and 25 per cent centres would be Anganwadi-cum-creche centres. The general creches assisted by the Fund would be on the pattern of the Creche Scheme of the Department of Women and Child Development and would provide children below five years, services which would include day-care facilities, supplementary nutrition, immunization, medical and health care and recreation. Children of parents whose monthly income does not exceed Rs 1,800 are eligible for enrolment. The voluntary organizations/ Mahila Mandals selected for opening the creches are required to open creches in schools or in places close to schools, in rural areas and urban slum areas dominated by SCs/STs. The creches have a maximum of 25 children and normally work for eight hours a day. The voluntary organizations/Mahila Mandals are encouraged to involve the community in the implementation of the scheme so that the creches become self-supporting.

Great deal of importance is attached to efforts which, trigger changes in societal attitudes towards women. An integrated media campaign projecting a positive image of both women and the girl child through media and film is the most important component of the governments communication strategy. A large number of TV spots, quickies, documentary films, radio programmes with positive messages about the girl child and women, have been produced by the department to undertake publicity and coverage.

Gender Sensitization: The Women's Development Division (WDD) of the NIPCCD, New Delhi organizes training programmes with a focus on gender issues under the DANIDA Bridging Arrangement as well as its regular activities. These training programmes were organized at national, regional and state levels. Some of the important programmes include para legal training; training of elected women representative of Panchayats; leadership of organization, training of voluntary agencies reaching women; awareness and gender sensitization programmes; incorporation of gender issues in development programmes, etc. The participants of these programmes include government officials, representatives of voluntary agencies, academic and technical institutions.

Under legal literacy, para legal training programmes were organized by the WDD in collaboration with these agencies working for women's emancipation. The major objective of these training programmes were to sensitize the participants about the constitutional, political and legal provisions relating to rights of women; to inform participants about legal structure and procedures; to create awareness about existing support schemes of government and non-governmental agencies and to conscientize them about the scope of rights, their potential to act as pressure groups, to access the entitlements of women. These programmes were organized in West Bengal, Delhi, Himachal Pradesh, Bihar and Haryana.

In the field of training for Panchayat members, training programmes were organized for women elected representatives of

Panchayats in Orissa, Karnataka and Madhya Pradesh. About 300 elected women members were trained. The main objectives of these training programmes were to sensitize the leadership qualities among elected women members, to enable them to understand the structure, function and responsibilities of Panchayats and make them aware about various development programmes implemented at the grass roots level.

Besides, the WDD also organized training programmes on leadership and organization of grass roots level women, incorporating gender concerns in Prime Minister's Rozgar Yojana, courses for superintendents of remand homes/jails on custodial justice to women and children sensitization programmes for law enforcement machinery, media campaign on pilot project on gender issues in credit and support services, orientation training programmes for police personnel on atrocities against women, issues and interventions, consultation on women in human settlement development, awareness generation on constitutional and legal rights for women, consultation on violence against women, etc.

Awareness, Generation Projects for Rural and Poor: The programmes of Awareness Generation Projects was introduced in 1987-88. It aims at identifying the needs of rural and poor women and generating awareness among them of their status in the family and society and to activate them to work for achieving their rights and to deal with social issues, like community health and hygiene, technology application and environment, etc. The camps organized under the programme provide a platform for rural poor women to come together, exchange their views and ideas and in the process develop an understanding of their problems and come out with ways to tackle them.

The programme of Education Work for Prevention of Atrocities Against Women, started in 1982, extends financial assistance to research and academic institutions like universities, colleges/women's study centres and institutions of higher learning etc., and voluntary organizations for various items of education work, propaganda, publicity and research work such as production of publicity materials, research studies on particular aspects of violence/ atrocities against women; awards for best films, short stories, poems and other creative efforts, etc. Dissemination of information/publicity materials in regional languages is also envisaged under this programme. The focus is on those women who are subjected to deprivation, brutality, extortion and exploitation.

Welfare Programme for Children

The ICDS - gift to millions of children and mothers living in the most backward rural, tribal areas and urban slums all over the country - aims at improving nutritional and health status of preschool children, expectant and nursing mothers and adolescent girls through a package of services, viz., supplementary nutrition, immunization, health checkup, referral services, treatment of minor illnesses, pre-school education and nutrition and health education. Started in 1975-76, with 33 projects, the scheme has expanded gradually and reached, by June 30, 1997 to 5,614 ICDS projects by covering 3,663 Community Development Blocks and 260 major urban slums. Of the 5,614 projects, 3,397 are under Central sector projects and the rest of the 510 projects (including 316 TINP projects) are in the state sector. These projects benefit around 198.44 lakh (19.84 million) children and 35.37 lakh (3.54 million) mothers/women.

Of the total 5,614 ICDS projects, around 1000 projects located in Andhra Pradesh, Bihar, Madhya Pradesh and Orissa are receiving assistance from World Bank to enrich the services with innovative activities.

It is proposed to universalize ICDS at the earliest to cover all Child Development Blocks/urban slums. Of these, 500 Blocks/ slums are being taken during the current year, while the balance of over 1400 Child Development Blocks/slums are proposed to be covered during 1996-97 or in future years depending on the resource position and capacity of the States to operationalize the new Blocks.

For the first time in India, a special intervention has been devised for adolescent girls using the ICDS infrastructure. The scheme of adolescent girls focuses on school drop-out girls in the age group of 11-18 years and attempts to meet the special needs of nutrition, education, literacy, recreational and skill development of adolescent girls. It attempts to make the adolescent girl a better future mother and tap her potential as a social animator. The scheme for adolescent girls has been sanctioned in 507 Child Development Blocks and, when fully operationalised, would benefit about 4.50 lakh girls.

National Commission for Women: In January, 1991, the government constituted a statutory body called National Commission for Women (NCW) with a specific mandate to study and monitor all matters relating to the constitutional and legal safeguards provided for women; review the existing legislation to suggest amendments wherever necessary; and to look into complaints involving deprivation of the rights of women. Similar Commissions have also been set up in nine States. The NCW has taken up a number of activities which include (a) Setting up of 11 expert committees to tender advice on various women's issues; (b) conducting Pariwarik Lok Adalats, to which nearly 35,000 cases were referred; (c) Complaints and Pre-litigation Cell; (d) Legal awareness; (e) Welfare of women prisoners under trials; and (f) Action on issues of women and children.

Legal Literacy Manuals: Ten legal literacy manuals were brought out in 1992 to educate women about the laws concerning their basic rights. These manuals have been written in a simple and illustrated format so that even semi-literates and neoliterates are able to comprehend them. They cover a wide range of subjects, namely, laws relating to working women, child labour, contract labour, adoption and maintenance, Hindu, Muslim and Christian

Marriage Laws, including right to property, dowry, rape, kidnapping and police procedure. The manuals have been distributed to State governments and NGOs for wider dissemination and are being translated into many of the Indian languages.

The National Plan of Action of Children (1992) and The National Plan of Action for the Girl Child (1991-2000 AD): The two Plans of Action are both integrated and multi-sectoral in their approach to ensure survival, protection and development, of children with an ultimate objective of building up a better future for children. While the Girl Child - being an integral part of the total target group of children - is expected to derive full benefits from the general Plan of Action, her gender-specific needs will be taken care of by the Plan of Action for the Girl Child with a focus on the adolescent girls.

National Resource Centre for Women: Government is also finalizing a proposal to set-up the National Resource Centre for Women and three State Resource Centres for Women which will act as an apex body for promoting and incorporating gender perspectives in policies and programmes of the government. A pilot project to test the concepts and methodologies underlying the National Resource Centre has been successfully implemented.

For the first time in the history of demographic records, an attempt was made to capture women's work in the informal sector in 1991 census. The provisional data of 1991 census on 'Workers and their Distribution', has shown that there was a substantial increase in the female work participation during 1991 census compared to that of 1981.

Reservation for Benefits for Women Under Poverty Alleviation Programme: Under various poverty alleviation programmes of rural development sector, 40 per cent of benefits have been reserved for women belonging to the below poverty line groups (families whose annual income is about Rs 6,000 to Rs 11,000).

Reservation for Women in Grassroots Democracy: The (73rd and 74th) Constitutional Amendment Bills passed in 1992 by the Parliament marks a holistic event in the lives of Indian women as amendments ensure one-third of total seats (33.3 per cent for women in all elected offices in local bodies whether in rural or urban areas). As a result of this, women have been brought to the centre-stage in the nation's efforts to strengthen democratic institutions at the grassroots level. About 0.8 million have emerged as leaders/decision makers at grassroots levels and entered into public life through the existing 0.23 million all over the country. Of these, about 76,200 are at the village, Block and district levels.

Training in Leadership Development: A massive country-wide training programme was launched in 1993 to extend leadership training for eight lakh women Panchayat members/chairpersons, emerging as a result of the elections to Panchayats and urban local bodies since 1993 when the 73rd and 74th Constitutional Amendment Acts came into force.

Voluntary Action: India has a rich tradition of selfless voluntary action. While the governmental interventions in this sector are operationalized largely through NGOs, the initiatives that the latter have themselves developed are rich and diverse. These efforts have often demonstrated success of alternative models of empowerment and development. Whether it is in the field of credit of poor women or women's health or women's awareness generation or women's literacy, or participatory rural appraisal involving women or organizing women's self-employment groups in traditional and non-traditional sectors of the economy. The Central Social Welfare Board, which is an apex agency of voluntary organizations at national level promotes voluntary action and community participation through its country-wide network of more than 12,000 Voluntary organizations at the grassroots level. Besides these, there are many more voluntary organizations working at block/ district/ state levels in the field of women and child development.

Empowerment Schemes

Holistic Development: The major approach for the future will be to bring in holistic approach for women's development. This underscores harmonization of various efforts in different fronts - social, economic, legal, political and cultural. This calls for consolidation of various programmes and efforts in different sectors of the Government and their integration in a logical fashion to converge various services and facilities required by women. A Sub-Plan approach to package all relevant resources and benefits for women's development will be laid down to ensure their systematic focus on women.

The over-arching strategy component for women's development in the Ninth Plan will comprise mobilization and convergence orchestrated by women's groups and supported by Panchayati Raj institutions. The organization of women will by itself empower them and provide them a forum for articulating their needs and contributing their perspectives to development. This will also give them experience in participatory decision making, thereby building up a cadre of grass root leaders, capable of effective participation in institutions of local government.

This capacity building has to start in the womb, without any deprivation, for the mother of the child, particularly the girl child. Her survival, protection and development as identified in the National Plan of Action for the Girl Child (1992) has to echo through all sectoral programmes. Access-to education, health, information and resources are, therefore, the vital areas of concern, that need to be effectively addressed in future to attain many of the goals for the next millennium.

The thrust in the future has to be on identifying traditional sectors of employment that are shrinking due to technology changes or market shifts, and retrain the women to take up jobs in the new and expanding areas of employment.

The provision of support services is another critical input that can greatly improve women's enhanced economic participation. Promoting women's labour market mobility through an expanding network of working women's hostels, the provision of toilet facilities for women in places of work and widespread provision of creches for working parents are essential if women are to derive maximum benefits from the economic liberalization process.

Keeping in view the aforementioned experiences, the following specific programmes could be considered for adoption in the future: (i) Expansion of education and training among women; (ii) EDP training; (iii) Provision of child-care support facilities for men and women workers so that either parent can avail of this facility at the work-place and not make it a cost on women's employment; (iv) Provision of hostel and residential facilities to enable women take up employment away from home; (v) Special employment and placement services which should seek to promote employment of women in non-conventional sectors through dissemination of information, counselling, etc.; (vi) Legal protection and legal aid services, (vii) Promotion of women workers organizations through voluntary effort; (viii Protection against flexibility. Considering the new trend towards economic liberalization such protection cannot be ensured through statutory means and should, therefore, be attempted, through negotiations and collective effort. The State, the employers as well as the workers must have separate layers of protection against loss of employment, (ix) Introduction of flexitime, multi-entry, conducive personnel policy on leave, transfer and promotion and training opportunities, to help women retain their jobs or move to new and higher areas of work, (x) Conducive credit policy to access credit to women through appropriate organizational and institutional mechanisms including self-help groups, and (xi) Improvement of the bargaining strength of women workers by encouraging their participation in trade-unions.

The DWCD has recently launched the IMY which is intended primarily to mobilize the women around an integrated delivery system. IMY is a major step towards participation of women in the planning and development processes of their areas. It is also a mechanism that can establish a system of coordination and integration of the sectoral activities. In order to put the need perceptions and the sequential priorities of these women into the Sub-Plans, women would be organized into groups and empowered to participate in the planning process. A sub-plan, consisting of the women's components, would emerge through an interactive process of discussions at the district, block and Panchayat/local levels.

Different developmental schemes and programmes already have quantified components of SCP and TSP. In a like manner, these schemes and programmes could also have a "Mahila Plan" component. It will therefore, be helpful if all Central Plan schemes/ programmes, Centrally sponsored schemes/programme, State plan schemes/ programmes and non-plan schemes/ programmes identify a Mahila Plan component, with both physical targets and financial outlays. For plan schemes/programmes, such a component should exist for both the Annual and Five-Year Plans.

The basic approach to women's development and empowerment should continue to be based on the theme of convergence, i.e. convergence of the development programmes of different departments of the government to target women through a single delivery system as well as convergence of the efforts of both the government functionaries and community or NGOs in achieving a common objective.

This Women's Day there was reason to rejoice. The Ninth Plan draft document has said that 'empowerment of women' is one of its prime objectives. While this is significant, what is also important is the sub-Plan that was evolved in the run-up to the preparation of the Plan, the fact that a think tank of women was set up to evolve a document that spelt out the specific demands of women in the country. Way back in 1974, the report of the Commission on the Status of Women had called for a sub-Plan, one that would address gender inequities but it was not taken seriously. So while some attempts were made in subsequent Plans to give women a place in the developmental process, it tended to be sectoral and haphazard.

The think tank, comprising academicians, activists and researchers held consultations with the Planning Commission, the Department of Women and Child Development, various ministries and women all over the country. The focus was on building consensus with a view to understanding what women wanted and what is perhaps even more important on what was working and what was not.

The concerns voiced were varied, but the key ones were the right to information about changes, opportunities, options, schemes, services and technologies, the gender sensitization of government functionaries particularly the police and the local administration in the areas of health, agriculture and animal husbandry, and the right to work and employment guarantee schemes.

Liberalization, it was pointed out, is here to stay but women were losing out and will continue to lose out because they have neither the skills nor the legal safeguards to be included.

Other important demands were gender analysis and gender audit of all plans, policies and programmes, the elimination of violence against women and girls through the strengthening of institutional capacity and legal provisions and the decentralization of democracy so that decisions can be taken at levels that are ipso facto more accessible to women.

Happily, if one is to go by the Ninth Plan draft, there is a veritable sea change in Plan perspectives. Until now women's development, to quote the document, was primarily 'welfare oriented'. The focus was always on health, nutrition, education and in the early nineties, on training for employment. Demands that they be recognized as participants in development made little headway. The approach was patronizing and chauvinistic.

The draft is therefore significant promising, as it does, "to create an enabling environment where women can freely exercise their rights within and outside homes as equal partners along with men". It goes on to add that "this will be realized through the early finalization of the 'National Policy for the Empowerment of Women, which lays down definite goals for targets and policy prescriptions along with a well-defined Gender Development index to monitor the impact of its implementation in raising the status of women from time to time. Also significant is the fact that the Ninth Plan directs both the Centre and the States to adopt the 'women's component plan' through which no less than 30 'per cent of funds and benefits are earmarked to the women related sector.

To quote Madhu Dandavate, Deputy Chairperson of the Planning Commission "Women have moved from 'footnote' to an 'objective' in the Ninth Plan" but a lot more will have to be done to ensure that policies are evolved along the lines of the Plan initiatives. Perhaps, as Anita Anand, a member of the think tank suggests, an autonomous body on the lines of the National Organisation of Women in the USA should be set up. Bandhs and dharnas will no longer suffice and a much more sophisticated approach is required in which people with expertise in policy analysis and advocacy will lobby for change. In fact, it must work in tandem with the Planning Commission to ensure the economic and political empowerment of women and gender sensitizing of issues.

The tendency all along has been to direct jobs, resources, political positions, credit et. al., to men especially in the macro sector. The assumption was that the benefits would percolate down to the women and children but, in actual fact, it has only further marginalized them. Panchayati Raj will of course go a long way in remedying these aberrations. Since the passing of the 72nd and 73rd amendments four years ago, almost a million women have come into local politics and in Haryana and Kerala there are all women Panchayats. But, the issues raised by them at the grass roots level will have little success if women's representation in the upper echelons of democracy remains low. Studies conducted in the US on disparities between the blacks and whites have shown how important it is to have a 33 per cent reservation. Anything below this has proved to be ineffective. This is why it is absolutely imperative that the 81st Amendment Bill providing for 33 per cent reservation for women is reintroduced and passed in the next session of Parliament.

9

Action Plan

In the words of India's first Prime Minister:

> We talk about a welfare State and direct our energies towards its realisation. That welfare must be the common property of everyone in India and not the monopoly of the privileged groups as it is today. If I may be allowed to lay greater stress on some, they would be the welfare of children, the status of women and the welfare of the tribal and hilly people in our country. Women in India have a background of history and tradition behind them, which is inspiring. It is true, however, that they have suffered much from various kinds of suppression and all these have to go so that they can play their full part in the life of the nation.
>
> —Jawaharlal Nehru: Foreword to *Social Welfare in India*

Indian planners have generally seen development as a process comprehending the entire social system. According to the Planning Commission on the First Five-Year Plan:

> Maximum production, full employment, the attainment of economic equality and social justice constitute the accepted objective of planning ... plan for development must place balanced emphasis on all these.

> Development touches all aspects of Community life and has to be viewed comprehensively. Economic planning thus extends out into extra economic spheres- educational, social and cultural. Second Five-Year Plan.
>
> This broad approach to development was to give shape to the policy of transforming India into a welfare State, as directed by the Constitution.

The overall development process envisages a share in the development generated by the Plan equally for women and men. Since the Constitution stresses the need for promoting with special care the educational and economic interests of the weaker sections of the people, the welfare and development of women received particular attention from the beginning.

The Planning Commission's 'Plans and Prospects for Social Welfare in India, spells out social welfare services as intending to cater for the special need of persons and groups who by reason of some handicap-social, economic, physical or mental-are unable to avail of or are traditionally denied the amenities and services provided by the community. Women are considered to be handicapped by social customs and social values and therefore social welfare services have specially endeavoured to rehabilitate them.

The Planning Commission defined three major areas under which they have paid special attention to women's development: (a) education, (b) social welfare, and (c) health. The development of education for women has been already discussed. In this Chapter we shall examine the policies, provisions and programmes for women's development, in the fields of social welfare and health including the administrative agencies created by the Government of India to implement the overall policies regarding women's development, in order to assess the achievements in this regard.

The *First Plan* emphasized that, in order to fulfil women's legitimate role in the family and the community, adequate services needed to be promoted for her welfare. Well organized social service departments were needed in the States to initiate comprehensive programmes of women and child welfare. It recognized that the problem of high infant and maternal mortality was mainly due to malnutrition and undertook to develop (a) school feeding schemes for children and creation of nutrition sections in the State Public Health Departments; (b) maternity and child health centres; and (c) family planning.

The *Second Plan* emphasized the need for special attention to problems of women workers, since they were comparatively less organized and suffered from certain social prejudices and physical disabilities. They were also paid less because of the feeling that they were less suited to heavy work and were more vulnerable in situations which produced fatigue. The Plan stated therefore that women should be protected against injurious work, should receive maternity benefit and creches for children. It also suggested speedy implementation of the principle of equal pay for equal work, provision of facilities for training to enable women to compete for higher jobs and expansion of opportunities for part- time employment.

The main thrust of the *Third Plan* as regards social women's development was on the expansion of girls' education' in social welfare, the largest share was provided for expanding rural welfare services and condensed courses of education for adult women. The health programmes for women mainly concentrated on provision of services for maternal and child welfare, health education, nutrition and family planning

The approach in the *Fourth Plan* was a continued emphasis on women's education. As regards social welfare, the approach was to let the voluntary sector operate the bulk of departmental Programmes. Governmental efforts were confined to the provision of institutional services for destitute women and women rescued from prostitution. The basic policy was to promote women's welfare with the family as the base of operation.

The outlay on family planning was stepped up to reduce the birth rate from 40 to 25 per 1000 through mass education and motivation, and with cooperation of voluntary agencies and local leadership. High priority was assigned to immunization of pre-school children and supplementary diet for children and expectant and nursing mothers.

The *Fifth Five-Year Plan* indicated that priority was given to training women in need of care and protection, women from low income families, needy women and dependent children and working women. A programme for functional literacy to endow women with necessary knowledge and skills to perform the functions of the housewife (including child care, nutrition, health care, home economics, etc.) will be launched for the age group 15-45. Special steps will be taken for the Placement of follow-up of successful candidates under the exciting scheme of condensed courses, of education and the socio-economic programmes.

In addition to production-cum-training units, managerial and sales training will be introduced to promote the marketability of goods produced in different units. Under the Health programmes, the primary objective is to provide minimum public health facilities integrated with family planning and nutrition for vulnerable groups, children and pregnant and lactating mothers. The plan emphasizes the need to correct regional imbalances and provide services to meet the minimum needs of the community.

An examination of the Five-Year Plans reveals that in spite of the policy emphasis on welfare or investment in human resources, the share of investment in the social services in terms of the actual allocation has been steadily declining in successive plans. The objectives emphasized in the various plans, as well as the share of allocations indicate that among programmes specifically designed for women's development, the order of priorities up to the Fourth Plan has been education, then health, and lastly other aspects of welfare because it was generally assumed that all other programmes will benefit women indirectly, if not directly.

Progress and Welfare

Programmes for women's welfare and development may be classified as follows :

Programmes under Statutory Obligations: The suppression of Immoral Traffic in Women and Girls Act, 1956 provides for institutional custody and after-care programmes. The Maternity Benefits Act, 1961 has a provision for leave and cash benefits. Under the protective laws, women in organized industries are entitled to provision of creches and family welfare facilities.

Programmes for Development: Under this category can be included the largest number of programmes which provide essential services and opportunities to women for development, such as education, health, maternity and child welfare, family planning, nutrition, socio-economic training and certain community organizations.

Programmes for Special Group: These vary from State to State. Some special assistance programmes have been initiated to serve groups like widows, the aged and the destitute, in the way of pensions or homes. A programme to provide hostels for working women in urban areas was initiated in the Second Plan, and has been continued over all successive Plans. For girls from backward communities, Scheduled Castes and Scheduled Tribes, there is provision for scholarships, and free residential schooling in Ashram schools.

While there have been additions and shifts in emphasis regarding the concept of women's welfare and development under the various Plans, and in some cases programmes have been expanded or integrated with others under a new nomenclature, the nature and content of the programmes have not changed.

Agencies at Work

In pre-independence India, while provisions of health and educational services had been increasingly demanded from the

State, social welfare programmes were administered mainly, by voluntary agencies. There was no comprehensive nation-wide programme to provide welfare services. After the attainment of independence, it was felt that social and economic uplift of the masses required Government assistance to strengthen the services rendered by voluntary agencies. The administrative structure inherited from the colonial Government was clearly not equipped for this task. The Central Government therefore created a new agency-the Central Social Welfare Board in 1953 to promote welfare and development services for women, children and other underprivileged groups by providing assistance to voluntary agencies, improving and developing welfare programmes and sponsoring them in areas where they did not exist. Following the creation of the Central Social Welfare Board, the State Government set up, at the request of the Central Social Welfare Board, State Social Welfare (Advisory) Boards for the same purpose. This was necessary, as welfare is a State subject.

Even after creation of these Boards, there is no clear pattern in social administration. The responsibility for planning and administering women's welfare and development is scattered in various departments and other agencies of the government. The federal framework, and the need to involve voluntary or community organization in this task generally results in a three-tier structure of administration, with agencies at the centre, the State and the local level.

Agencies at the Centre: At the Centre, the major responsibility for planning and implementing women's welfare and development programmes rests mainly with the following: (i) Planning Commission; (ii) Ministry of Education and Social Welfare with its two specialized agencies - the Central Social Welfare Board and the National Council for Women's Education; (iii) Ministry of Health and Family Planning; (iv) Ministry of Home Affairs; (v) Ministry of Labour and Employment.

Agencies at the State Level: At the State level, there is no uniform pattern. Programmes for women's and children's welfare and development are administered by a large number of departments. All States have separate departments for Health, Family Planning and Education. With the exception of a few States, the Department of Agriculture and Community Development also is responsible for some women's programmes. In some States, the department of Local-Self-Government is involved in these programmes. Social Welfare departments or directorates as well as Social Welfare (Advisory) boards have been set up in most States. In some cases, they exist independently while in others they have been combined with education, tribal welfare, etc. A few States have set up separate directorate for Women's Education, or Women's Welfare.

The Committee endeavoured to collect information from all Central and State Departments concerning their special programmes for women's welfare and development. 12 Ministries of the Central Government indicated that they have some programmes for women's welfare. 19 States and one Union Territory indicated the existence of similar programmes. The replies were not comprehensive and often did not provide full answers to our questions. Two things, however, clearly emerge from these replies:

(a) These programmes, even when they have common objectives, are supervised and implemented by many Government departments without any effective machinery to coordinate their functions.

(b) Government departments, by and large, are not at all clear in their understanding of what constitutes welfare or development for women. Some adopt a comprehensive view, some a very limited one. A few regard improvement of earning power as essential for any development. Most are, however, content to adopt a somewhat charitable approach to welfare and equate it with assistance to women in distressed condition.

Since the major responsibility for social welfare and development lies with the Ministries, of (a) Health and Family Planning and (b) Education and Social Welfare, we have examined them in some detail. The rest are only briefly enumerated.

Assessment

It was impossible to use quantitative indices to measure progress in the implementation of these programmes. Owing to data particularly in the field of development, programmes specifically meant for women are very few and do not give a total view of governmental effort to improve the condition of women. The general programmes, designed for all sections of the population, do not maintain separate records of allocations or expenditure for women, nor has any attempt been made so far to evaluate their impact.

We were, however, surprised to note that with the exception of the Second Plan, all the others have confined their concern for women's development to only education, health and welfare. Conspicuous by its absence is any reference to the need for generating and improving employment of women. Even the Fifth Plan, which gives highest priority to employment generation, appears to accept the present low representation of women in the labour force as a natural order of things, which will continue unchanged in the years to come. This expectation appears to be in direct contradiction to the Planning Commission's own view, that utilization of idle manpower would be a tremendous force to speed up the process of development. It is also a denial of the Government of India's stated objective of the total involvement of women at all levels of national development.

It is interesting to note that all the agencies engaged in programmes exclusively for women, inevitably attach the highest priority to increasing women's earning power. But since these programmes are classified as welfare and therefore non-productive, they invariably enjoy lower priority.

This ambiguity and confusion springs from traditional middle class attitude regarding women's roles in society. It will continue to affect both planning and administration of women's welfare and development unless the objectives of such policies are clarified and given concrete shape.

Health Front

According to the World Health Organization, health is "a state of complete physical, mental and social well-being and not merely the absence of disease and infirmity." Health is both an important factor in the achievement of status as well as an indicator of social status, particularly for women, whose health is conditioned to a great extent by social attitudes. The health status of women includes their mental and social condition as affected by prevailing norms and attitudes of society in addition to their biological and physiological problems. Societies delineate women's roles partly according to their biological function and partly from prevailing attitudes regarding their physical and mental capacity. These social attitudes also influence the provision and use of preventive and curative health care, including maternal care. The health care facilities offered by a community in the form of medical, particularly maternity services for women, is a significant index of the emphasis that community places on the health of its women. Some studies in both the developed and developing countries have shown a definite link between low status of women and deficiencies in the knowledge and utilization of preventive health services.

In 1957 a study was made of the percentage distribution of ailing males and females both adults and children according to expenditure for treating the illness in six rural communities covering six districts in Maharashtra State with a total population of 37,000. The survey revealed that in the year under study there were 730 ailing females and 513 ailing males in the age group below 15 years. The percentage of males getting medical treatment was higher than females. The study also showed that more adult women had to be content with free or traditional treatment or no treatment as compared to the medical facilities used for the males.

Cultural Norms and Attitudes: The cultural norms that particularly affect women's health are the attitudes to marriage, age of marriage, the value attached to fertility and sex of the child, the pattern of family organization and the ideal role demanded of the women by social conventions. They determine her place within the family, the degree of her access to medical care, education, nutrition, and other accessories of health. In India, marriage is almost a universal function because of cultural and religious influences. The age at marriage and fertility rate have important demographic implications. The largest number of children are born to women who marry at the age of 19 years. Cultural insistence on the marriage of women in the early phase of their child bearing period leads to high fertility rate and each additional child is a burden on the mother, affecting her physical and mental health. Barrenness is regarded as a curse and the woman is always blamed for this. Though the desire for many children may not be, the desire for sons is widespread. The joint family system also has in many ways contributed to high fertility in India. It encourages early marriage and large sized families which appears as a source of collective economic security as well as emotional security.

The lower status of woman is the result of her dependence and lower educational and social position. Tradition idealizes her role as the mother, housewife and the distributor of food. It is customary in all Indian households for the women to serve the family first and then to eat whatever is left. According to our survey, 48.53 per cent of persons stated that in their families males eat first. In families affected by poverty, this generally results in still greater malnutrition for the women. The young girls as they grow up are taught subservience and self-effacement.

The process, therefore, starts at an early age and has very adverse consequences on women's health particularly at the time of pregnancy and child-birth. From their childhood, girls are taught to be uncomplaining and to maintain strict secrecy about their physical troubles. With menstruation, taboos are enforced and restrictions placed on their movement. They are unable to either discuss their health problems, if any, or even visit the doctor. Later as a mother, with children depending on her for care and attention, the woman has a tendency to carry on until ailment overtakes her. Reluctance to visit a doctor, particularly a male doctor, arises out of these restrictions imposed on women from the beginning. Such social attitudes, therefore, lead to a general neglect of women's health and in view of their child bearing role, they are the greatest sufferers as compared to men.

A study of data from particularly the developing countries indicates that other health problems of women-the higher maternal and infant mortality, maternal morbidity, lower expectation of life at birth, malnutrition, mental disorders, suicide rate and certain sex-selective diseases are linked to their status and role in the society. Child bearing and rearing is still the dominant role assigned to most women in developing nations. In the context of low socio-economic status of the bulk of the population, this factor becomes adverse to good health-in the case of women. All the developing nations are faced with rapidly growing population. Inadequate housing sanitation and poor medical facilities adversely affect the vulnerable segment of the community. Maternity, therefore, constitutes a special problem. The bulk of the stress and strain falls in the women who suffer from extremely poor health.

The indicators of women's health status in India are drawn from two sources: (a)Demographic trends, and (b)Access to health services. They should be examined separately.

Demographic Trends: We have already drawn attention to the adverse and declining sex-ratio, higher mortality rate and lower life expectancy of women. The high birth and fertility rates, beyond doubt, contribute to the low health conditions of women. Starting with 1871, almost every census report has emphasized: (i)The crucial role of female mortality; (ii)The significant contribution of mortality in the age group 15-44 to aggregate female mortality; (iii)The crucial role of neglect of female health in determining female mortality; and (iv)The insignificant role of under numeration to explain the adverse sex-ratio.

Neglect of women was proved by customs like female infanticide then prevalent in certain parts of the country. Child marriage, premature consummation resulting in early childbearing, overwork and malnutrition were cited as other causes of women's poor health. The census of 1931 drew attention to higher female mortality in the age group 5-10, and "at the reproductive age".

The apparently low sex-ratio of deaths (female deaths per thousand male deaths) is actually due to large under-reporting of female deaths as compared to male deaths. The doubtful accuracy of SRS data on age-wise and sex-wise mortality rates has been demonstrated in a recent study. The difference between estimated and reported deaths of females is sometimes said to be as high as 75.69 per cent for rural areas and 59.07 per cent for urban areas in the lowest age group; 46.57 per cent and 35.47 per cent in the age-group 1-19; 58.56 per cent and 37.94 per cent in the 20-49 age group; and 50.2 per cent and 28.54 per cent in the 50+ age-group. This difference in the case of males is consistently lower.

All the available evidence leads us to conclude that female mortality infact is higher for all the three age groups, namely, during infancy, childhood and during the productive age particularly in rural areas. The inference from this is that female mortality is due to the consistent neglect of female health.

It is observed that the maternal mortality rate is high enough to raise the overall death rate for females and accounts for the low sex ratio. It was reported to be 252 per 1,00,000 live births in 1964 for the country as a whole, but for rural areas, it is as high as 573 in 1968. It is unfortunate that no later figures are available for this.

The SRS data for 1968 and 1969 also reflects the same pattern as reported in the various censuses, namely that female mortality continues to be higher in the age groups 0-4 and 15-34.

Factors Contributing to Women's Ill-Health: Recent medical research has tried to identify particular contributory factors to the problem of women's ill-health and higher mortality. Since maternal mortality in India continues to be so high, it is understandable that the bulk of this research has concentrated on this aspect of women's health. The specific factor that has been identified by various studies is firstly pregnancy wastage, caused by abortions and still births. The incidence of this phenomenon has remained constant over the period 1957-68, a period which witnessed intensification of family planning activity. In fact there was even an increase in actual numbers. Such foetal wastage prevails more in low income groups. One study reported that pregnancy wastage of malnourished mothers was 30 per cent as late as in 1972. Still births are reported as constituting 11 per 1,000 live births. Much of this pregnancy loss and prenatal mortality and still births result from premature births, itself a consequence of maternal malnutrition, particularly iron deficiency during pregnancy. Haemoglobin estimations carried out on about 5,000 pregnant women in different parts of the country show that 30 per cent of them are anaemic, i.e., they have haemoglobin levels below 10 per cent. There is evidence that this is largely due to iron deficiency. Premature births have consistently been a very high proportion among the cause of infant deaths.

A second group of causes for both infant and maternal mortality relate to higher birth orders. Frequency of pregnancies causes protein malnutrition of the mothers. As it is, the majority of Indian women are victims of malnutrition. 10-20 per cent of maternal deaths are known to be due to nutritional anemias. This has been borne out by a series of studies of the National Institute of Nutrition.

It has been estimated that if causes of maternal mortality are eliminated female mortality will decline substantially, since pregnancy complications still constitute 16.44 per cent or the second highest contributor to female morbidity. The Bhore Committee had observed that even psychiatric morbidity among Indian women was the result of malnutrition, frequent pregnancies and anaemia. While data on this aspect of women's health is scanty, a WHO Report indicates that psychiatric morbidity is more prevalent among women than men.

All the demographic indicators thus point to a low health status of women. In particular they suggest that child bearing in India, for the majority of women, is more a health hazard than a natural function.

The broad objectives of the health programmes so far have been to control and eradicate communicable diseases, to provide curative and preventive health services in rural areas through the establishment of primary health centres in each block, and to augment programmes for the training of medical and para-medical personnel. In the Fifth Plan the main thrust was to improve the deficiencies in building, staff, equipment, drugs and medicines in the primary health centres and to integrate family planning and maternity and child health services. Health is a basic component of the proposed minimum needs programme. Any assessment of the impact of these programmes on the health of women has to take both quantitative and qualitative factors into account. A comparative assessment of available basic medical facilities in selected countries of the world indicates that India's position is more backward than even some of the developing countries.

In spite of the achievements during the last Four Plans figures indicate that medical care remains inaccessible to a large section of the population.

Any increase in personnel or medical facilities is nullified by increase in the population. The quality of the existing health services is reduced by inadequacy of staff, medical supplies and equipment, by overcrowding. In rural areas not even the minimum medical facilities by trained personnel is available in all districts. Distance and inaccessibility remains a major problem, particularly in hilly and difficult areas.

The lowest unit of the Health Service structure or its rural arm is the Primary Health Centre which is supposed to provide integrated and comprehensive curative and preventive health services in rural areas. The Bhore Committee which proposed the setting up of primary health centres had recommended that, to start with, each centre should cater to a population of 40,000 with a 30 bedded hospital to serve four Primary Health Centres. It visualized district level hospitals with a strength of 500 beds. Among other staff, primary health centres were to include four public health nurses, two medical officers, four midwives and four trained dais. Describing these requirements as the irreducible minimum, the Committee had recommended the key importance of developing preventive health services, with 'the country-side as the focal point.'

The Mudaliar Committee reiterated these recommendations, adding further the provision of three specialists in medicine, surgery, obstetrics and gynaecology, and 75 maternity and 50 paediatric beds to each district hospital.

In fact, when the primary health centres were established, the 'irreducible minimum' requirements were not provided. They had to serve a far larger population of 60 to 70,000 with only one lady health visitor and four auxiliary nurse-mid-wives (ANM), six beds and three sub-centres. Each sub-centre was put in charge of one ANM. Their functions were wide, including medical relief, maternity and child-health, control of communicable diseases (including the major national programme of Malaria control), school health, environmental sanitation and health education. By 1961, 2,800 primary health centres had been established.

Though the recommendations of the Mudaliar Committee were not implemented due to shortage of trained personnel and funds, from 1963 family planning services were initiated with additional staff (one woman medical officer, one extension doctor, one ANM, and two family planning workers to supervise four sub-centres). The sub-centres were to cater to a population of approximately ten thousand and were more than doubled in number, but with family planning as their major activity. The emphasis on family planning was strengthened further in 1966 by treating it as a crash programme, providing additional staff, and delinking it from Malaria control activities. In most States, the existing four health assistants were transferred to the family planning side.

Though the number of primary health centres increased from 67 to 5195 and the sub-centres from 17,522 to 32,218, their impact on the health of the rural population has not been substantial. An expert Committee observed that apart from West Bengal and Kerala, where utilization was 50 per cent, in other States like Bihar, Rajasthan, UP, Orissa, Madhya Pradesh and Jammu & Kashmir, the net utilization in primary health centres was hardly between 5-15 per cent. The reasons for this under utilization were: (a) apathy of the staff, (b) the status barrier that separates the doctor and his team from the village population, particularly the lower socio-economic groups, and (c) absence of lady doctors in many centres. Emphasizing the need to improve maternity and child health services, the committee recommended the provision of domiciliary maternity services as essential.

Critics of the present pattern of health services feel that they have deviated from the basic recommendation of the Bhore Committee, to emphasize preventive services in rural areas as the keystone of public health. Under the present system, the expenditure on curative services is thrice that on preventive services, but most of it is concentrated in urban areas. The 10 per cent of hospital beds meant for the four-fifths of the population living in rural areas are ill-staffed, ill-equipped, and ill-financed. In the sphere of women's health in particular, while all the expert Committees emphasized greater attention to maternity services, the actual position shows wide regional variations in the provision of this crucial service.

According to the estimate of the Study Group on Hospitals, earlier there were only 45,000 maternity beds in 493 maternity hospitals and wards of general hospitals. The total number of beds at that time was 2.75 lakh, i.e., maternity beds constituted less than 17 per cent of total hospital facilities. It should also be noted that most hospitals in India provide no separate beds for women.

The All-India Statewise life expectancy at birth, during the years 1951-95, projected that Kerala, which stands out for provision of maternity services also, has the highest expectancy of life for women, which was 60.7 for 1991-95, and the lowest infant mortality rate. Uttar Pradesh, with the lowest provision for such services has a female life expectancy of 53.7, which is nearly the lowest in India, and the highest infant mortality rate.

There is no doubt that improvement of maternity services has a definite impact on life expectancy of women. States like Tamil Nadu, Andhra Pradesh, Punjab, Assam, Karnataka and West Bengal which have given some attention to these services, have helped to improve their women's expectation of life. The impact, however, cannot be uniform, because of the operation of other factors, like education, employment, general cultural norms, etc., which exert considerable influence on women's utilization of these services.

An important cultural norm which has a direct impact on women's health is the age of marriage. No district in Kerala has below 15 as the average age at marriage and only 3 districts (33 per cent) have an average below 20. In the case of Bihar, Rajasthan and UP, the picture is just the opposite, where 71 per cent, 65 per cent and 48 per cent of the districts respectively have an average below 15 per cent, 35 per cent and 31 per cent of the districts in Andhra Pradesh and West Bengal also come into this category.

Kerala also has the highest female literacy rate which is 53 per cent in rural areas, and 60.6 per cent in urban areas. Tamil Nadu, though well behind Kerala, is still the second highest State in female literacy, which is 19 per cent in rural areas and 45.4 per cent in urban areas. Uttar Pradesh, Bihar, Rajasthan stand out for their low female literacy rate.

We may infer from this that the availability and utilization of medical care for women reflects the general social attitude to women in a region. There is also no doubt that the female literacy rate is an important determinant for utilization as well as supply of medical and health care for this section of the population. This is particularly true of maternity and child care.

Apart from regional variations, the accessibility of health services is also affected by rural-urban and social-economic differentials, including a broad pattern of sex differentials. For example, uncontaminated water is available to 40 per cent of towns, but only 9 per cent of villages. Since about two-thirds of the total number of doctors and nurses, and most hospitals are concentrated in urban areas, the four-fifths of the population living in rural areas get a much smaller share of these services. The National Sample Survey (19th Round, 1964-65) found that 46 per cent of all births in urban India are attended by trained medical personnel, as compared to 9 per cent in rural areas. The household consumption data of the same Round also shows that average per capital private monthly expenditure on medicines and medical services is Rs 1.01 in urban areas, and about half that in rural areas. Majority of doctors in urban areas are private practitioners, charging high fees. Their services can be used only by the upper and middle income groups. Private nursing homes and paying hospitals, with private doctors, are almost totally out of reach of the poorer sections of society.

A recent study on rural health services brings out the peculiar tension created by scarce supply of medical personnel in the villages. On the one hand is the unmet felt need for the services of the Auxiliary Nurse Midwife at the time of child birth. Villagers are keen to have the ANM's services because they consider her to be more skilful than the traditional *dai*. Whether the ANM's have provided the services, the dais' role has become less significant. During our tours we were repeatedly informed of the inadequacy in the number and services rendered by ANMs. Apart from their small number, the area covered by these personnel is too large, with consequent transport and accommodation difficulties. Nighthalts and the problem of security create difficulties for most of these workers in rural areas, and effect their functioning.

Such problems very often obstruct an ANM from really attending to her duties in all places under her charge. Secondly, for an outsider to live and work in rural areas, a degree of social acceptance and security is essential. Protection extended by influential members of the village community ensures this, and prevents her from being handicapped by their hostility. The result very often is that her services are monopolized by the dominant, or relatively well-to-do section of village society. It should also be remembered that the social and educational background of the NMs is likely to be closer to the dominant, or well-to-do groups in the village, rather than the poorest.

This sort of cornering widens the gap between the ANM and the masses of women who need her services. The overall image of the ANM in villages, particularly in North India, is that of a person who is distant from them, meant only for special people or for those who can pay for her services. She is not for the poor. She can be called only when there are complications and then also she has to be paid.

As for sex differentials, they are deep rooted in social attitudes regarding the needs of women for care and assistance during ailments. In many areas we were told that rural society does not always care to report women's ailments, or seek medical aid. Women themselves often prefer to be silent in such matters. The studies in nutritional deficiencies of women indicate that their requirements are often sacrificed to provide a little more nutrition to others in the family. The incidence of diseases caused by malnutrition is higher not only among adult women, but even among female infants. At the same time hospital records reveal that more male children are treated for such diseases.

The two sets of indicators demographic trends, and access to medical care, both reveal the same situation regarding the health status of women.

This increase in comparative neglect of female lives as an expendable asset, observed to persist and increase over several decades, is a matter of serious concern.

Birth Control

If the masses of Indian women are to be freed from their status as 'expendable assets', some of the obvious and immediate answers lies in releasing them from the bondage of repeated and frequent childbirth, providing them with some choice in the size of their families and in ensuring adequate medical facilities to protect them during and against maternity.

Propagators of the family planning movement in India have been keen to emphasize the improvement in the status of women as one of the direct consequences of acceptance of family planning. The birth control movement in India, from its inception, was associated with the feminist movement, and women's organizations were among the first to start a voluntary campaign for spread of birth control techniques among women. Even now they are active partners of the government's programme to persuade more and more women to accept family planning methods.

Recent researches in this field however make it extremely difficult to establish such an *a prior* relationship. All recent studies seem to agree more on the obverse of the relationship, viz. that improved status of women, with rise in the age of marriage, education, employment, better living conditions and greater general awareness, have a direct impact on the adoption of family planning methods.

There is no doubt that knowledge of family planning methods enables a woman to regulate her biological function and thus gives her a greater control over life and future. This certainly helps to build up her confidence in herself and can enable her to pursue various other ways to develop her personality, e.g., training, career interests and fulfil responsibilities to herself, her family and the wider society. Above all, such control has a direct impact on her health, Ability to prevent frequent and excessive drain on her physical resources undoubtedly helps to preserve her health, and since health is a basic necessity for any kind of development for a person, ability to plan her family ultimately contributes to such improvement of a woman's personality. A third consequence, which is sometimes emphasized is the possible change in husband-wife relationship, leading to improved position of the woman in decision making within the family.

All these results could certainly lead to a general improvement of a woman's status. But each of them are integrally connected with other socio-economic factors and developments, and the relationship between family planning and status improvement depends, in the ultimate analysis, on the presence and behaviour of such variables as social attitudes and opportunities for women's education, employment, pursuit of independent interests and career, size and sex of the family, accessibility of health services, and general economic development.

If the sexual role were the main determinant of male dominance and authority in a society, there would have been no communities in the world where the women are dominant, or equal members. The status of women in any society depends on a complex set of social, economic, demographic and political variables, among which the woman's ability to control the size of her family could be a contributory factor. But in our view, emphasizing it as a direct cause of improvement of women's status is somewhat exaggerated, and ignores the evolution of women's status in different societies. The matriarch of many ancient civilizations and primitive communities certainly enjoyed a much higher status than the women with complete control on the size of their families in the developed, modern societies of the West today. Knowledge of family planning techniques may have liberated Western women from excessive pregnancies, but it has not basically changed their status in these societies either economically or politically. Even in the sphere of social attitudes, with all the progress in education, and different types of social freedom and changing roles, their image as sex-symbols has been intensified, not eliminated.

In India, there has been an enormous volume of research on degree of acceptance of family planning, to assist the continuous evaluation of the Family Planning Programme. In one such research by the Ministry of Health and Family Planning, it was concluded that:

> The focus of evaluation of the Family Planning Programme at present is on the purposive assessment of impact of the programme, identification of areas of success and failures and reasons thereof, and feeding back this information for motivation and improvement or programme implementation. Family Planning Programme can be evaluated in terms of its objectives, viz., (a) the immediate objectives, including efforts and performance, objectives set for developing resources and activities for achieving the decision made; (b) the intermediate objective of spreading knowledge, developing favourable attitudes towards encouraging practice of family planning methods; (c) the ultimate objective, which is reduction of fertility so as to bring down the birth rate to 15 per thousand.

Apart from continuous assessment of information received from the States, regarding the success of the programme in quantitative terms, i.e., actual number of couples protected by various methods, provision of services in the way of personnel and equipment, etc., the evaluation includes field surveys on knowledge, attitudes and practices (KAP Studies). The Central Family Planning Institutes, the National Sample Survey, the various demographic and communication action research centres in the country, as well as a large number of individuals and institutions in the university system have been engaged in periodical assessment of the impact of this programme at both local and national levels since its inception. As a result, family planning is now the most heavily documented and evaluated among all major programmes of the Government of India.

One common trend in the results of these studies has been to expose the differentials in knowledge, acceptance and practice of family planning methods between different sections of the population. The results from the national survey conducted by the Operations Research Group, Ministry of Health and Family Planning indicate that the percentage of couples using any family planning method increases with:

(i) Age of wife (from 7 per cent among those below 25 years of age to 17 per cent among those aged 30 years or more);

(ii) Number of living children (from 2 per cent among those without any living child to 25 per cent those with 5 or more living children);

(iii) Education of wife (from 10 per cent among wives without any education to 56 per cent among those who have gone to college);

(iv) Family income (from 10 per cent among those with monthly income of Rs. 100 or less to 30 per cent among those with monthly income of Rs. 1,000 or more);

(v) Size of city or village (from 10 per cent among those living in villages of 5,000 or less to 32 per cent among those living in cities of 1 million or more);

(vi) Community trends that the percentage of current users among the Hindus is higher than among the Muslims.

The survey revealed notable differences in the characteristics of current users, past users and non-users of contraception.

In our discussions with Muslim women in different parts of the country, we did not get the impression that there was any organized resistance to family planning on religious grounds. Some of the very poor women told us that they had heard about the religious propaganda but they could not see their children starve. In every state we asked the lady doctors about the response to family planning from different sections of society. The answers were interesting. Those doctors who had some kind of social commitment and sympathetic attitude invariably said that women from all classes and all regions came to them for advice while the others complained that Muslim women and women from the poorer sections of society were not interested.

Our general impression has been that men, particularly, Muslims, are not very much concerned about family planning, though in Kerala an enthusiastic collector informed us that in the Family Planning Camps a number of Catholic and Muslim men came to him for vasectomy but they did not want anyone to know about it and requested that the operations may be performed at night. He agreed to make the necessary arrangements and the response was good. According to him there was no significant difference in the percentage of acceptors from different communities. In a village in West Bengal while a B.D.C. was complaining that Muslims were not coming forward for family planning, an old, poor Muslim woman came up and asked where she could take her daughter-in-law for advice, so that she would stop having any more children. She already had 5 children. In Kashmir, the educated and working women are very much interested in family planning and we did not come across any group of women expressing disapproval on religious grounds.

An analysis of variance in five factors, viz., educational level of spouses, family income, number of children, urbanization and exposure to mass media simultaneously has shown that the effect of each of these factors on the use of family planning methods is significant at 1 per cent level. Some studies have suggested that the differential in adoption and use of family planning methods between States may be due to the differences in socio-economic characteristic of couples in actual implementation of strategies or combination of both.

While some of the studies occasionally contradict findings of previous research, one factor which is generally emphasized by most is education, particularly the education of women. The Regional Fertility Survey conducted by the Demographic Research Centre, Lucknow, indicated that mean number of live births varied inversely with the mother's education. The educational level of both husband and wife was found to have a very large influence on their attitudes towards family planning.

The Delhi Fertility Survey conducted by the Demographic Research Centre, Institute of Economic Growth, Delhi based on a total sample of 9,000 households, indicated the inverse relationship between a couple's educational level and average number of live births in a pronounced way only when both husband and wife were educated beyond matriculation level, the variation being 2.73 for this group and 4.47 for literate couples. The Mysore Population Study reported that among the social and economic factors studied, the one which appeared to be the most significant in relation to fertility in Bangalore City was educational status, but education below the high school or university stage was not found to be related significantly to the average number of children born.

Education may affect fertility in two ways: (i) by increasing knowledge and advantages of family planning; and (ii) by generating deliberate efforts for a planned family.

The first is effective at lower educational levels, while the latter operates probably when a sufficiently high level of education is achieved by the couple. The National Sample Survey indicated that the percentage of husbands desiring additional children after 2, declined from 60 when they were illiterate to 41.59 when they were intermediate and above. However, the decline was neither consistent nor pronounced when the educational level was below intermediate and above.

The Dharwar Surveys on the attitudes towards family planning undertaken by the Dharwar Demographic Research Centre indicated that educational level was the most important factor associated with awareness about family planning.

Role of Education: While all the major surveys found a positive relationship between education and knowledge, acceptance and practice of family planning, most of them have revealed the existence of other associational factors which may have influenced this relationship. Education is generally associated with one or more of the following: (a) rise is the age of marriage; (b) diversification of consumption pattern of people, involving both material and non-material aspects which can lead to a decline in the psychic utility generated by the birth of children; (c) urbanization; (d) possible increase in work force participation of women; (e) higher socio-economic status of the couple; (f) higher mobility; (g) higher exposure to mass media and (h) more diversified knowledge of family planning methods. It has been found that couples with primary level education or below have very limited knowledge of family planning and are most often aware only of sterilization and IUCD (Intra Uterine Contraceptive Device).

Methods of Contraceptions: Most of the methods for contraception affect women directly, and acceptance by them would indicate the success or failure of a method.

IUCD: This was introduced in 1965 and initially was very popular. Later the level of acceptance showed a reverse trend. Various studies indicate that the failure of IUCD was largely because enough information on certain side effects of the insertions was not adequately published.

During our tours, the doctors and field workers told us that this method was unpopular and it was a failure. Their observations were as follows: (1)The careless handling of IUCD insertions by the paramedical staff led to complications and there was a whispering campaign everywhere that it was harmful for the health of the women. (2)Proper arrangements were not made for a follow-up treatment in case of bleeding or other side effects.

We found, however, that wherever it was handled by properly trained personnel, e.g., in Haryana and Punjab, it was found to be the most successful method, specially because it was reversible and inexpensive.

Sterilization: This has been performed as part of the family planning programme. Tubectomies accounted for two-thirds of all sterilizations and they exceeded the number of vasectomies, but since then the number of vasectomies has increased more rapidly, and they accounted for more than 80 per cent of all sterilizations. We would like to point out, however, that the validity of these figures has been often questioned.

Since sterilization is a terminal method which is often believed to have consequences on the health of the woman, the possible constraints that may develop in taking recourse to this method are obvious. During our tours we received evidence of this apprehension from a large number of women. They were reluctant to end their chance of child bearing because of an underlying fear regarding the survival of their existing children. They were also apprehensive of the possible consequence of their health. This fear has occasionally been aggravated by the experience of the mass tubectomy camps which very often did not provide adequate medical care or follow-up measures.

Two specific arguments regarding sterilization were brought to our notice by women doctors. A group of these doctors in West Bengal mentioned a number of cases of 'post ligation syndrome' where the women developed psychological disturbances after tubectomy, particularly if any untoward incidence like illness or death of a child happened in the family. In their view, this was due to the tremendous hold of traditional values on the minds of these women, who developed a sense of guilt and regarded these tragedies as being the consequences of their 'unnatural' act. Yet another argument by doctors in the rural areas of Rajasthan was the impossibility of undertaking sterilization for a large number of women, particularly tribal ones, because of their extremely anaemic condition.

Other Methods: About 2.3 million couples are estimated to be using various other types of conventional contraceptives. This is 2.3 per cent of the estimated couples protected in the reproductive age group. For women the most significant is the use of oral contraceptive pills. A number of trials have been conducted to study the medical and social acceptability of oral contraception among Indian women. The pill as a method of oral contraception is useful for the educated urban rather than rural women. It is also comparatively more expensive and constant medical supervision is necessary to check the side effects.

Abortions: The objectives of the Medical Termination of Pregnancy Act 1971 is to reduce the incidence of criminal abortions which pose grave risks to pregnant women by liberalizing the provision of the Indian Penal Code which restricted medical practitioners from terminating pregnancies legally. The Shanti Lal Shah Committee has estimated that for every 73 live births, 25 abortions take place of which 15 are induced. "In a population of 500 million, the number of abortions per year would be 6.5 million, 2.6 million spontaneous and 3.9 million induced." From hospital records it has been observed that 15 to 20 per cent of the direct obstetric causes of maternal deaths are from abortions. Of these, 98 per cent were from septic abortions usually resulting from abortions undertaken by unqualified persons. According to the Registrar General Census (vital statistics); abortions form a high percentage of causes of all deaths due to child birth. According to two studies of the National Institute of Nutrition, Hyderabad, pregnancy wastage from miscarriage and abortions ranges from 16 to 19 per cent to 32 per cent among poor income groups.

The Act allows termination of pregnancy on: (a)Therapeutic grounds where the continuance of pregnancy would involve a risk. (i)to the life of the pregnant mother or, (ii)of grave injury to her physical and mental health. (b)Genuine grounds where there is substantial risk that the child, if born, is likely to suffer from such physical or mental abnormalities as to be seriously handicapped. (c)Humanitarian grounds, where the pregnancy has been caused by rape; or (d)Social grounds: (i)where the pregnancy in a married woman is the result of contraceptive failure, or (ii)that the environment of the pregnant woman during the continuance of pregnancy at the time of childbirth and thereafter, so far as is foreseeable, would involve risk of injury to her health.

Termination can be done only by registered practitioners certified for the purpose in approved places, mainly government hospitals.

While the Act emphasizes its importance as a health measure, the permission granted under section 3(2) to permit such termination for married women in cases of contraceptive failure, has emphasized its importance as an instrument of population control. This has given rise to a strong difference of opinion among medical personnel who are averse to using abortion for such a purpose. Many of them insist on tubectomy as a condition for abortion. In their view, based on experience, abortions often lead to frequent pregnancies, apart from its health hazards.

There is considerable evidence that the measure is being used more for birth control than for other reasons. According to a study undertaken by the Government and Children Hospital, Egmore, Madras, out of 7,957 abortions only 11 were for therapeutic reasons and 617 were cases of induced abortions admitted to the hospital only after complications had set in.

A study undertaken by the International Research Fertility Programme revealed that 88 per cent of abortion cases were among married women, of whom 55 per cent were between the age of 25 to 33, 81 per cent were urban, 19.1 per cent rural; 37 per cent had three or four children. In another study it was found that 72 per cent were married, of whom 60 per cent were in the 20 to 29 age group. The average total pregnancy of these groups was 4.3, where the average number of living children 2.5 and 0.8 had previous abortions. 50 per cent of all the patients had a previous abortion in their record and 17.8 per cent had 2 to 5.

All the studies indicate "that most pregnant women who go in for induced abortions are fully motivated for small family norms if not planned parenthood. These people are very amenable and can be fully motivated for adoption of family planning methods, more often sterilization, if they have two or more living children or other temporary methods of spacing children."

We have given serious consideration to this matter and discussed it with several representatives of the medical profession. While we appreciate the ethical considerations which make some of them reluctant to perform this operation, we feel that it is a woman's right to have control over the size of her family. At the same time it is important that doctors should have the authority to discourage such operations when it possesses a definite risk to the health of a particular patient.

We, however, feel that the condition being imposed in many hospitals, that abortion will only be performed if the patient agreed to sterilization, should not be compulsive, particularly where a woman has only one child. It would be far better to adopt methods of persuasion through expert counselling rather than compulsion. Compulsive conditions of this kind will only drive women to unqualified persons, thus defeating the main purpose of this Act.

We have been informed that there are serious psychological hazards posed by both pregnancies as well as sterilization. It is, therefore, imperative to organize systematic research on this field, to ascertain the impact of these situations and operations on the physical and mental health of women.

The difficulties placed before us by medical personnel regarding the recording procedure and paper work involved in these operations, lead us to suggest that these procedures need to be simplified. It is also necessary to extend facilities for authorized termination of pregnancies, particularly in the rural areas. We have also been informed that though the law does not require it, many hospitals insist on the husband's consent before performing these operations. A special effort needs to be made to convince the medical profession of the social value of this law, from the point of view of both individuals and society.

We have also been informed that most doctors are reluctant to perform these operations in the case of unmarried girls. It is necessary to clarify the point that rape is not the only ground to justify termination in cases of unmarried girls nor is there any legal obligation on the doctor to inform the police of an abortion done in a rape case. We note that the All India Medical Council has introduced this Act in the syllabus for medical jurisprudence, with the object of setting up new norms for the medical profession. This will go a long way in breaking down the resistance of doctors.

Recommended changes in Law: We would also like to recommend the following changes in the Law: (a)According to Section 4(a) of the Act - consent of a minor girl is not required for operation, while in other surgical operations on children above 12, such consent is necessary. In our view this distinction is uncalled for and may lead to guardians' compelling young girls to undergo this operation even when they do not want it. The consent of the patient should be essential. In the case of a minor girl nearing majority if the doctor and the patient are in agreement, the consent of the guardian may be dispensed with. In all such cases, greater discretion should be permitted to the doctor; (b)Section 8 of the Act provides an overriding protection to the doctor for any damage caused by the operation. Since no such protection is given for other operations, this seems an unnecessary clause and may lead to negligence. It may, therefore, be dropped.

New Policies and Programmes

During the First and Second Five-Year Plans, Government's approach to the problem of population growth, and the need for family planning, was a long-term objective, depending as much, if not more, on 'improvement in living standards and more widespread education especially among women', as positive measures for 'inculcation of the need' and techniques of family planning. Admitting that rates of population growth could only be altered over a period, it was agreed that programmes to restrain population growth had to complement a massive development effort.

From the Third Plan, however, restraint of population growth received a much greater emphasis and priority, with time-bound targets for reducing the birth rate and heavy investment in the administrative network to mount the programmes on the lines of a military operation, and the adoption of practices like mass sterilization camps, financial incentives and appointment of promoters, to make sterilization acceptable to the people. The legalization of abortions in cases of contraceptive failure was also a step to promote reduction in the birth rate. Some State Governments even adopted measures to deny maternity benefits to Women Government Servants after the third child. We feel strongly about this measure, for the denial of maternity benefits to a working woman is likely to affect both the health of the mother as well as that of the child. In Madhya Pradesh, we met a group of women teachers who complained bitterly that this measure has resulted in a number of them having to work till the day before the child was born. We have already pointed out the results of the absence of this benefit to construction workers.

The result of this change in emphasis was to put excessive reliance on the clinical rather than the welfare approach to family planning. Heavy investment in services, personnel and propaganda, exclusively devoted to family planning, led to a relative neglect of the other health and welfare services. In the case of women, the maternity and child health services, family welfare, adult education, and economic progress, all suffered relative lack of attention and resources, and Family Planning came to be described as the most important governmental programme for women.

The Fifth Plan had changed the emphasis again, mainly in view of a growing realization that the programme is becoming increasingly unpopular among many sections, and is failing to achieve the unrealistic targets. It is also admitted that a purely clinical approach cannot overcome the socio-psychological resistance caused by poverty, ignorance, low survival rate of children among the poor sections, and the economic and social dependence on children.

Though integration of family planning with maternal and child health care was suggested in the Fourth Plan, the policy of integration could not be achieved, since the family planning services had been already placed under a different administrative machinery from the other health services. A new strategy evolved for the Fifth Plan visualizes the integration of family planning into the general health services, particularly its maternal and child care component including nutrition. The principle of integration will be extended to other fields, in particular to efforts at mass motivation through the existing channels for functional training programmes to train multipurpose health workers to deliver the integrated health care services under the Minimum Needs Programme. The impact of this decision to see family planning in its proper perspective is clearly visible in the allocation of resources proposed for the next Plan. According to the Draft Five-Year Plan:

> The primary objective during the Fifth Plan is to provide minimum public health facilities integrated with family planning and nutrition for vulnerable groups - children, pregnant women and lactating mothers. It will be

> necessary to consolidate past gains in the various fields of health, such as communicable diseases, medical education and provision of infrastructure in the rural areas.

During our tours we found that wherever the medical personnel and the village level workers were mature and sympathetic in their approach and worked with a sense of social commitment, their persuasive power evoked a great degree of response. On the other hand there was considerable criticism of the 'motivators', most of whom are very young and inexperienced as well as purely untrained persons. It was a frequent observation that they were responsible for criminal mistakes like persuading extremely young persons both male and female to undergo sterilization, or bringing elderly women who were long past the child bearing age for the same, entirely because of the financial incentives. According to Banerjee:

> Perhaps the greatest mistakes in the formulation of family planning programmes has been a gross overestimation of the effectiveness of the motivators and equally gross underestimation of the resistance to be encountered motivating a community as a whole.... Motivation techniques were viewed as some sort of a magic which would be applied by a person to induce another to accept family planning.

We understand that it has been decided to introduce community incentives and group awards for the programme personnel with a view to increasing the involvement of the community and strengthening the commitment of the staff and institutions in order to improve the quality of the services. Most of the doctors and the women with whom we discussed problems of family planning were of the opinion that while payment to acceptors should continue particularly for daily wage workers, the payment to motivators is not only a waste but has been responsible for much of the unpopularity of this programme. There were also severe criticisms of the lack of adequate follow-up measures. We also came across large gaps both in areas and communities where the family planning services have not reached. One group of women whom we met in Bangalore had never heard of family planning.

During the course of its tours in the States, the Committee met a number of health and family planning officials, social workers, as well as a cross-section of rural and urban women. An analysis of the tour reports reveals that the message of family planning has reached almost everywhere, but access to health and family planning services was most inadequate. Even in slum areas of big cities, there were no family planning clinics in the vicinity, and the women did not know where to go though they were anxious to avail themselves of the information. In the rural areas, there was an acute shortage of maternity facilities, and trained medical personnel.

In Bastar district, and in some tribal areas of Himachal Pradesh, we were informed that the birth rate is 29 per 1000, which is well below the national target for the Vth Plan, and yet we found money being spent on family planning projects in these areas. There were huge hoardings and posters advocating the small family norm, when this money could very well have been utilized for other welfare activities in these extremely backward areas.

In our view, the inadequacy of qualified medical personnel and mature counselling presents the greatest internal drawback to the success of this programme. We are entirely in agreement with the Draft Fifth Five-Year Plan, that integration of family planning with more positive health services like maternal and child health and nutrition, and improvement in the life expectancy of children and mothers, will provide a far greater incentive to the adoption of family planning measures than the hitherto adopted negative approach.

Programmes for women's welfare and development can be classified under the following broad base

A. Programmes in the rural areas: Welfare Extension Projects, Family and Child Welfare Projects, Organization of Mahila Mandals, Training Schemes for Workers.

B. Programmes in urban areas: Welfare Extension Projects, and Working Women's Hostels.

C. Other Programmes: Grants-in-aid to voluntary organizations, Condensed Courses of Education for Adult Women, Adult Literacy and social education for women. Craft training centres, Socio-economic programmes, Nutrition Programmes, Social Defence Programmes, Border Area Programmes, Homes for Women.

Rural Areas: The concept of rural development as conceived in India covers a wide field and history. Both Mahatma Gandhi and Rabindranath Tagore had seen rural development as an important method of social mobilization which could build the social infrastructure for independence. According to Tagore, it was an effort to make the village a self-reliant and self-respectful unit, with knowledge of its culture and history and to enable the people to make use of modern resources for their full upliftment - physical, social, economic and intellectual. Gandhi viewed rural development as aiming to make every village a 'Republic', in which no person would be unemployed, and everyone would enjoy sufficient nutritious food, houses with adequate hygiene and sanitation, and enough khadi for their clothing. Thus, rural development was not seen only in its micro-dimension, but as a new philosophy for society, which was to bring social consciousness or a revolution among the rural people. Tagore's Shriniketan and Gandhi's Village Construction Programmes were the forerunners of rural development that was to be taken up by the government after independence. The Community Development Programme undertaken by the Government of India drew heavily from the Gandhian concept.

The application of Gandhian ideas to the field of women's development had been done by the Kasturba Memorial Trust after the death of Kasturba Gandhi, which had been given a concrete form in the objectives and activities of the Kasturba Memorial Trust. This Trust was born with the objective of serving rural women by providing: (i) education for women and children; (ii) medical and health services; and (iii) socio-economic programmes in the form of khadi and village industries to relieve economic distress.

The Trust trained a number of gramsevikas and mid-wives and the training centres were specially conceived to train and mobilize village women, specially widows and deserted wives. The health programmes aimed at prevention of diseases as well as promotion of positive health through maternal and child welfare programmes.

When the Central Social Welfare Board decided to launch the Welfare Extension Projects in 1954, this threefold approach was adopted as the basic framework for provision of services. The activities included Balwadis, maternity services and general medical aid, social education and craft training for women. The original Welfare Extension Projects (WEP) were to serve a unit of 25-40 contiguous villages, with a population of 25-30 thousand through five centres. At the end of the Second Plan, there were 420 such projects with 2004 centres. Eight of these projects, with 40 centres, continue to be operated by the Central Social Welfare Board, while others have either been closed or handed over to Mahila Mandals and voluntary organizations which receive 75 per cent financial assistance.

Since the general objectives and methodology of this programme were similar to those of the larger programmes of community development initiated by the government during the First Plan in 1952, and to eliminate duplication of work, it was decided that Welfare Extension Projects should be started in Community Development Blocks on a coordinated basis. All original Welfare Extension Projects were converted into this pattern as soon as the area was covered by a C.D. Block. These projects covered a block of 100 villages with a population of about 60,000 through 10 centres. The work and the functionaries were supervised by a Project Implementing Committee which consisted of representatives of block officials and local voluntary workers. For the first year the budget was shared by the Central Social Welfare Board, the State Government and Community Development Block in the ratio of 12:65 and at the end of 5 years the total expenditure was shared in the ratio of 24:12:5. Later, there were 264 projects with 2,800 centres.

Since greater importance was increasingly attached to the role of voluntary organizations in the continuance of welfare programmes, 1,629 centres of the Welfare Extension Projects (original and coordinated pattern) were handed over to Mahila Mandals. 442 Mahila Mandals, who have taken over one or more activities of this project were given a grant of Rs. 25.69 lakh.

On the recommendations of the Central Social Welfare Board and an Evaluation Committee of Social Welfare on the Welfare Extension Projects, it was decided to revise services existing in rural areas in different patterns aiming to develop a countrywide programme of integrated welfare services for children. Thus the Family and Child Welfare (F&CW) scheme was initiated, whereas extension projects provided services for women and children, the Family and Child Welfare Projects aimed at integrated development of the pre-school child, training to young mothers and all services that were necessary for the proper growth and development of the child and rural family.

The family and child welfare projects were funded by the Central and the State Governments in a 75:25 ratio and aided by UNICEF with equipment, stipends and training facilities. They have progressively taken over the functions of the earlier projects of the Central Social Welfare Board and the Ministry of Community Development. The services provided are: (a) Integrated services to rural children; specially preschool; (b) Basic training to women and young girls in home management, health education, nutrition education, child care. General health and maternity services for women were also to be provided with the aid of the Primary Health Centres. Similar collaboration was also envisaged for nutrition. (c) Assistance to women through Mahila Mandals, specially established centres and existing welfare agencies, for getting supplementary work to augment their income. (d) Cultural, educational and recreational activities for women and children.

Initially, there were 221 projects in existence and later, 20 coordinated welfare extension projects were added to this scheme, bringing the total to 240. On 31st March, 1973, 281 projects were functioning.

Maternity and Child Welfare Services: With the integration of the First Plan, Maternity and Child Welfare Services were taken up by the Ministry of Health as part of the overall development programme in health. These services were augmented by WHO and UNICEF. A number of Maternity and Child Welfare Bureaus were established in States, staffed by qualified women medical officers. At the same time, the then Community Projects administration also undertook these services in the Community Development and National Extension Service Blocks. Other Ministries like Railways, Defence and Labour also promoted Maternity and Child Welfare Programmes through the Ministry of Health. The number of Maternity and Child Welfare Centres increased and these services were given an important place in rural development programmes. The Union Government assisted the States in establishment of primary health centres and sub-centres covering a C.D. Block. At present 5,195 centres are functioning in the country. Maternity and Child Welfare Services are also undertaken by the Ministries of Railways, Labour (under Labour Welfare and the various Acts in this section) and public sector undertakings.

Mahila Mandals: Practically from the beginning it was realized that the objectives of these rural development programmes could not be achieved without the active participation and leadership of the local community. Government functionaries, however, efficient and dedicated, can only provide some stimulus and act as catalytic agents to train and release efforts for self-help of the people. This was particularly true of women who had been paralysed by generations of social oppression, and denial of basic rights. Both the Central Social Welfare Board and the department of Community development concluded that the proper agency for the success of this programme would be a committee of local women. The organization of Mahila Mandals thus became one of the objectives of these rural development programmes.

The declared objective of community development is to enable rural women to organize themselves at the village level to assemble on a regular basis to learn from each other and from workers appointed by the Government. The basic idea is to create opportunities for rural women to improve their status as housewives and to take part in public affairs. The department therefore organizes Mahila Mandals, imparts training facilities to their members and provides incentive awards for performance.

Mahila Mandals, were organized in villages and blocks for promoting women's programmes. Nutrition, education, health, mother and child care, home improvement, adult literacy, recreation and cultural activities and training and house and family planning were part of their programmes. There were about 53,000 Mahila. Mandals with a total membership of 14,00,000 averaging 11 Mahila Mandals per block. Under the Applied Nutrition Programme, additional facilities are being provided for the promotion of economic activities of Mahila Mandals towards, development and management of kitchen and school gardens, organization of fishery units, etc. During the Fourth Plan 7,500 awards in various categories were given to Mahila Mandals.

The Central Social Welfare Board and the State Social Welfare Advisory Boards also realized the importance of Mahila Mandals and now they are being given grants up to 75 per cent for running some programmes of the Board. Subsequently, 442 Mahila Mandals received a grant of about Rs 25.69 lakh. They are also running some Welfare Extension Projects of the Board.

Voluntary-agencies like the Bhartiya Grameen Mahila Sangh have also established a large number of Mahila Mandals. The representatives of the Village Mahila Mandals form the District Mahila Samities and the representatives of the District Mahila Samities constitute the State panel or State branches. According to the Bhartiya Grameen Mahila Sangh, its branches in the 17 States now cover 7,000 villages.

Training Scheme for Workers: The various functionaries required for these rural development schemes are trained at centres located in different parts of the country. The training is organized by some government agencies like the Directorate of Extension of the Ministry of Agriculture and various schools of social work, non-governmental organizations like the Kasturba Memorial Trust, Visva Bharati, Jamia Millia with assistance from the Central Social Welfare Board.

The Department of Community Development in the Ministry of Agriculture has a programme for training associate women workers to enable members of Mahila Mandals to come forward to become organized. The members of Mahila Mandals get to know about the organization of Balwadis, health and nutrition, education, nursery, kitchen gardening, etc. About 20,000 women received training in the Third and Fourth Plans and a sum of Rs 11.17 lakh was spent during the Fourth Plan.

The Directorate of Extension of the Ministry of Agriculture also provides training for village level workers of Community Development Block at 25 centres. The emphasis is on the protection of Agricultural production and nutrition education. In service, training facilities are provided after 2-3 years service and two week refresher courses are given to Mukhya Sevikas. Refresher courses are also given to Instructresses for Gram Sevika and Mukhya Sevika training centres for six weeks. Associate workers such as Gram Lakshmis or Gram Kakis are also given one month's training. Under the nutrition education scheme, training was given to associate women workers.

Farm Women's Training Courses for one week are organized at about 100 training centres for farm women. This farmers' training was started in a few districts and is now being implemented in almost all districts. The emphasis is on agricultural production, reproduction patterns of high yielding variety cereals, stock managements, nutrition, etc. Radio broadcasting is also used for educating the farm women and organizing discussion groups.

The Bhartiya Grameen Mahila Sangh also holds various training camps for rural women. Among these are leadership training camps sanctioned by the Department of Social Welfare in border areas. Similar programmes have also been sponsored by the CSWB. The increased agricultural production programme is a seven-day camp sanctioned by the Ministry of Food and Agriculture for training in improved agricultural methods and covered 650 villages. The Ministry of Health has sanctioned the family planning orientation programme to train village women in methods of family planning.

Scene in Towns

The structure of welfare programmes in urban areas varies from region to region. The municipalities and local administration are responsible for providing basic formal education and health facilities like schools, hospitals, dispensaries, etc. Welfare programmes as such have already been left to voluntary organizations, which in some cases receive grants through the Central Social Welfare Board or the State Governments.

In 1958 the Central Social Welfare Board started Welfare Extension Projects in the urban areas to meet the needs of people living in the slums, particularly in new industrial areas. These projects provided balwadis, creches, arts and craft classes and family planning and maternity advice for women; they also do placement of destitutes. 65 such projects were in existence at the end of the Plan. They were reduced to 33. Later, Welfare Extension Projects received Rs 2.78 lakh benefiting approximately 70,000 families.

Working Women's Hostels: An increasing number of women are leaving their homes and entering employment. The problem of accommodation in metropolitan areas, particularly impelled the Central Social Welfare Board to provide grants for hostels for working women as one of its services. The Board viewed this service as a preventive measure against the possibility of young girls in urban areas being exposed to undesirable and anti-social influences.

The scheme was started during the Second Plan and the Board sanctioned grants to voluntary welfare institutions willing to provide healthy accommodation at reasonable rates for working women of lower income groups. At the end of the Plan, 101 grants amounting to Rs 9.76 lakh had been sanctioned. Later, 29 hostels received a grant of Rs 66,000 from the Board. The Department of Social Welfare initiated a scheme for financial assistance to voluntary institutions for the construction of hostel buildings in capital cities and cities with a population of over ten lakh. The pattern of assistance is under review at present and in the current Plan a sum of Rs 15 crore has been set aside for hostels for working women.

Condensed Courses of Education for Adult Women: The very high percentage of illiteracy amongst women as well as various difficulties in imparting education to them gave rise to the condensed courses of education for adult women which are being implemented by various governmental and non-governmental agencies. The programme was initiated by the Central Social Welfare Board with the dual objective of opening new vistas of employment for needy women and to create a band of trained workers for various projects in the rural areas.

Under the scheme, adult women between the ages of 18 and 30, who have some schooling, are prepared for middle schools, matriculation or equivalent examination within a period of two years. Grants up to Rs 35,000 per course for two years are given for maintenance, stipends, salaries to teachers and educational equipment. Women who complete these courses can go in for vocational training as nurse, mid-wife, gramsevikas, etc. In the Second Plan Rs 58.82 lakh were-sanctioned for 271 courses, though only Rs 28.88 lakh was released. In the Third Plan, a provision of Rs 150 lakh was made for 500 courses. Up to the end of February 1973, 1,386 courses had been started and Rs 3 crore were spent. Of 33,000 women enrolled about 25,000 completed their studies. The programme has been extended to wives of Jawans killed or disabled in action. The Community Development Department also has established adult literacy centres in blocks which cover women.

Socio-Economic Programmes: It was realized at an early stage of the welfare programmes that they would not have the desired impact unless the women were imparted some craft or technical training. This was a part of the three pronged approach of the earliest programmes. While health received some attention and resources from the Ministry of Health, and Family Planning, as well as welfare agencies, the economic schemes did not receive corresponding attention from the concerned governmental agencies. On a very minor scale, some socio-economic schemes were initiated by the Central Social Welfare Board and its grants-in-aid schemes and also organized on a small scale by the Department of Community Development and some voluntary organization. Initially started by the Ministry of Rehabilitation for refugee women, it was taken up by the Central Social Welfare Board, to provide leisure time employment to women in lower income groups and help them supplement their income. This was undertaken in cooperation with the Ministry of Commerce and Industry which provides them necessary assistance in technical training, finance and marketing. The scheme was working in co-operation with State Governments and State Social Welfare Advisory Boards. 95 demonstration-cum-training centres, set up on 26 pilot projects for industries in the Community Development Project areas have benefited women.

At present the socio-economic programme of the CSWB provides financial assistance to voluntary welfare institutions and

Co-operative Societies for setting up small production units where needy women or handicapped persons are given initial training and subsequently provided with employment. In the implementation of this programme, the Board as well as voluntary institutions and Cooperative Societies obtain technical assistance from the National-Small Industries Organization and regional offices of the All-India Handicrafts Board and All-India Handloom Board. The categories of the scheme that are being implemented under this programme are: (1) Production units of small-scale industries, such as manufacture of toys and articles, printing books, binding, fruit preservation and canning, bakery, confectionary, ready-made garments, etc. (2) Handicrafts training-cum-procurement and production units; for example, cane and bamboo articles, mat-weaving, traditional embroidery, etc. (3) Handloom training-cum-production units; (4) Units ancillary to large industries; and (5) Industrial co-operative societies set up under the voluntary welfare programmes started by the Board.

Up to the end of March 1972, the Board had approved grants to 130 institutions for setting up production units with an employment potential of about 4,000 under various categories of schemes. An amount of Rs 54.60 lakh had been sanctioned for 140 approved units with an employment potential of 4,235.

The Annual Report of the Central Social Welfare Board mentions that the attention of the State Governments have been drawn to the need for extending some sort of protection or patronage to socio-economic units run by voluntary institutions buying their products. The problem of marketing remains unsolved and unless this is overcome, the objective of a number of socio-economic programmes will remain unfulfilled. A number of Ministries such as Railways, Ministry of Labour, apart from the Ministry of Agriculture and Community Development have small schemes for providing craft training to women. The Mahila Samities of the Ministry of Railways have handicraft centres to help women in learning some trade to enable them to supplement the family income. Some public sector undertakings have Mahila Mandals which also provide such training. While the emphasis on these programmes to improve women's earning power indicates awareness of the dimension of women's problems, it is doubtful whether these programmes are having the desired impact, since most of these women are unable to obtain the raw-material or market the finished goods. It is also remarkable that the governmental agencies responsible for promoting industrial development have completely ignored the reality of the problem that they are trying to solve.

Nutrition Programmes: The Plan emphasized nutrition as a major problem particularly in rural areas, and among the lower income groups. The Department of Social Welfare and the Central Social Welfare Board, the Ministry of Health and Family Planning, the Department of Community Development of the Ministry of Agriculture and the Ministry of Education are all operating various nutrition schemes for women and children.

The Special Nutrition Programme of the Government of India was introduced in 1970-71 to provide supplementary nutrition to children in tribal areas and urban slums, by the Department of Social Welfare. This scheme covers a number of pre-school children in 0-6 age groups and nursing the expectant mothers. Over 19,600 feeding centres have been set up in the tribal areas and about 7,500 in urban areas. The Department of Social Welfare also implements a nutrition programme for children in the age group 3-5, through the Balwadis and day-care centres run by the CSWB, the Indian Council of Child Welfare, the Harijan Sevak Sangh, and the Adimjati Sevak Sangh, covering 2,00,640 children and 5,577 instructions. The Balwadis of the Family and Child Welfare Projects were generally excluded from this Programme because provision for nutrition was already provided in the scheme. The Board, however, feels that it has not been possible to build up adequate machinery for implementation and supervision of this programme at the State and Central levels and it requires greater provision by the Government.

The Directorate of Extension of the Ministry of Agriculture has been running a Composite Nutrition Programme since 1969-70, to provide nutrition education in areas not covered under the Applied Nutrition Programme. It includes nutrition education, through Mahila Mandals, strengthening the supervisory machinery for women's programmes, encouragement of economic activities of Mahila Mandals, training of associate women workers and demonstration feeding. The Applied Nutrition Programme of the Department of Community Development was introduced in collaboration with UNICEF, FAO and WHO. It was intended to educate the rural people in improved nutrition by promoting the production and consumption of protective foods like fruits, vegetables, fish and poultry. From 1966-67, steps were taken to coordinate the operation of the Applied Nutrition Programmes with other schemes like the Mid-Day Meal Programme of the Ministry of Education, and Family and Child Welfare Projects of the Department of Social Welfare. The ANP covered 221 blocks and it covered, 1,101 projects and spent Rs 1.46 crore for this purpose. Under this programme, demonstration, in cooking and feeding is held, particularly designed to give- direction on nutrition through the Mahila Mandals, and to train women workers.

The Ministry of Health has increasingly emphasized nutrition particularly for pregnant women, lactating mothers and pre-school children of the weaker sections, through an integrated programme of supplementary feeding, health care, immunization as well as nutrition education. Now, concentrated attention will be given to these vulnerable sections in rural areas, urban slums, tribal development blocks and school going children of the weaker sections. Within the resources allocated, it should be possible to cover about 11 million additional beneficiaries in the Plan. This programme is under the budgetary control of the Department of Social Welfare.

The Fourth Plan Special Nutrition Programme for pre-school children and expectant and nursing mothers has been redesignated and included in the Integrated Child

Development Programme in the current Plan. The services include supplementary nutrition feeding, immunization, health check-up and referral services, health and nutrition education. The entire expenditure for the ICDP during the Fifth Plan will be made by the Centre and implemented through the State Governments and Union Territories. It is proposed to cover about 7,000 nursing and expectant mothers in each project. Women between 15-44 years numbering approximately 23,000 will be provided nutrition and health education. In the tribal areas 2,450 nursing and expectant mothers and 7,000 women in the 15-44 age groups are the target population for each project. The ICDP depends on interdepartmental coordination between the Ministry of Health, State Health Departments, Community Development Department and the Department of Social Welfare. The existing 33,000 feeding centres of the Special Nutrition Programme and Balwadi nutrition programmes are in operation in organized slums, tribal areas and other rural areas. They will initially be included into ICDP centres in the project areas.

Social Defence Programmes: Among the services available in the country for the correction and reformation of persons who come into conflict with the law are the following which apply directly to women: (a) Suppression of Immoral Traffic; (b) After care services; and (c) Welfare Services in Prisons.

These services are provided by the Department of Social Welfare and Rehabilitation Directorate at Central level.

The Suppression of Immoral Traffic in Women and Girls Act of 1956 provides for protective homes and reception centres. There are at present 33 protective homes and 68 reception centres and district shelters in the country. A scheme for short stay homes for rehabilitation of women and girls facing moral danger was approved in 1969-70 and two pilot projects - one in West Bengal and the other in Madhya Pradesh were provided grants of Rs 1.10 lakh in 1972-73. During the Second Plan, programmes were drawn up under Social and Moral Hygiene and After Care Programmes not only for those under the SIT Act, but also those discharged from Correctional and non-Correctional Institutions. The State Governments were assisted to set up special homes such as protective homes.

We visited some of these protective homes. In the Protective Home in Lucknow and in the Nari Niketan in Delhi, efforts are made to rehabilitate the inmates by providing training in sewing and embroidery. There is no formal procedure for marketing of these products, nor are the inmates given any training either to organize production or marketing. We were informed that sewing machines are presented to the inmates when they are discharged to help them to become self-employed. This practice was reported to be prevalent in many States. According to reports by social workers in different parts of the country, most of these young women find it difficult to earn an adequate livelihood from this occupation. Quite a number are compelled to dispose of the machines, and revert to their original profession. We were rather distressed to find that these homes house women rescued from immoral traffic as well as young girls sent under the Children's Act. Even insane women are housed in these homes. We consider this to be a very unhealthy and undesirable situation. We also feel that the training provided for rehabilitation in these homes is not adequate and requires much greater attention and planning as well as resources. We were informed that in some of the homes, efforts are made to return these young women to their families wherever possible, or to arrange marriages for them.

There has been considerable discussion on these programmes for rehabilitation of victims of immoral traffic. During a recent Judicial Seminar on Correctional Services, the speakers, who included representatives of the Association for Social Health, the Director of Social Welfare, Delhi Administration and members of the staff of the Delhi School of Social Work, pointed out the inadequacy of the arrangements for the employment of these young women. Without economic rehabilitation, much of the efforts made for their rescue is wasted. Some social workers have suggested to us that the best way for rehabilitation would be to set up production-cum-marketing centres along with these homes. It is also necessary to diversify the types of training provided to the inmates, since over-dependence on tailoring and embroidery has led to considerable waste. Economic independence is the only way to protect these women from the clutches of persons who have a vested interest in this traffic.

Homes are also provided for the aged and destitute women in various States though the total number of such homes is inadequate in terms of the population to be covered. A scheme for the welfare of destitute women between the ages of 18-44 and 45-65 providing for basic amenities of food, shelter, clothing, besides education and training in craft to enable the younger group to become self-reliant, as also services for dependent children up to 7 years was finalized in 1970-71. For the first group, residential institutions to accommodate 200 persons were to be provided. The scheme was to be implemented by giving grants-in-aid to voluntary organizations up to 75 per cent of the expenditure. The total Fourth Plan provision was Rs 100 lakh. We regret to note that the scheme remains unimplemented.

Grants-in-aid: Grants-in-aid are extended to registered voluntary institutions working for welfare of women, children and handicapped persons. Under the grants-in-aid for women's welfare during the First and the Second Plans, assistance was provided for expansion, development and improvement of activities of voluntary organizations. On the basis of the recommendations of the grants-in-aid Committee, the Board decided to limit the assistance during the Third Plan to consolidate and improve the activities initiated during the First and the Second Plans. Generally all grants except those given for developing special schemes were given on a matching basis.

The amounts allocated to these schemes during the four Plans indicate that while the First and Second Plans brought in a number of voluntary institutions within the network for administration of welfare services, Government's dependence on these bodies has registered a decline during the Third and Fourth Plans.

Social Work

Voluntary welfare services in India have always been an integral part of the cultural and social tradition. The bulk of the social services were provided by the voluntary sector prior to independence. Social welfare services have always been present in some form or the other for the well-being of the weaker sections of society who, because of various handicaps, social, economic, physical, etc., could not make use of, or were traditionally denied, normal facilities. The weaker sections included women, children, the aged, infirm and handicapped, Scheduled Castes and Scheduled Tribes.

Voluntary organizations may opt for several alternative roles according to their objectives and composition. They may be innovational and experimental activities in fields where government has not entered. They may co-exist with the public sector and the private sector for social development because they may have some advantages over the former or they can provide the government with a supportive base, i.e. they can work like agents of the government at local levels and operate programmes of the government as their own.

Soon after independence, on the basis of a survey made by the Planning Commission, it was estimated that there were about 10,000 voluntary organizations in the field of social welfare. In order to strengthen and encourage these agencies the Central Social Welfare Board was established in 1953, with a nationwide programme for grants-in-aid. It was realized that the voluntary organizations, with the qualities of flexibility, of experimentation, human touch, nearness to the clientele, sensitiveness to the new problems and capacity to discover new ideas could be of great assistance, since it was impossible for any government to take care of all the welfare needs of the people. The voluntary agencies could also mobilize resources from within the community for social welfare.

The relative importance of the role of the State and the role of the voluntary agencies has been engaging the attention of policy makers, planners, social thinkers, administrators and voluntary workers. In 1959, a Study team on Social Welfare and Backward Classes, appointed by the Planning Commission, recommended that whereas all programmes of social welfare arising out of the statutory responsibility of the State should be sponsored by State departments of Social Welfare, other social welfare services to meet local needs, should be implemented through voluntary organizations. A seminar on Social Administration in Developing Countries held in New Delhi in March, 1964, felt that the cooperation of the State and voluntary agencies in meeting social needs would always bring out better results in promoting welfare services on a larger scale.

We met representatives of some national voluntary organizations working for women's welfare and the welfare of socially deprived groups. We also met representatives of voluntary welfare organizations in every State during our tours. Most of the women's voluntary organizations have been confined to the urban areas, with its membership drawn mainly from educated urban middle-class women. Their main activities are conducting literacy classes, adult education centres, Balwadis, promoting women's cooperatives, small savings, handicrafts, etc. Some of these organizations have also taken up family planning programmes. In times of emergency, such organizations have organized canteens, blood banks and other services. These organizations seek to raise the status of women in the social, economic, political and educational fields. They have passed numerous resolutions for the uplift of Indian women, but their constructive activities have suffered from limitations of resources, personnel, and failure to reach rural areas.

Only a few organizations have endeavoured to work amongst rural women, to improve their living conditions, promote leadership and assist them to take part in developmental activities. The government has given grants for some voluntary welfare activities. In some cases, the grant has been for administration and maintenance while in other cases it has been allotted for programmes only.

Apart from the Central Social Welfare Board's grants-in-aid programme, there is no machinery to coordinate and distribute the services provided by these bodies, to ensure greater efficiency and even distribution. Nor are the resources of the majority of these organizations adequate to maintain trained workers for their complex types of work. Initially, the important organizations were able to act as pressure groups in directing the attention of the government to social problems, and to mobilize support for social legislation. Our investigation has shown that these laws still remain unknown to the large mass of Indian women, who have not been able to take advantage of them. Most of these organizations operate independent of each other and as such have not been able to fully benefit the community.

Role of Government

Expenditure for welfare programmes, including programmes meant for women is low in comparison to other sectors, since it has been viewed as a non-productive item in comparison to the economic sectors. In times of stringencies, financial cuts are made first in this sector, since returns from investments are not immediate. A break-up of allocations indicates that a major part of the expenditure is on maintenance and establishment charges, leaving only a small percentage for actual services. The administrative tradition in India has tended to emphasize maintenance of law and order, and economic development, and departments dealing with welfare programmes generally occupy a relatively less important position in the governmental structure. The training imparted to the administrators also emphasizes the same aspects. It has now been realized that administration must also be welfare oriented and recently a working group has been set up to frame a syllabus for social administration for the training of service probationers at the National Academy of Administration and other State level training institutes.

The administration and handling of welfare programmes has become increasingly technical. Administrators have to acquire technical orientation for successful implementation of social welfare programmes. The lack of emphasis on the required technical competence and the limitation of resources have had an adverse impact on the quality and success of welfare programmes.

Certain factors impede realization of a high degree of rationality in organization and flexibility in operation. The federal nature of our policy vests responsibility for implementing social policy and programmes with State and local authorities, but resources and agencies for planning are at the Centre. The weakness of local authorities further complicates the problems. There is dire need for greater coordination between voluntary agencies and organizations built up by Government, between activities of States and the Central Government and of the district or local level organizations and the States.

State Level: At present the majority of the States have a Minister-in-charge of Social Welfare, though this portfolio might include other subjects. State governments give still lower priority to social welfare programmes, and are reluctant to allocate sufficient resources. It has also been found that in the operation of the democratic process, the interests of the weaker sections are sometimes neglected, as they are relatively less vocal and less powerful than the dominant section of the population. Due to existing social prejudice and attitudes towards women, any policy regarding their welfare and development is limited either to education or welfare of special groups like handicapped or destitute women. Therefore, though social welfare is a State subject, the major share of the State's allocations go towards the maintenance of the existing social welfare activities initiated generally by the Centre.

As an illustration, it may be mentioned that during Shri Charan Singh's tenure as Chief Minister in UP, all women's welfare programmes of the Government were summarily discontinued. The State Social Welfare (Advisory) Board was however allowed to continue because of strong representation from the State Finance Department that its abolition would result in stoppage of Central assistance. The closure provoked a protest from the women functionaries whose services were held up as a model to other States, because of their success. The result of the closure has left only skeletal services for women in the States.

Most State governments do not have any machinery for collection of data or planning of welfare services. The State Social Welfare (Advisory) Boards, which might have fulfilled this role, serve mainly as a link organization to supervise, implement and report on the working of aided voluntary organizations in the State as an agency of the Central Social Welfare Board. The relationship between Central and State Governments, the Central Social Welfare Board and the State governments are also not clearly defined and the status of the State Boards differ from State to State.

Local administrations have shown even less interest in women's welfare programmes in general and local bodies authorized to allocate resources have given very low priority to them. Everywhere we were told that the Mahila Mandals were being starved of funds and not being provided even with accommodation. The process of co-opting women into the Panchayats has also not been very successful as their small numbers have prevented them from being more effective in emphasizing the needs of women. As a rule, they have not had an effective voice in policy making or the allocation of resources. The male members of the rural elite, are by and large not favourably disposed towards improving and changing the position of women and consequently women's programmes are prone to be neglected.

The neglect and indifference to welfare activities by the local and State Governments has led to an increase in the role of central agencies in this field. Within the federal framework the Central government's role should normally be planning, monitoring progress of activities, stimulating particular activities to ensure a national minimum standard, and guiding States through policy directions, giving advice and providing technical and financial help. The reasons for this increase in the role of the Centre can, therefore, be summed up as follows: (a)Limitation of resources of State Governments; (b)Indifference and low priorities for welfare programmes on the part of most State Governments; (c)Absence of proper welfare agencies in most of the States.

The experience of the Central Social Welfare Board suggests that the Coordination Committees as envisaged at the local level of some of the projects of the Board were not very useful since local administrations were not willing to take up women's welfare programmes. The State Boards were not in a position to function autonomously and the State Governments were disinterested in women's welfare programmes.

Under the system of financial relations between the Central and the State Governments, the Centre provides assistance for development programmes during a Plan period either on sharing or on full basis. At the end of the Plan period full responsibility for continuing the programmes devolves on the States. In the case of the women's programmes initiated by Central agencies, State Governments have not always been willing to accept the responsibility for continuation. In such cases, these programmes have had to be discontinued or re-designated as a new programme so that Central assistance could be continued.

The concept of a local need-based approach to social welfare has gradually been overshadowed as a direct consequence of this centralizing trend. Programmes and policies are initiated at the Centre, and there is increasing distance between the level of policy making and the levels of implementation. National programmes are framed without adequate reference to local variations and needs and this defeats the very purpose of social welfare. It particularly affects the initiative of the local community and the voluntary sector, and leads to increasing bureaucratization. It has also prevented the State Governments from admitting their responsibility in the field of welfare.

Because of this bureaucratization and centralization, the authority and initiative of the field staff is considerably impaired. As an example, the field staff at the State level are not taken into confidence nor are their suggestions considered at the level of policy and planning. For a number of schemes of the Central Social Welfare Board, the State Boards have little authority for initiating and reviewing the programmes.

The delays inherent in routine procedure and functioning of the Government hampers the progress of the programmes. Government organizations and procedures, with rigid rules governing sanctions and expenditure by their very nature, are not suited to the essentially informal and personal approach required for welfare work. Generally the approach of the voluntary workers and organizations is more flexible and personal. Once funds have been allotted for a particular project, they cannot be diverted for any other purpose and these agencies have to function within the rigid framework of the government sanction.

An examination of welfare and development activities undertaken in the country so far indicates that there is a multiplicity of programmes, agencies and functionaries. A large number of these programmes have very similar objectives and functions.

These programmes are run by different departments, have separate allocations, and the field staff belongs to different agencies. Areas of implementation in many cases are not rationally demarcated. Since most of these are Central programmes, planning and policy making is carried out by separate Ministries and Departments at the Centre. There is very little or no coordination between these Ministries and Departments, except where a coordinated programme has been envisaged (as in the case of Integrated Child Development Programme). This leads to a waste of funds in the duplication of administrative machinery, leaving a relatively small amount for the actual implementation of the programmes.

There is very little coordination at the State level also. Even though the State Social Welfare Advisory Boards have some government officials as members, this has failed to ensure any substantial coordination of governmental effort in the welfare of women. At the project level, the functional committees and implementation committees are constituted with representatives of the State Governments and State Boards. They have to work in collaboration with the Panchayats or other local organization. The experience of these committees has not been always happy. Besides, their scope of activities is limited, only to the programmes of the Board.

There is little justification for the vast number of agencies for implementing welfare programmes with almost similar objectives. A division in administrative agencies can be justified on one of the three following grounds: (a) territorial distinction, i.e., each agency functioning in clearly demarcated territory; (b) methodological distinction, i.e., if the method of work has to be different; (c) functional distinction, i.e., if the objectives of the agency are such as to warrant a separate organization.

The present allocation of work amongst various agencies has followed no such principle of clear distinctions.

As one of the most important agencies for the implementation of social welfare activities, the status of the Social Welfare Boards is currently under consideration. Though in practice the Board has enjoyed some autonomy, legally it has no independent existence. It was given the status of a charitable company in 1969 to meet audit objections in the way of giving grants. This has not solved its problems and its relationship with the Department of Social Welfare in regard to policy, planning and approval of programmes and financial allocations clearly indicates its status as a subordinate agency of the Department.

The justification for creating an agency outside the ministerial framework of the Government lay in the peculiar nature of welfare work, which required a flexible, personalized and committed approach, not easily possible within a government department because of procedural rules and regulations. The intention of the government was thus undoubtedly to create a specialized agency with its membership drawn from the ranks of social workers, with direct experience of voluntary welfare activities. Some other specialized agencies created by the government have been given statutory autonomous status. The unfortunate vagueness of the status of the Central Social Welfare Board, created administrative difficulties and led to its registration as a company in 1969. This arrangement has been admittedly unsatisfactory, and there is an increasing demand for a more autonomous status.

It may also be noted that at the time of the creation of the Central Social Welfare Board, the Government of India had no central department responsible for social welfare. With the establishment of the Department in 1966, and its increasing role in planning and execution of various welfare programmes, the Central Social Welfare Board's position has become still more anomalous. Uncertainty regarding its ultimate status and consequently of the State Boards has had a very adverse effect on their functioning.

At a Conference of State Ministers of Social Welfare held in July, 1992, recommendations were made for the reorganizations of the Central Board. This reorganization was dependent upon the adoption of a general enabling enactment. The State Governments, who had been advised to implement recommendations of this Conference with regard to the State Welfare Boards, were asked to defer action until the reorganization of the Central Social Welfare Board.

At a second Conference of the Social Welfare Ministers and Secretaries held in January 1974, discussion covered four major points. In regard to functions of the Central Social Welfare Board, it was decided that in addition to its executive functions, the Central Social Welfare Board should be responsible for the following: (a) To advise the government on the problems and provision of measures for the welfare of women, children and handicapped; (b) To promote investigation into the study of problems in specific areas, particularly those affecting women and children; (c) To arrange training for social workers at all levels for promoting the involvement of women in national activities; and (d) To provide technical guidance to voluntary organizations for effectively rendering welfare services.

In regard to the composition of the Central Social Welfare Board, the Conference urged that all the Governments of States and Union Territories by rotation, should be represented on the executive committee and the General Council of the Central Social Welfare Board. In conformity with their demand for greater control over the State Boards, the States and Union Territories wanted a greater voice in the nomination of State Board members. With regard to relationship between the Central and State Social Welfare Boards, some States wanted them to be set up by State Governments, while others wished to register them as independent societies.

Difficulties Faced by Field Agencies: Because of the present variations in status and functions of these multiple agencies for welfare and development activity, the field staff experiences many difficulties. The procedure for the release of grants to a voluntary agency often takes about six months and a great deal of hardship is faced by the voluntary agencies whose meagre resources often do not permit continuation of the programme. The uncertainty felt by the staff seriously hampers their work. Many voluntary agencies informed us that they do not have trained workers to manage the accounts in the manner required by the government.

The ad hoc nature of the programmes, their frequent conversion under the various Plans, and the reluctance of State Governments to take over maintenance have also caused a great deal of uncertainty among the field staff. For example, in the case of the Family and Child Welfare Projects, at the end of the Fourth Plan period, 13 States and 3 Union Territories have agreed to accept the responsibility. Six States have not agreed and the continuation of 74 projects are now uncertain. It is proposed to absorb them in the Integrated Child Development Programme. The feeling of the Board in this matter is clear. "With more time, more projects could have been started in consultation with State Governments. The proposed change in the nomenclature and contents of the programme and transfer of all the programmes from the Board to the State Governments, without ensuring continuity by allowing sufficient time for the existing schemes to achieve their objectives, only tend to confuse the rural population."

The staff of the Central Social Welfare Board and the State Boards are not considered on par with government employees and do not enjoy the same facilities and benefits. Their status at the field level is also temporary and dependent on the allocation for the year or the life of the projects. They have a feeling of uncertainty because of the temporary nature of their appointment which is dependent on the continuance of the scheme. They face a number of difficulties, particularly accommodation problems.

We met a large number of these field workers in various States. In our experience, the workers from voluntary organizations and the Board's staff have, on the whole, established better relationship with the village community, since they are better motivated and dedicated to welfare work, as compared to government functionaries who are more concerned with their service conditions, promotion, etc. The Board's cadre are more knowledgeable about the programmes in their areas and can give a better idea about the difficulties with regard to their implementation.

In recognition of this problem, the Department of Social Welfare has, recently examined the service conditions of the staff of the Board, and some of recommendations of the Third Pay Commission have been made applicable to employees of the CSWB. An officer on special duty was appointed by the CSWB in 1973 for drafting service regulations for its employees. The draft is now under examination by the Department of Social Welfare and is expected to be finalized in the near future.

Deficiencies of the Programme: While most programmes for women have emphasized acquisition of knowledge and skills to improve their efficiency as housewives and mothers, and to improve their earning power, they have neglected the dissemination of information, particularly regarding their rights and duties, which could increase their awareness and improve their participation as citizens. The objective of improving their earning power has also not been adequately fulfilled.

Role of Voluntary Agencies: Though it would be difficult to demarcate territories, the relationship of the voluntary and the Government sector should be all along complementary and mutually supportive. The present relationship between these two have not been very satisfactory and a number of complaints have been voiced on both the sides. Ideally the Voluntary Sector should provide services for implementation of welfare programmes, while the financial contribution should come from the Government. Further, the voluntary agencies have a surveillance role to play to see to what extent social legislation and the Government have contributed and can contribute to social welfare.

Voluntary organizations complain of lack of involvement with Government programmes since they are not consulted at the planning stage. Being totally outside the decision-making process, they have been reduced to the level of grant receiving agencies. Due to paucity of funds many voluntary agencies have come to rely heavily on the Government and in this process, the initiative and humanitarian impulse of voluntary welfare work has been considerably reduced. The basic concept of social work is that it should arise out of the local community needs. Voluntary agencies have repeatedly stressed that they should be equal partners with the Governments in the fields of welfare and accountable only for rendering proper accounts for grants. At the policy planning level, voluntary agencies desire that their experience and advice should be taken into account.

The voluntary agencies also express difficulties faced by them because of lack of training of their workers. Training facilities should be provided by the Government, if possible. Without technical and organizational competence, they are unable to utilize resources in the most productive manner. One of the representatives of a voluntary organization needed to review their organizational structure with a view to improving the managerial and professional competence of their workers.

The rising cost of living has reduced funds from private sources. It has also affected the ability of women to devote the same time and resources to voluntary work. Consequently, the area of constructive work of most of these voluntary agencies is limited to their neighbourhood.

The Conference of State Ministers and Secretaries of Social Welfare held in January 1974, earmarked the following programmes as of interest to voluntary organizations: (1) Socio-economic programmes organized broadly on a cooperative basis; (2) Condensed courses of education for adult women; (3) Functional literacy for women; and (4) Integrated Child Development Service Programme.

It was also agreed that the procedures and rules for making grants should be liberalized, and new ways found for raising and training voluntary workers, to ensure greater coordination amongst them and to improve the dialogue between governmental and non-governmental sectors at all levels, particularly at the district level. This can succeed only with a change in the approach to the voluntary sector.

Suggestions

Health and Family Planning: While welcoming the proposed integration of family planning and maternity and child health services in the Fifth Plan, we wish to offer certain suggestions with regard to its organization at different levels, so that the objective of integration is not defeated by organizational separatism.

1. The rank of the Chief Executive for the integrated maternity and child health services, including family planning, should be upgraded to at least that of an Additional Commissioner, so that this service does not again become subordinate to Family Planning. This procedure should be adopted at all levels of the administration at the Centre and the States.

2. A separate budget head for maternity and child health services should be created, drawing on the provisions now made for family planning and the general health services. It is important to increase the provision for these services to avoid their being neglected, as has been the trend so far. Since programmes for immunisation and nutrition of infants yield better results when they form a part of general maternity and child health services, we see no difficulty in increasing the allocation for these services.

3. At the level of the primary health centres, the maternity and child health services should be separated for purposes of administrative supervision, provision of medical personnel and budget. While they may share the same buildings and equipment, a separation of the administrative structure required for maternity and child

health services will ensure greater priority of treatment. It has often been found that the services of the lady doctor, lady health visitor and the auxilliary nurse-mid-wife, are unavailable to the poorer sections of the rural community. The primary health centres have to cater to the whole population, and women and children do not always get the priority of treatment in the way of medical attention or medicines and other facilities. Separating the MCH Unit will limit the clientele to the women and children, and make the services more accessible to these weaker groups. The allotment of facilities in the way of maternity beds, equipments for immunization of children and family planning for women could be allocated to the MCH Unit. The PHC could be responsible for sterilization operations for men along with other general health services. The proposed Integrated Child Development Programme calls for a coordinating agency at the implementation level, to coordinate all the nutrition and immunization measures which form a basic component of the programme. If the MCH Unit is separated as suggested above, these functions could be allotted to it.

Yet another function that could be undertaken by these Units with suitable provision of staff, is that of maintenance of fertility and morbidity statistics for women and children, the absence of which has made it impossible to undertake any substantial research and evaluation in these fields.

4. We recommend that each MCH centre should collect this data which should be studied and evaluated at the district level by persons of required competence. This will call for a health statistics section at the district level.

The separation of the MCH Services with family planning as a component at all levels will be a step towards a system of health services which would be reasonably accessible to women and children for preventive, diagnostic and supportive treatment, no matter at which point or stage the patient enters the system.

5. We recommend the abolition of the present practice of providing financial incentives to promoters of family planning.

6. We also recommend that incentives to women who accept family planning should be in the shape of a token or certificate to ensure them higher priority in health care facilities for both the mothers and their children. Such a step will promote greater acceptance of family planning and correct the social attitude towards these practices. Compensation for loss of wages during sterilization operations should however be paid to daily wage earners. Others should be given paid leave for this purpose.

7. The qualifications prescribed for recruitment of personnel for these services in rural areas need to be gradually raised. Until women of requisite higher qualifications are available, the present requirements may continue, but they should be reviewed and progressively increased after every 3 years. Attempts should also be made to obtain the services of older and mature women for these services in the rural areas.

8. We further recommend the promotion of research in the field of female disorders, e.g., puerperal psychosis and the ill-effects of family planning methods on their health.

9. We disapprove the denial of maternity benefits to women in government service after three children, as adopted by some State Governments, and recommend rescinding of such orders.

10. We also recommend that mass campaigns for family planning should also aim to correct prevailing social

attitudes regarding fertility and metabolic hereditary disorders, and the sex of the child for which the woman is generally blamed. Correct information in these matters would go a long way to improve the status of women.

Welfare and Development

1. Any programme for women's welfare and development must have an integrated approach. In order to prevent any ambiguity in the understanding of what constitutes women's welfare and to prevent the development of policies that sometimes go against the basic objective, we recommend that the Government of India should evolve a National Policy on women's development in the light of the Constitutional Directives and pledges made to the women of this country and to the international community from time to time.

   We also feel that in the absence of a general policy for social development, the weaker sections of society tend to receive inadequate attention. Economic development has sometimes contributed to elimination of social inequalities, but has also aggravated them. Adoption of a policy for social development would clarify matters, and provide a frame of reference for assessment of governmental and voluntary effort in these fields.

2. In view of the need to maintain links between governmental and voluntary and community effort for promotion of women's welfare, and to assist the process of government planning with actual knowledge and experience of the problems and needs of women at different levels, the following steps are recommended:

   (a) Reorganisation of the Central Social Welfare Board as a statutory and autonomous specialized agency for planning, co-ordination and management of welfare and development programmes for women and children.

(b) Reorganisation of the State Social Welfare (advisory) Boards as statutory autonomous agencies at the State level with similar functions. In addition, the State Boards may also serve as links among the Central agency, the State Government and the local bodies.

The Acts in Force

The existing legislations should be reviewed so that equality and social justice can be ensured to women of all communities and creeds. Where this involves amendments to existing personal laws of the minority group, initial efforts should be concentrated on arousing a desire for change from among the members of such minority groups. A vigorous campaign should be made to educate women about their rights, and to generate among all communities, a desire for a common civil code, to be achieved by the end of the UN Decade for Women in 1985.

Legal aid should be organized for women in need with the active assistance of the Bar Councils.

The setting up of family courts should be considered for speedy and effective adjudication in all cases concerning the family. Women, particularly in rural areas, should be protected against harassment.

The practice of dowry should be eradicated. The legislation should be strictly enforced. This is a social evil which requires sustained action not only on the part of government agencies, but also on the part of voluntary organizations and public leaders.

The provisions of the existing Child Marriage Restraint Act should be reviewed. Special attention should be given to streamlining the enforcement machinery and involving local authorities and voluntary organizations in the implementation of the Act. Active public support should be mobilized by governmental agencies, voluntary organizations and public leaders against child marriage, particularly in rural areas. Simultaneously, systematic programmes of education and training should be developed for girls till they marry.

Steps by Government

Education: Education is the greatest known catalytic agent for social change. All out efforts should therefore be made to achieve the goal of universal primary education as early as possible. The ideas of equality between the sexes and participation by women in development should be woven into the fabric of the educational system.

The employment of women teachers should be actively promoted. The existing employment procedures, including those for part-time, employment, should be reviewed and, where necessary, relaxations in age, etc., made so that more women teachers, can be employed and husbands and wives are posted in the same schools or at the same station.

The content of education should be strengthened in terms of both life and work relevance. Attention should be given to vocationalization and diversification of courses which should not only be limited to traditional women's vocations but also give emphasis on the preparation of women for participation in modern sectors of industrial production. Polytechnics (including mini-polytechnics) should be started for girls in the smaller urban centres to provide training facilities in trades crafts which will prompt self-employment.

At the stage of higher education special incentives like, freeships, scholarships, hostel facilities, and book loans should be made available to girls from rural, backward and hilly areas, from backward classes and from poor families. A greater diversification in the courses offered should be made to enhance work opportunities in non-traditional vocations in modern sectors of industrial production.

Adoption of multiple entry in education, non-formal part-time education facilities, condensed courses for education, correspondence courses and courses for continuing education should be made available in a larger measure to women in semi-urban and rural areas, and to working women in urban and semi-urban areas. Adult education and functional literacy programmes should be vigorously pursued through both official and voluntary agencies.

Employment: Equal Remuneration Act, 1976, has been passed, providing for payment of equal remuneration to men and women workers and the prevention of discrimination on grounds of sex. Special steps should therefore be taken to review recruitment, promotion and other personnel practices in all public and private sector undertakings to ensure that there is no discrimination against women candidates. Women apprentices should be taken without discrimination in industries. Representatives of women's voluntary organizations, should be associated, in the machinery set up to ensure adequate participation of women in employment.

Village industries which provide scope for the employment of women should be further promoted-Special training services should be organized and credit, marketing facilities, etc., extended, specially in regard to crafts which can have a ready export market, through modernization of design, etc. Integrated pilot projects to cover training, production and marketing should be started.

The existing requirement procedures and employment conditions should be reviewed to encourage the re-entry of women into the workforce. For this purpose, the provisions relating to maximum age of entry into services should be reviewed. Part-time employment of women should be promoted wherever feasible. Refresher courses and training programmes should be organized for adult women to make them fit for re-employment.

Organizations entrusted by the government with the task of promoting self-employment opportunities should develop special women's entrepreneurial training motivation programmes and provide special assistance to women entrepreneurs and to women's co-operative in terms of credit, licensing, etc.

The existing legislation in regard to maternity benefits should be reviewed. It should simultaneously be ensured that there is no consequent adverse effect on the employment of women.

Health Care, Nutrition and Family Planning: Maternal and child health care facilities should be expanded, particularly in semi-urban and rural areas, and coverage provided to high risk pregnant women. Ante-natal and post-natal clinics should be started in every Primary Health Centre and district hospital.

Nutrition supplementation should be provided to high risk pregnant mothers. Simultaneously, nutrition and health education should be given to girls and to mothers through all available media and institutions (school, hospitals, PHCs, etc.).

Family welfare planning services should be expanded and measures intensified to educate and prepare couples to avail them, specifically in rural, backward and tribal areas. The facilities under the Medical Termination of Pregnancy Act, 1971 should be made available in semi-urban and rural areas and information regarding the provisions disseminated among women, immunization facilities should be gradually extended to all children.

Facilities of Working Women: The establishment of day care centres, creches, and balwadis should be promoted on a large scale in rural, semi-urban and urban areas to help working mothers and active women social workers discharge their duties, and enable the older children to attend school.

Hostel facilities for working women of the lower income groups should be expanded.

Care for the Socially Disadvantaged: Women without any means of support, and the physically handicapped should be provided services for education, training and rehabilitation so that they can become self-reliant. Old age homes should be opened for the aged and the infirm. Special programmes should be developed for unmarried mothers and their children.

The provision of the Suppression of Immoral Traffic Act (1956) should be reviewed to facilitate their more efficient implementation. Comprehensive rehabilitation programmes for victims of immoral traffic and their children should be developed. Special steps should be taken to prevent vulnerable young girls and women from becoming victims of this social evil.

Promotion of Voluntary Effort: The growth of voluntary organizations, especially in rural, backward and tribal areas and in urban slums should be promoted to mobilize public support for different programmes of welfare. Training facilities should be provided on a large scale to voluntary workers. Leadership training programmes, particularly for women from weaker sections, should be developed so that they can function effectively as agents of change. The establishment of Mahila Mandals should be promoted in every village so that they can function as field level agencies for social and economic transformation. Voluntary organizations have critical role in mobilizing public opinion in favour of equality among men and women and eradicating superstitions, social evils and waste.

A vigorous campaign of education and action should be launched in favour of community sanitation and hygiene. Public utility services for women should be expanded wherever called for.

Machinery for Implementation: In order to ensure that the Resolution unanimously passed by the two Houses of Parliament is acted upon and the implementation of the Plan of Action is ensured, it is proposed that:

(i) A Standing Advisory Committee should be set up at the national level which will review the progress every year so that a report is submitted to Parliament annually. The Committee may be called 'The National Committee on Women'.

(ii) To service the above Committee a special bureau should be set up in the Ministry of Education and Social Welfare (Department of Social Welfare). The Bureau will keep in touch with the implementation of the various programmes by the Central Ministries, State Governments and non-official agencies.

(iii) At the State level similar committees should be set up under the chairmanship of the Chief Minister. These Committees should also have adequate administrative support.

In Area of Education

In realization of the importance of education in general and the need for equality in opportunities for the intellectual development of men and women, successive Five-Year Plans have consistently placed special emphasis on the acceleration of women's education. The emphasis with regard to women's education has all along been to equip her for the multiple roles as citizens, housewives, mothers, contributors to family income and builders of the new society. Efforts have been made during the past two decades of planned development to enrol more girls in school; to encourage girls to stay in schools; to continue their education as long as possible; and to provide non-formal education opportunities for women. The Draft Fifth Five-Year Plan has declared that "the outlays for the education of girls will be stepped up.". The fulfilment of the constitutional directive in respect of providing free and compulsory education up to the age of 14 years has been included as one of the components of the Minimum Needs Programme.

These efforts have had a significant impact on the progress of women's education in India. For example, there is a primary school within easy, walking distance from the home of almost all the children. This has resulted in an increase in the enrolment of girls in classes I-V as a percentage of total enrolment in these classes from 28.1 in 1950-51 to 37.6 in 1973-74. In respect of classes I-VIII, IX-XI/ XII and university education also there has been an appreciable increase in the percentage of girls' enrolment to total enrolment, between the years 1950-51 and 1973-74. In fact, girls' enrolment is observed to be growing at a faster rate than those of boys.

Despite these encouraging trends and marked progress made in respect of women's education, the educational status of women is still far from satisfactory for the following reasons:

(a) Literacy among women is generally lower than that among men. According to the 1971 Census data, only 13.4 per cent of women in this age group of 25+ are literate.

(b) Enrolment of girls in classes I to V is only 66.4 per cent of girls in the corresponding age group, i.e., from 6 to 11 years; while in respect of boys the relevant percentage is 100.2.

(c) Drop-out rate is also very high in classes I to V. A recent study has shown that the drop-out rate especially accentuated in the case of girls from rural areas and from the less privileged sections of society, is as heavy as 42.85 per cent between classes I and II.

(d) In classes VI to VIII, percentages of enrolment of girls and boys to the total girls and boys in the relevant age group (i.e., from 11 to 14 years) are 22.2 and 48.3, respectively.

(e) At the secondary stage, i.e.., from classes IX to XI the girls enrolled constitute only 12 per cent of girls in the relevant age group 14 to 17 years as against 31 per cent in respect of the enrolment of boys in this age group.

(f) Enrolment of girls in Post-Matric classes constitutes only 2.3 per cent of girls in the concerned age group 17 to 23 years, while the enrolment percentage of boys in this age group is 7.5.

Factors Retarding the Progress of Women's Education: Girls and women in India have thus not been able to take full advantage of the available opportunities/facilities for intellectual development. This is mainly because of several social and cultural factors in addition to various other reasons. Action plans and strategies for women's education should, therefore, aim at neutralizing the effects of the factors which have retarded the progress of women's education in India. With a view to facilitating the formulation of such a plan of action, in what follows, some of the major reasons which have operated against girls/women in taking full advantage of educational opportunities/facilities are listed below:

(a) General indifference to education of girls.

(b) Social resistance arising out of fears and misconceptions that education might alienate girls from traditions and social values and lead to mal-adjustments, conflicts and nonconformism.

(c) Early marriage and social inhibitions against girls pursuing education after marriage.

(d) Prevalence of child labour among girls belonging to weaker sections and the hard domestic chores which some of the unmarried girls - even in the middle-class families - are required to perform.

(e) The prevailing notion that the sole occupation of women is to bear children, look after her husband and children, and thus be restricted to domestic work.

(f) Discrimination effected by employers against women labour in both organized and unorganized sectors in matters of recruitment, training and promotion.

(g) Many girls and their parents find that the school curriculum do not conform adequately to their needs and interests.

(h) Unsuitable and inflexible school timings and inadequate facilities for girls in schools, particularly in the co-educational schools.

Major Objective of Women's Education: It should be recognized here that the general objective of any policy towards women's education cannot be different from those relating to men. However, in view of the social and cultural handicaps that have operated against women in general and in view of the multiple role that women are required to play, the need for a set of objectives specific to women's education is imperative. The following major objectives are, therefore, considered here:

(a) Prepare women to fully participate in socially productive work, fully aware of family planning needs with a view to achieving her full integration with the democratic and developmental efforts of the country.

(b) Help break down overt covert biases against women.

(c) Make women aware of the various legal, social and economic rights, provisions -and privileges available to them and the way they can take advantage of them, for their advancement.

(d) Enable women to be self-reliant to achieve economic independence.

(e) Impart the idea of equality between the sexes and participation by women in development through the educational system.

(f) And above all, to find full expression for her talent, ability and personality and for this purpose, enable her to adopt a discriminating attitude so that she can escape the bonds of superstition and obscurantism.

Action Plans: Action plans here are evolved within the general framework of major objectives mentioned above. In addition, the action plans have taken into consideration other objectives which are specific of educational categories like elementary education, middle stage education, secondary stage education, university education and non-formal education. For the sake of convenience, in what follows, action plans specific of each age group of girls, are all mentioned separately.

Elementary Education-Girls in the Age Group 6-11 years: Girls in this age group constitute the population of girls of primary school going age. Action plans for this age group will need to be in two directions:

(a) To universalize primary education for girls, and

(b) To strive for the retention of girls already enrolled.

Towards this end, the following action plans are suggested:

Administrative and Structural Measures

(i) State Governments should take note of the habitations without primary schools as indicated by the Third Educational Survey and make arrangements for providing primary school within a distance of 1.5 km of all habitations within next five years.

(ii) Mobile schools should be provided for children of all nomadic tribes, migrant labour and construction workers.

(iii) Girls in this age are often required to look after younger children and attend minor household duties, particularly in the rural areas and among weaker sections of the society. As this is one of the major reasons that holds such girls from attending school, special efforts should be made to enlarge the scope and coverage of pre-school education programmes like Balwadis and Anganwadis, where the older girls can be given practical work experience and child care.

(iv) These pre-school education programmes should, wherever possible, be attached to primary schools or at least located in the vicinity of primary schools, as that would help in cultivating a school going habit right from the childhood.

(v) Supervision and inspection of primary schools should give particular attention to the problem of enrolment of girls, their retention, involvement of the community, etc.

(vi) Special and sustained persuasive and motivational campaign and organizational drives should be undertaken among regions/communities which have shown markedly a low achievement in girls enrolment. Voluntary organizations at local levels like Mahila Mandals and local bodies should be fully involved in this programme.

(vii) Promotion and support to girls' education should also be tackled through a multipronged programme of incentives - both for bringing girls to schools and for retaining them in schools. The incentives can be in the form of mid-day meals, free supply of books and reading materials, scholarships awards, etc. Active collaboration of voluntary organizations may be sought in this regard.

(viii) The primary teacher training course should undergo a major revision with a view to adequately preparing the teacher for the promotion of girls' education. Emphasis should be more on the use of such non-formal methods of imparting education that would interest and attract more and more girls to attend schools.

Education for Girls in the Age Group 11-14 years: Population of girls in this age group constitutes girls of middle school going age. This group can be divided into three sub-groups:

(a) Girls students attending middle schools;

(b) Girl drop-outs at various stages from classes I to V; and

(c) Girls who have not attended school.

The objectives of education and training are different for each of the sub-groups.

Action Plan: Action plans for education of girls in this age group should be concerned about:

(i) encouraging further enrolment of girls at this stage;

(ii) retention of girls already in middle schools; and

(iii) rendering the curriculum more relevant.

The following action plans are suggested:

(i) The content should be more oriented to the needs of girls in the village communities so that both the parents and the girls see relevance of this education for their own lives. The curriculum of the middle school stage needs to be given a strong work experience orientation, introducing girls to crafts and skills which will be of direct use to them in the family, community and farm, and help them in rural employment and self-employment. It should also introduce girls to scientific knowledge, principles of home-making, family life education, nutrition and diet, environment education and civic education.

(ii) Women Teachers: It is very important for the promotion of girls' education to employ women teachers in schools. Infact, the general view is that women are more suited to be teachers and larger number of teachers should be women, However, the problem may come up in different ways. More number of men may be qualified and trained women may not be in a position to accept employment as full time teachers due to personal problems; women also have difficulties in working in rural areas.. There has to be relaxation from age restrictions. The States may consider reserving a certain number of posts of teachers for women and where there are not adequate number of trained teachers, untrained persons may be recruited and deputed for training. The question of giving posting to husband and wife both of whom are teachers in the same place may be considered.

It may also be worthwhile in those areas which have schools without women teachers, to select educated women in that area and send them for training and appoint them in the schools in that area. Where educated women are not available for posting in a school, local women may be selected and posted as school matas (school mothers) to keep the girl students company and induce parents to send their girls and children to schools. The rules relating to age and qualification of recruitment and service may have to be relaxed in these cases and the deficiency made up through in-service training.

Women should not be discriminated against in matters of recruitment. Selection and recruitment should be made on merit. No qualified meritorious woman candidate should be overlooked. State Governments may contemplate providing for 50 per cent of teachers in schools being women and to look into this aspect while sanctioning grants to institutions.

In single teacher institutions (the exact position will be brought out by the Third Educational Survey), it may be desirable to ensure that where there are two teachers, one of them should be a woman. If locally educated women are available, they can be recruited. Husband wife teams can be posted.

(iii) The primary teacher training course needs to undergo a major revision to adequately prepare the trainees for their special responsibility for the promotion of girls' education in rural areas, especially in adapting the content to suit the needs and interests of girls, in adopting non-formal methodologies and in linking with community and developmental activities.

(iv) Supervision and inspection of schools should be given particular attention to the problem of enrolment of girls, their retention, factors contributing to wastage and stagnation, revision of curriculum, involvement of the community, working conditions of women teachers, etc.

(v) School timings should be flexible, as many of the girls in this age group are required to help their mothers in routine domestic chores.

(vi) Adoption of multiple entry and part-time courses is recommended.

(vii) Incentives like mid-day meals, scholarships, free school uniforms, free books and study materials, stipend, awards, etc., should be extended to all girls in the rural areas and slums in the urban areas.

(viii) For school drop-outs of girls, pre-vocational training programmes should be organized on an extensive scale to cover all girls in the rural areas and in the slums of urban areas. The objectives of such training should be to render them self-sufficient in home management, and help them to achieve economic independence. With this in view, such training programmes should include courses in sewing, knitting, cooking, nutrition, minor repairs of the house, motherhood, child care, etc.

(ix) For the non-student girls in this age group, the objective should be to provide adequate preparation in life through a combined three-year course in general education and vocational training. Vocational training should be on the lines of pre-vocational training mentioned above.

(x) Such training programmes should be extended to all girls in the rural areas. In the urban areas, preference should be given to girls in slum areas and destitute girls.

Education for Girls in the Age Group 14-17 years: Girls in this age group also can be classified into three groups:

(a) Girl students with motivation to attend secondary school;

(b) Girl drop-outs from classes VI to VIII; and

(c) Non-student girls, i.e., students who never attended schools.

Girl Students

The action plans under this category should emphasize more on:

(i) facilitating more girls to pursue education at the secondary stage, and

(ii) strengthening the content in terms of both life and work relevance.

Administrative and Structural Measures

(i) Separate girls schools or separate sections should be started where the social/ cultural environment demands them.

(ii) In co-education schools special attention should be given to the provision of adequate toilet, rest and recreation facilities, separately for girls.

(iii) State Governments which have not yet made high school education free for girls should do so on a priority basis.

(iv) Multiple entry system and part-time education may be provided.

(v) All courses of training in vocational and technical schools at the secondary stage should be open to both boys and girls. There should be no discrimination in this regard.

(vi) Liberal incentives in the form of book allowances, book-bank facilities, etc., should be extended to encourage more girls in rural and backward areas to pursue secondary education.

(vii) Separate hostel facilities should be provided particularly in rural areas and residential scholarships should be offered.

(viii) The curriculum should be more diversified taking into consideration the various occupational opportunities available to women and the interests and aptitudes of girls.

(ix) Condensed courses of education started in 1958 were found very useful. Under this scheme women in the age group 13-30 years who have had some schooling are prepared for middle school, matriculation or equivalent examinations within a period of 2 years' duration. The minimum age limit here should be reduced to 15 years. This scheme should be extended to cover all rural areas and weaker sections of the urban community.

(x) The condensed course should be organized for smaller groups, say 5 to 7 persons, using the community resources like girls' high schools and girls' colleges.

(xi) Apart from imparting general education, condensed course should also aim at imparting job-oriented training with the active co-operation of existing vocational training institutions.

(xii) Correspondence courses and self-study programmes may be introduced.

(xiii) Efforts should be made to cover at least about 215 lakh of girls in the age group 15-30 under the condensed courses programme during the Fifth Plan period.

(xiv) Fourth Plan introduced a programme of functional literacy with the objective of imparting elementary general education and vocational training-related to the functions performed to men and women in the rural areas who never attended schools. This programme should be expanded to cover all rural areas.

(xv) Apart from imparting general elementary education and knowledge about farming technologies, the curriculum for women should include courses of training in occupational skills like kitchen gardening, food processing, poultry keeping, animal husbandry; and household, arts like cooking nutritional values of foods locally available, sewing, knitting, etc., and motherhood, child care and family planning as also electronics and like fields.

(xvi) Similar programmes should also be designed for girls in this age group and under this category belonging to urban areas.

Education for Girls in the Age Group 17 Years and Above

Education for girls in this age group also can be divided into three groups, as in the case of other age groups:

(a) Education for girls at the higher education stage;

(b) Education for girl drop-outs from the educational system beyond the secondary stage; and

(c) Education for non-student girls - girls who never had any education.

In respect of the last category here, i.e., education for non-student girls, action plans are the same as those concerning non-student girls in the age group 14-17 years. Hence, this category is not dealt with separately here.

Education for Girls at the Higher Education Stage

Action plans in this area should aim at:

(a) Making higher education available to the less privileged sections of the society, particularly girls from the rural areas; and

(b) Making the curriculum more relevant and responsive to the cultural and occupational needs of women.

The following action plans may be taken up for consideration:

Administrative and Structural Measures

(i) The general policy here should be to discourage separate institutions for women and to promote co-educational institutions for women and to promote co-educational facilities. However, in areas where separate institutions are required to promote education of women, they may be permitted on the merits of such cases.

(ii) Vocational counselling and guidance services should be organized in a more meaningful way to help girls in colleges and universities opt for suitable courses relevant to their talent, interests and needs.

(iii) Incentives like scholarships, freeships, etc., should be provided to enable girls from rural areas to pursue higher education.

(iv) For girls belonging to weaker sections, in addition to freeships and scholarships, bursaries should also be provided to meet their expenses on food and lodging.

(v) Provision of self-cooking facilities in hostels for girls should also be considered.

(vi) Girls pursuing higher education should be provided easy access to textbooks and other reference material through book-bank facilities.

(vii) Girls should be encouraged to enter professional courses. If necessary, reservation of seats for girls in professional courses may be considered.

(viii) Diversification of courses at the junior college level and undergraduate level should be undertaken on a priority basis with a view to preparing the girls for the various employment opportunities open to them.

Education for Girl Drop-outs

Girls in this age group drop-out of educational system for various reasons. Marriage is one of the reasons which force girls in this age group to discontinue further formal education. Economic hardship is another reason which forces some girls to drop-out and seek jobs, with a view to supporting their families. Social prejudices and cultural attitudes also force some of the girls to leave the formal educational system. For girls in this category, therefore, the policy should be to extend non-formal educational facilities on a large scale.

The following action plans are suggested:

(i) Facilities for part-time self-study and correspondence courses should be expanded on a large scale to enable working girls and non-working married and unmarried girls to enhance their educational qualifications.

(ii) In addition to course leading to degree/diploma, short courses in specific subjects through summer schools/ sessions, ad hoc programmes like seminars, laboratory work, workshop experience, etc., should be organized for working girls, with a view to upgrading their professional skills and qualifications. Facilities for further education not necessarily leading to a degree but for upgradation of knowledge and skills could be provided.

(iii) While the initiative for organizing such programmes should be taken by the Central and State Governments, the employees should also be increasingly involved.

(iv) Pre-examination training facilities should be organized on a large scale for educated women from the rural areas and those belonging to weaker sections with the objective of equipping them to successfully compete in examinations for public jobs.

(v) Entrepreneurship development programmes should be organized separately for educated women in the age group 18-30 years with a minimum of matriculation level of education.

The objective of such training programmes should be:

(a) Make them aware of the various opportunities for self-employment;

(b) Motivate them to take up self-employment;

(c) Impart needed skills/training; and

(d) Promote achievement motivation among them.

Administrative Measures: To make the various action plans successful and to achieve a real breakthrough in women's education, there is an urgent need for a matching and effective administrative set up, both at the central and state levels. With this in view, the following suggestions are made:

(i) In the Union Ministry of Education and Social Welfare, a special unit/cell may be set up to be in charge of women's education to review and initiate follow-up action.

(ii) In each State education department, a senior officer should be placed in charge of girls' education in order that it may receive adequate emphasis, execution and co-ordination.

(iii) As the district is the operational unit for all educational programmes and as the needs of girls vary in extent and kind from area to area within a district, a separate cell for girls' educational – formal and non-formal may be created within the purview of the district educational officer at the district headquarters.

(iv) School supervisory system should be staffed with more women.

(v) A suitable machinery may be set up at the Centre and the States to help in the formulation of plans for women's education - formal and non-formal to monitor, co-ordinate and evaluate progress of women's education from time to time, to create public opinion in favour of women's education, etc.

10

Educational Support

Education is the most important instrument for human resource development. Education of women, therefore occupies top Priority amongst various measures taken to improve the status of women in India. In recent years, the focus of planning has shifted from equipping women for their traditional roles of house-wives and mothers to recognizing their worth as producers, making a major contribution to family and national income. Efforts have been made over the past three decades of planned development to enrol more girls in schools and encourage them to stay in schools, to contribute their education as long as possible, and to provide non-formal educational opportunities for women. The fulfilment of the Constitutional directives in respect of providing free and compulsory education up to the age of 14 years has been included as one of the components of the 'Minimum Needs Programme' and given overriding priority.

Education in India is constrained by the socio-economic conditions of the people, their attitudes, values and culture. During the pre-British era, education was linked to the socio-religious, institutions, reinforcing the patriarchal social structure. During the British period, education became a tool of colonial power, enabling a small minority to have access to education, and all the benefits it entailed. The social reformers of the nineteenth century raised the demand for women's transformation but to make them more capable of fulfilling their traditional roles. Since Independence, the policy makers have argued for universal education and for making education as a tool for bringing about social equality.

In spite of concerted efforts to improve the enrolment of girls and provide adult education for women, their educational status is still far from satisfactory. Female enrolment in educational institutions is low as compared with males and drop-out rates are higher. There are also regional and inter-group disparities.

The factors which do not permit the closing of the existing gap between the education of men and women are many. While undertaking a review of the educational system at the time of formulation of the National Policy on Education 1986, if was noted that the system is caught in a state of ambivalence, aiming at creating an equal society, while at the same time not disturbing the class, caste and gender relationships. Issues in women's education are, therefore, not issues only of educational sector, but they extend to issues of environment, employment production processes. Indeed, the entire gamut of social and, economic policy has a bearing on women's education. The need for educating girls is not considered worthwhile. In urban areas, by and large, there is a greater acceptance of its need than in rural areas. Some other factors responsible for low enrolment are:

(i) The requirement for older girls to stay at home to take care of siblings when mothers are away at work;

(ii) Need for girls to work in order to help in augmenting the family income;

(iii) Early marriage of girls;

(iv) Social customs that hinder female mobility after puberty;

(v) Lack of relevance of school curriculum; and

(vi) Lack of facilities in the form of school buildings, hostels and women teachers, etc.

Assessment and Planning

Women's education has assumed special significance in the context of the country's planned development.' This is because women constitute nearly half the nation's population representing a valuable human resource and play an important role in the development of the community and the national economy. Education enables women to acquire basic skills and abilities, and fosters a value system which is conducive to raising their status in society. Recognizing this fact, great emphasis has been laid on women's education in the five-year plans. The First Five-Year Plan advocated the need for adopting special measures for solving the problems of women's education. It held that women "must have the same opportunities as men for taking all kinds of work and this presupposes that they get equal facilities so that their entry into the professions and public services is in no way prejudiced". It further added that "at the secondary and even at the university stage it should have a vocational or occupational basis, as far as possible, so that those who complete such stages may be in a position, if necessary, to immediately take up some vocation or other". Accordingly the educational facilities for girls continued to expand in the subsequent plans. The major schemes undertaken encompassed elementary education, secondary education, university education, postgraduate education and research, technical education, scholarships, social/adult education and physical education. The Second Plan continued the emphasis on overall expansion of educational facilities. The Report of the National Committee on Women's Education (1959) made a strong impact on the Third Five-Year Plan. It launched important schemes like condensed school courses for adult women, Bal Sevika training and child care programmes. Subsequent plans supported these measures and also continued incentives such as free text-books and scholarships for girls. This trend continued in the Fourth and Fifth Five-Year Plans.

Although there was a large-scale expansion of facilities for education up to the Fourth Plan, vast disparities existed in the relative utilization of available facilities by boys and girls at various stages of education. Hence, the major thrust in the Fifth Plan was to offer equality of opportunities as part of the overall plan of ensuring social justice and improving the quality of education imparted. To promote enrolment and retention in schools in backward areas and among underprivileged sections of the population, in addition to the incentives like free distribution of textbooks, mid-day meals, etc., girls were to be given uniform and attendance scholarships. In spite of these schemes, it was noticed that insufficient numbers of women teachers resulted in low enrolment of girls. To remove this bottleneck, scholarships were given to local girls to complete their education and training leading to a teaching career. Besides, condensed and correspondence courses were organized for the less educated women. Emphasis as also laid on the need for orientation of the curriculum to meet the special needs of girls.

A landmark in the Sixth Plan was the inclusion of women's education as one of the major programmes under Women and Development which was an outcome of the publication of the report of the Committee on the Status of Women in India. The programmes for universalization of elementary education were specially directed towards higher enrolment and retention of girls in schools. It was envisaged to promote Balwadi-cum-creches attached to the schools to enable girls responsible for sibling care at home to attend schools. Women teachers, where necessary, were to be appointed in rural areas to encourage girls education. Science teaching in girl schools and colleges had to be strengthened to achieve greater participation of women in science and technology.

Streamlining the admission policies to promote greater enrolment of women in engineering, electronics, agriculture, veterinary fishery and forestry courses was stressed. For boosting the education of women belonging to backward classes, the number of girls' hostels were to be increased. Instead of adding more separate women's polytechnics, which were developed as multipurpose institutions for imparting training in arts, crafts, etc. coeducational institutions were encouraged as far as possible. The adult education programme too received a fillip.

The Seventh Plan envisages restructuring of the educational programmes and modification of school curricula to eliminate gender bias. Enrolment of girls in elementary, secondary and higher education courses, formal as well as non-formal, has been accorded high priority. At the elementary stage, education has been made free for girls. Sustained efforts are to be made through various schemes and measures to reach 100 per cent coverage in elementary education. Financial assistance schemes to voluntary agencies to run early childhood education (pre-school centres) as adjuncts of primary/middle schools are to be expanded, particularly to help evolve innovative models suited to specific learner groups or areas. Efforts are to be made to enrol and retain girls in schools, especially in rural areas, and also to enrol children belonging to Scheduled Castes, Scheduled Tribes and other weaker sections. Teacher training programmes are to receive continued priority with a view to increase the availability of trained women teachers, and thereby to enhance girls' enrolment and retention in schools. Incentives by way of distribution of uniforms, free textbooks and attendance scholarships to needy girls are to be continued. Non-formal elementary education is to be expanded to benefit girls in the age group of 6-14 years. Talented girls are to be encouraged to pursue higher education. It is also proposed to expand the 'Open Learning System', including correspondence courses for them. In order to promote technical and vocational education for girls, more women's polytechnics are to be set up and programmes for vocationalization of education are to be expanded.

To expedite education among the girls of the Scheduled Castes and Scheduled Tribes, additional facilities will continue to be provided under the "Development of Backward Classes" sector. Girls above the matriculation stage will get higher scholarships/ stipends than male students. Financial assistance is envisaged for construction of hostel buildings for girls at the district level and for purchase of equipment, furniture utensils, books and periodicals in these hostels.

Under the National Sports Policy, participation of women and girls in sports and games is to be encouraged. Stress is to be laid on the identification of sports talent among women, and provision made for sports scholarships, coaching and nourishment support for promising girls with a view to improve the standards of their performance in competitive games. Besides, the schemes for encouraging traditional folk, tribal and hill arts and cultural activities are to be expanded and strengthened.

Notwithstanding the planned objectives and endeavours, actual progress in upgrading the educational status of women has been slow. The literacy level among women has risen from 7.9 per cent in 1951 to 24.3 per cent in 1981 (excluding Assam). Among males, the corresponding rise was from 24.9 to 46.3 per cent. Thus the gap in percentage literacy points between male and female literacy increased from 17 in 1951 to 22 in 1981. In absolute terms too, the number of illiterate women has increased during the period, from 158.7 million to 241.7 million (excluding Assam). Women comprised 57 per cent of the illiterate population in 1981, and girls formed 70 per cent of non-enrolled children in the school age group.

There are disturbing regional variations in the levels of literacy in the country. The literacy rate for women varies from 65.7 per cent in Kerala, as per 1981 census, to 11.4 per cent for Rajasthan. The gap between male and female literacy, rates in percentage points is only 9.5 in Kerala, but 24.9 in Rajasthan. States like Madhya Pradesh, Uttar Pradesh and Bihar are also lagging behind in girls education. Certain ecological constraints like difficult terrain, variety of dialects as in Arunachal Pradesh, migratory habits due to unfavourable weather as in parts of Jammu & Kashmir, etc. have also been instrumental in perpetuating low levels of literacy in such areas for the population as a whole and particularly for women.

Stages in Education

High Priority has been accorded to elementary education in the National Development Plans to fulfil the requirements under Article 45 of the Constitution for universal, free and compulsory elementary education for children upto the age of 14 years.

By the end of the Sixth Plan, it was apparent that in order to achieve universal elementary education, an additional enrolment of 255.3 lakh is required of which the girls constitute 140.7 lakh, i.e., a little more than 55 per cent. Besides, there is a sharp fall in the number enrolled at the middle level, viz., from nearly 332 lakh to 91 lakh indicating a large dropout rate, wastage and stagnation. The enrolment ratio falls from 76.7 to 36.3. The retention of girls in schools from classes I to VIH, therefore is a task requiring urgent attention.

Among Scheduled Tribes particularly, the enrolment of girls is far below that of boys. At the primary stage, the enrolment of Scheduled Tribes boys is almost double the enrolment of girls, and the difference increases at higher stage. Girls belonging to Scheduled Castes communities are also lagging behind boys. The ratio of Scheduled Castes boys to girls in the elementary classes is 2:1. In the VI to VIII classes, 61.9 per cent of girls in the general Population are enrolled, whereas among Scheduled Castes this proportion is only '20.9' per cent; The reasons for Scheduled Castes and Scheduled tribes girls lagging behind boys. The ratio of Scheduled Castes boys to girls in the elementary classes is 2:1. In the VI to VIII classes, 61.9 per cent of girls in the general population are enrolled, whereas among Scheduled Castes this proportion is only 29.9 per cent. The reasons for Scheduled and Scheduled tribes girls lagging behind the boys are mainly rooted in socio-economic conditions and environmental constraints such as inaccessibility of schools in tribal areas. Irrelevance of formal education curriculum to the immediate environment is also responsible for low initial enrolment and subsequent drop-out rates. Among the urban and rural poor, the compulsion on girls to assist in household chores including care of younger siblings, and on children of both sexes to work for their own survival and contribute economically to the household income, forces them to remain outside the education system.

According to the Fourth Educational Survey (1978), in the plains 95 per cent of the rural population have access to a primary school within one kilometer of their habitation (having a population of 360 persons or more). Middle schools are available to 78.8 per cent of rural people within three kilometres from their habitation. But commuting to distant schools does pose a problem for girls. There are very few separate schools for girls. The parents, particularly in rural areas, are reluctant to send their daughters to co-educational schools. Moreover, in most schools, the teachers are male. Despite considerable emphasis in the plans, the proportion of women teachers continues to be low Provision for accommodation for women workers including teachers is far from satisfactory.

A large number of primary and middle schools, in rural areas especially, lack facilities such as a proper building, adequate number of teaching rooms, drinking water and toilets for girls. More than 85 per cent primary and 70 per cent middle schools in rural areas do not have these facilities, according to the Fourth All India Educational Survey (1978). Hostel facilities for girls continue to be meagre.

There is a progressive rise in the rate of enrolment in secondary education of girls during the various Plan periods as seen below:

The enrolment ratio of girls in the age group 15-18 years for secondary classes is 14.3 per cent as against 29.3 per cent for boys. Secondary education continues to be more or less confined to urban areas, and is affordable and accessible largely to the higher castes and the upper and middle economic strata. Although a large number of secondary schools have come up in rural areas, their enrolment particularly, in respect of girls is low. The main constraints in improving secondary and higher level education among girls have been a lack of availability of trained lady teachers, dearth of separate institutions for girls and lack of hostel facilities.

The 10+2+3 system of education has been introduced with the aim of establishing a uniform pattern of education all over the country in terms of its structure, curriculum and mobility across the States. This system has laid a common foundation for higher education without differentiation between boys and girls. Both girls and boys under the new system Will learn the rudiments of science and mathematics, social sciences and humanities up to matriculation and thus gain a holistic base education which will equip them to play an active and meaningful role in the employment market.

In the higher educational courses, girls constitute 24 to 50 per cent of the students enrolled depending upon the type of courses. The most popular course with girls has been teachers training where they already constitute nearly fifty per cent of those enrolled. The number of girls in science courses had risen to 41 per 100 boys in 1984-85. In engineering and technology courses, however, the enrolment of girls is only 6 for 100 boys. This Proportion has to be enhanced through suitable incentives in the form of scholarships and other facilities for girls studying for these courses.

Girls enrolled for higher education, particularly those in science and technical courses, are mainly from the higher economic strata. There is a need to introduce positive measure to improve the enrolment to girls in higher education courses in rural areas and, among backward groups like SCs and STs.

Education out of School

The concept of adult education has found support in several Plan Programmes. However, until the Sixth Plan, no special emphasis was given to women's education. In the Sixth Five-Year Plan, adult education was included as a part of the Minimum Needs Programme and the goal of reaching 100 per cent literacy by 1990 was set under the New Twenty-Point Programme. Adult education centres exclusively for women were set up, which provided education in subjects like health, nutrition and family planning. An effort was made to build up an awareness about these sub among women through discussions, talks and distribution of relevant literature.

Under the Adult Education Programme, apart from increasing adult literacy, the content of education was to be modified to incorporate new value systems regarding the role of women in the family, and community. The Seventh Plan also envisages, among other schemes, the preparation of district level plans with local community participation, both for activating, and implementing the literacy programme, and the creation of special mechanisms to monitor the progress of implementation at the State level. The Integrated Rural Development Programme (IRDP), National Rural Employment Programme (NREP), Training of Rural Youth in Self-employment (TRYSEM), and other such programmes, are also to have a component of functional literacy for women beneficiaries. The programme of Functional Literacy for Adult Women (a component of the ICDS programme) was unfortunately abandoned, though the concept of utilizing Anganwari workers, who belonged to the villages and were in contact with young mothers, could have been an effective mechanism for imparting non-formal education. The scheme has since been revised to focus on issues of immediate relevance to women but has yet to be introduced.

The scheme of 'condensed courses of education and vocational training' for adult women was started in 1958 under the aegis of the Central Social Welfare Board, and was suitably expanded over the years to vocational training in areas with high employment potential. Measures are to be taken to enhance the competence of the teaching staff /training institutions involved in this programme.

The various programmes, however, have not yet been able to make any significant impact on literacy levels of the Indian population, particularly on women. According to a World Bank Report in 2000 A.D., there will be 500 million illiterates in India, constituting 54 per cent of the world's population of illiterates. As per the Seventh Plan, the total number of adult illiterates is about 900 lakhs of whom 580 lakh are women. Although it is encouraging to note that the proportion of women in the adult education centres has gone above 50 per cent (52.34 per cent in 1984-85), women still constitute about 5.7 per cent of the illiterate population. Among these, literacy levels of SC mad ST women are still worse. Even those treated as literates, have very low levels of literacy, scant opportunities for continuing education and use of literacy skills. Therefore they often relapse into illiteracy.

The National Policy on Education (NPE)-1986 is a landmark in the approach to women's education. It has attempted for the first time to address itself to the basic issues of women's equality. In the section titled "Education for Women's Equality", the policy states:

> Education will be used as an agent of basic change in the status of women. In order to neutralize the accumulated distortions of the past, there will be a well-conceived edge in favour of women. The National Education System will play a positive, interventionist role in the empowerment of women. It will foster the development of new values through redesigned curricula, textbooks, training and orientation of teachers, decision makers and administrators.

It gives overriding priority to the removal of women's inhibiting their access to and retention in elementary education. Emphasis has been laid on women's participation in vocational, technical and professional education at different levels as also to promote women's participation in non-traditional occupations and existing and emergent technologies.

The Programme of Action for Implementation of NPE (POA) spells out the meaning of women's empowerment:

> Women become empowered through collective reflection and decision making. The parameters of empowerment are:
>
> (a) Building a positive self-image and self-confidence.
>
> (b) Developing ability to think critically.
>
> (c) Building up group cohesion and fostering decision making and action.
>
> (d) Ensuring equal participation in the process of bringing About social change.
>
> (e) Encouraging group action in order to bring about change in the society.
>
> (f) Providing the wherewithal for economic independence.

The programme entails the following:

(i) A phased time bound programme of elementary education for girls, particularly up to primary stage by 1990 and up to the elementary stage by 1995.

(ii) A phased time bound programme of adult education for women in the age group 15-35 by 1995.

(iii) Increased women's access to vocational, technical, professional education and existing and emergent technologies; and

(iv) Review and reorganization of educational activities to ensure that they make a substantial contribution towards women's equality, and creation of appropriate cells/units therefore.

A number of measures have been suggested to achieve the state's objectives of the National Policy on Education. The Action Plan enunciates that every educational institution should take up by 1995 active programmes for the development of women. All teachers and non-formal education/adult education instructors should be trained as agents of women's development. Special programmes should be developed by research institutions to promote general awareness and positive self-image amongst women through programmes like discussions, street plays, wall papers, puppet shows, etc. Preference in recruitment of teachers up to school level should be for women.

National Literacy Mission (NLM) which aims at eradication of illiteracy in 15-35 age group by 1995 concretizes what is envisaged in NPE as regards literacy and adult education. The Mission document emphasizes the importance of imbibing the values of national integration, conservation of environment, women's equality, observance of small family norm, etc., and goes on to say that "the focus of NLM would be on rural areas, particularly women and persons belonging to the Scheduled Castes and Scheduled Tribes."

For universalization of elementary and adult education, the present programme of non-formal centres for girls needs to be extended to all educationally backward pockets of the country. Increased assistance should be given to voluntary organizations to run non-formal education centres for girls. In rural areas, special support services should be provided to relieve the girls from sibling care and other household work like fetching water, fuel, etc. Skill development linked to employment opportunities in the villages is required to be given priority so that there is an incentive on the part of the parents to educate girls. It is necessary to develop adult education programmes for women linked with upgradation of their skills and income generating activities. Skill development for girls should be a continuous process of learning and should be supported by programmes administered by others such as Polytechnics, Industrial Training Institutes (ITIs), Women's Centres in Agricultural and Home Science Colleges, etc. Centres should be set up in a phased manner vocational training, provide opportunities for retention skills and application of this learning for improving their living conditions. Their are 104 ITIs functioning exclusively for women and 97 wings in general ITIs reserved for women would need to be revamped during 1988-90 in terms of diversification of trades and courses, keeping in view the job potential and facilities for vocational counselling, imparting information about credit, banking, entrepreneurial development and women's access to technical education, etc.

Women's studies programmes would also have four dimensions, viz., teaching, research, training and extension. Women's issues would be incorporated in courses under various disciplines. Research would be encouraged on identified areas/ subjects. Seminars/workshops would be organized on the need for women's studies, and for dissemination of information and interaction. Educational institutions would be encouraged to take up programmes like adult education, awareness building, legal literacy, information and training support for socio-economic programmes of women's development, instructional programmes through media, etc., which directly benefit the community and bring about the empowerment of women.

All the foregoing endeavours will be planned, coordinated, and evaluated continuously both at the national and state levels. The Women's Cell in the National Council for Educational Research and Training would be revived and strengthened. National, Institute of

Educational Planning and Administration and Directorate of, Adult Education would have cells to plan and administer women's training programmes. The Women's cell in the University Grants Commission would, be strengthened to monitor the implementation of various programmes at the higher education level. It is proposed that women cells should be set up in all the States.

Current Scenario

The programmes for women's education will have to be implemented as a priority so that women attain a comparable level of education by 2020 A D. The strategy to be adopted for raising literacy levels and education among women has to keep, in view the vast cultural, geographical and ecological variations as also the problems relating to poverty and ignorance. The cultural and geographical variations call for decentralization of educational planning. Within the national perspective planning, implementation and monitoring of educational programmes has to be done at district and block levels, keeping in view the socioeconomic and geographic parameters of the area. The vocational and occupational components have to be designed in accordance with the availability of resources and job opportunities in the regions. Voluntary organizations and women's groups active in the area should be involved in the task.

In view of the social and cultural handicaps that have operated against women's education and taking account of the multiple roles that women are required to play, the need for adopting set of objectives specific to women's education is imperative. The objectives to be achieved by 2000 A.D. in regard to women's education are:

(i) Elimination of illiteracy, universalization of elementary education and minimization of the dropout and stagnation rate in the age group 6-14 years, to negligible proportions.

(ii) Ensuring opportunities to all women for access to appropriate level, nature and quality of education and also the wherewithal for success comparable with men.

(iii) Substantial vocationalization and diversification of secondary education so as to provide a wide scope for employment and economic independence of women.

(iv) Making education an effective means for women's equality by (a) Addressing ourselves to the constraints that prevent from participating in the educational process; (b) Eliminating the existing sexist bias in the system; (c) Making necessary intervention in the content and scope of education to inculcate positive and egalitarian and (d) Ensuring that teachers perceive this as one essential role.

(v) Providing non-formal and part-time courses to women to them to acquire knowledge and skills for their social, cultural and economic advancement.

(vi) Impetus to enrol in various professional degree courses so as to increase their number in medicine, teaching, engineering fields substantially.

(vii) Creating a new system of accountability, particularly of the basic educational services, to the local community, inter alia, by active involvement of women.

In brief, it is reiterated that the goals and strategies spelt out in the National Policy on Education, POA and the National Literacy Mission will ensure a much larger access for women to education.

High priority has to be accorded to creating awareness, through the various communication media, of the need for women's education and their active participation in economic and political development of the nation.

The curricula for school as well as university education have to be reviewed and revised so as to remove sex bias, inculcate among the masses a recognition of equality between men and women, and make women aware of their own potentials as well as provide them necessary opportunities to develop their capabilities in every field. Greater accessibility of educational facilities to girls is to be achieved by reducing the distance of schools from village habitations, and expanding non-formal elementary education, adult education, and the open school system. Appointment of lady teachers in schools would help draw more girls to schools and instil confidence among their parents. Towards this end, provision of quarters for lady teachers would be essential. Efforts should be directed at training local women as teachers. Provision of creche facilities and Balwadis near the elementary and secondary schools for girls would enable the girls to attend schools and ensure care of younger siblings. Incentives like midday meals, better rates of scholarships, freeships, etc., would go a long way in preventing dropout.

Above all, better health facilities, smaller families, and relief from drudgery through improved technology for household chores, are essential prerequisites for better enrolment of girls at school and higher educational institutions. Inputs from other sectors are, therefore, important. Greater coordination of health, employment, welfare and education interventions will have an effect on the status of women and girls.

According to Educational Statistics for 1984-85 published by the Ministry of Human Resource Development, the enrolment of girls at primary level, which covers the age group 6-11 years, is 331.9 lakh. Surveys and field research have pointed out that there is 25 per cent inflation in the enrolment figures, and 22 per cent enrolment is outside the age group. Thus the effective enrolment gets reduced by about 47 per cent. Accordingly, the coverage for 1984-85 for the 6-11 years age group may be estimated as 176 lakh. The population projected for the age group is 422.7 lakh. This means that only 40.7 per cent of the girls in the age group 6-11 are enrolled in schools. On a similar basis, the enrolment of 11-14 years age group gets reduced to 48.1 lakh (from 90.7 lakh) which is only 19.2 per cent of the population of 249.9 lakh estimated for the age group. The population projections for the girls in the age group 6-11 years and 11-14 years for 1989-90 are 462 lakh and 2,67 lakh respectively. In order to have full coverage, the additional enrolment required would be 286 lakh for 6-11 age group and 219 lakh for 11-14 years age group, the total being nearly 5 crore. The task appears to be stupendous. Along with enrolment, there is the problem of very high dropout rates. Stemming from highly inflated enrolment rates and subsequent dropouts in the 6-11 years age group, enrolment of 11-14 years age group girls, even at primary level, may not be possible even by 1995.

In view of the social and cultural handicaps that have operated against women's education, the need for adopting a set of objectives specific to women's education is imperative. These would need to encompass the elimination of illiteracy and measures for retention of girls in schools, substantial vocationalization and diversification to enhance economic opportunities for women, improvement in the quality of education in terms of the values it promotes and inculcates, and finally the provision of access to professional courses for women. Such measures would be necessary as also efforts to remove the inherent prejudices working against women's education.

Suggestions

1. Awareness needs to be generated among the masses regarding the necessity of educating girls so as to prepare them to effectively contribute to the socio-economic development of the country, to strengthen their role in society and to realize their own capacities. The media and various forms of communication have to be geared to this end.

2. A fruitful rapport has to be established between the community at large and the teachers and other

education personnel. As per the Programme of Action under National Policy on Education-1986, every educational institution should actively participate in bringing about such awareness.

3. Involvement of local leaders, voluntary agencies and women's groups is also necessary. Mahila Mandals need to be revitalized and reoriented to provide an effective forum for the purpose. One measure to achieve this could be to assign the responsibility to Mahila Mandals for ensuring that all children in a community attend school. An incentive scheme should be introduced to motivate panchayats to ensure 100 per cent enrolment of girls in their villages.

4. Early childhood care and education introduces children into the school system gradually and smoothly. When children get used to attending schools, it ensures in some measure retention of children, including girls, at elementary stages also. Hence there is needed to have a comprehensive and effective programme of early childhood care and education linked to an integrated package of learning for women. The most comprehensive example of this is the Integrated Child Development Services Programme which needs to be universalized.

5. For improving enrolment and minimizing drop-outs and wastage in case of girl students, it would be helpful if learning is made more attractive by providing adequate teaching materials in schools.

6. The number of teachers should also be increased so that the interaction between the teacher and the taught, which is so essential for good education also increases. This would help in the retention of girls in schools and would be more effective if teachers from the area are

employed. In single teacher schools, the teacher must be a woman. In Orissa all jobs of primary teachers have been reserved for women.

7. School curricula should be imaginatively developed to stimulate creativity 'largely through play rather than overburdening children' with formal or rote learning. Regional language should normally be the medium of instruction.

8. School timings should be flexible and fixed to suit local conditions and the needs of the working girls and must be available within the walking distance of the child. A substantial increase is required in the number of schools for girls.

9. In addition to incentives like free textbooks, free supply of uniforms, award of attendance scholarships and mid-day meals, facilities such as proper school building, safe drinking water, and toilet, etc., need to be provided to encourage school enrolment and retention of girls especially girls from educationally deprived social groups and from hilly, tribal, desert and remote areas and urban slums.

10. Local talent must be developed in order to meet the need for recruiting women teachers at the primary and elementary levels especially in rural and tribal areas. In this endeavour national agencies like CAPART and CSWB, voluntary agencies, Mahila Mandals and local self-government agencies can make a significant contribution. They can also play a useful watchdog function to ensure that educational and other programmes are run efficiently and effectively.

11. There should be a reservation of 50 per cent posts for women teachers in elementary schools. Women teachers

working in the rural areas should be provided suitable accommodation.

12. Multi-entry system for girls who cannot attend schools continuously should be adopted.

13. Wherever necessary, schools meant exclusively for girls may be set up. The recommended distance of 3 kilometres for locating a middle school is a handicap for many girls. To ensure participation of girls in middle schools, it is necessary to provide hostel facilities.

14. The Savitribai Phule Foster Parent Scheme of Maharashtra could be adopted in other States/Union Territories to help poorer families to at least complete primary school. Under the scheme, well to do persons and organizations are persuaded to adopt one or more out of school girls and contribute in cash or kind or both @ Rs. 25 per month for her education. The money can be spent on uniforms, stationery or anything else, needed by the girls or also partly used to alleviate the economic distress of the parents. The Zila Parishad, Block Education Officer and headmasters play a pivotal role in implementing the scheme, which is purely voluntary and if district level officers are appointed for coordination of programmes for women, they could also actively take it up.

15. Condensed courses of education at elementary and middle school levels for girls must be started in all the rural areas and for weaker sections of the urban community.

16. Many girls in the 11-14 years age group would first have to be brought into the primary stage through non-formal education. By devising alternative education approaches non-formal schooling and through like intelligent use of technology, the pace of middle school education can be accelerated. If retention up to 73 per cent is achieved up

to class V, universal elementary education may be possible in some parts of the country by 2000 A.D. Other backward areas would have to be given much more attention in, professional as well as financial terms to enable them even to universalize primary education for girls by 1995. The National Literacy Mission will need to address these issues on a priority basis.

17. Special efforts are necessary for bringing tribal children particularly, girls into the school system. Tribal dialects, extreme poverty, problems of commuting, rigidity of formal education and its irrelevance to the tribal culture and the tribal's distrust of the ways of the mainstream society, must be borne in mind in formulating strategies.

18. The educational forecasts, may look more achievable if the system is opened up for flexible non-formal education which 'the below average states' should be persuaded to adopt in a large measure. The existing educational infrastructure particularly, in tribal and rural areas should be made effective and responsible.

19. Non-formal education is an alternative to the formal system which has the potentiality of becoming the major programme of education for girls who cannot attend school during normal school hours due to various reasons. The Central Government is already implementing a centrally sponsored scheme under which grants to the extent of 90 per cent are provided towards maintenance of non-formal education centres exclusively for girls in nine educationally backward states. This programme should be strengthened further and extended to other states where education of girls is lagging behind. It should at least cover all the pockets of low enrolments of girls and areas of high dropout rate. Besides literacy, it must also provide relevant information on skill development and inculcation of positive self-image among girls.

20. Secondary education for girls should entail:

    (i) A ten-year course in general education learning and diversified higher secondary education which may be either terminal or lead to further professional preparation; and (ii) Diversified courses after Grade VIII in technical subjects, viz., agricultural technology, health services, food production activities such as dairy and poultry and non-traditional areas need to be untroubled. A legal literacy component is also recommended at this stage.

21. Diversified courses leading to occupational preparation should be of parallel duration to the general secondary courses. In addition, there should be a variety of short and long term, whole time, part-time and apprentice courses. The trend of thinking is now to place emphasis on the last. Keeping in view the rapid modernization and advancement in technology for agriculture, there is an urgent need for skilled artisanship, for promoting productive activities on the one hand, and a variety of learning programmes for adjustment of the rural society to socio-economic change on the other. Efforts should be made to ensure that girls have every opportunity to enter into apprenticeship in areas that are non-conventional, and incentives be provided for the same. Further, at least 30 per cent seats should be reserved for girls in apprenticeship training courses on a non-transferable basis.

22. General and vocational training courses should be combined so that prospects of a career immediately on completion of schooling may attract girls from weaker sections. While designing the vocational courses, available occupational opportunities as well as the need to overcome market stereotypes should be kept in view.

23. Since secondary education has remained almost beyond the reach of weaker sections, liberal incentives and other

facilities to release the girls from household chores appear to be essential. It would also help to locate the institutions in the areas of their habitation.

24. Multiple entry system should be introduced in the secondary classes. Part-time education facilities should also be made available.

25. Condensed courses should be organized in cooperation with local vocational training institutions to cover all rural areas and areas inhabited by weaker sections in urban areas. Such courses may be organized for small groups of girls, and combined with job training. Efforts should be made to cover atleast 215 lakh women in the age group 15-30 years under the condensed courses programme wherever possible the condensed courses of the CSWB should be expanded and strengthened. New programmes that are to be initiated must avoid duplication in the areas where the CSWB's programmes exist.

26. Correspondence courses and self-study programmes can be especially useful for girls desirous of continuing education but are unable to do so because of circumstances. Apart from imparting elementary education and knowledge about farming techniques, the curriculum for non-student girls should include courses of training in occupational skills. Similar programmes should also be designed for girls in the urban areas.

27. The open school system should be expanded extending the facility to all the girls in rural and backward areas.

28. Science education for girls has been neglected so far. Secondary schools for girls must be helped to build good science programmes over the Eighth Five-Year Plan. Special scholarships for girls opting for science courses need to be instituted at the secondary and higher education levels.

29. Special scholarship may also be offered to rural women, who opt for teachers' training, especially those who complete the condensed courses at the secondary stage.

30. There is a need to open more colleges and polytechnics for girls, especially in rural areas.

31. Incentives like scholarships, freeships, etc., should be provided to enable girls from rural areas to pursue higher education for girls belonging to weaker sections. In addition to freeships and scholarships hostels should also be provided to meet their requirements for food and lodging.

32. Girls should be encouraged to enter professional courses. Reservation of seats for girls in such courses may be considered to level out the existing bias in access to certain professional streams.

33. Vocational counselling and guidance service be organized exclusively in a more meaningful way to help girls in colleges and universities opt for suitable courses relevant to their talents and interests, and free of traditional bias.

34. Vocational and technical education for women, both formal and non-formal, should be a major feature of the programmes of rural universities. The women's wings of the universities could undertake large-scale extension programmes in order to activate girls and women in the surrounding areas to take advantage of educational and occupational facilities of various types, particularly those leading to meaningful employment, essential for reducing women's marginalization.

35. In order to increase the representation of rural girls in higher education courses, 30 per cent seats, may be reserved for girls to begin with.

36. All agencies, involved with preparation of curricula prescription of textbooks and organization of educational processes will have to evince awareness towards women's issues. University/College Departments of Women's Studies, appropriate voluntary agencies, women's groups, etc., should be involved in giving a new perspective to the various issues of content and processes of education. Women's universities and women's centres in colleges need to take an active role in women's development and in influencing the attitudes of Future generations.

37. Facilities for part-time self-study and correspondence courses should be provided on a large-scale to enable girls who are not in a position to join higher educational institutions on a regular basis, to continue their studies.

38. In addition to courses leading to degree/diploma, short courses in specific subjects through summer school sessions, and ad hoc programmes like seminars, workshops, etc., should be organized for working women with a view to upgrading their knowledge and skills, not necessarily leading to degrees.

39. Integrated learning programmes for women are recommended which will not only lay emphasis on literacy but on empowering women through awareness building on social issues, bringing about attitudinal change, promoting skill training for employment, providing information on healthcare, nutrition and hygiene as well as on legal rights. Such programmes are beginning and must continue to be designed and structured so as to be relevant for the vast majority of rural women. The revised scheme linked to ICDS known as the 'Women's Integrated Learning for Life', should be introduced as an integral part of the non-formal education system.

40. Entrepreneurship development programmes should be organized separately for education of women in the age group 18-30 years, with a minimum of matriculation level of education. The objective of such training should be to:

    (i) Make them aware of the various opportunities for self-employment; (ii) Motivate them to take up self-employment; (iii) Impart needed skills and training; (iv) Promote motivation for achievement among them; and (v) Create access to resources such as capital, credit, etc.

41. A large number of girls cannot participate in whole day education programmes. Provision of non-formal and part-time programmes, with flexible school hours and sensitivity to the agricultural cycle are, of particular importance. In addition to the primary and upper primary stages, distance learning opportunities need to be provided at secondary and higher secondary levels.

42. Adult education will have to be composed of three interrelated stands aimed at:

    (i) Continuous flow of new information especially to rural and tribal areas, particularly to inculcate positive attitudes towards women;

    (ii) Continuous training of the people in the use of modern tools and methods of production; and

    (iii) Acquisition of permanent reading and computation skills.

    Following from the above, three types of programmes may be offered to the learner:

    (a) Information and literacy.

(b) Information and training in new technology and literacy.

(c) Information and training in new technology with or without literacy. Continuous information flows relating to human affairs, gender relations and the use of science and technology for betterment of life would be the common factor in all the three programmes.

43. The growing availability of communication media should be directed towards keeping up information flows and portraying positive images of women in non-conventional roles. Audio-visual materials, combined with non-formal training arrangements, could impart to various population groups the kind of instruction they need in the use of new technologies. Involvement of mass media in motivating women to attend literacy classes is most essential.

44. Rapid strides in the development of technologies and tools for the reduction in women's drudgery and easy access to work places, water and fuel supply, child care, health services and population control can contribute significantly to the success of learning programmes for women. Women's literacy programmes would succeed better if they centre around women's concerns and also provide opportunities of recreation and sharing of experiences.

45. District plans should be prepared keeping in view literacy requirements of the learners and identifying agencies which can take up such programmes in districts.

46. All women working in industries or employed elsewhere should be made literate by the employers by allotting time from the working hours for their

education. Place of teaching, teachers and teaching material should be arranged by them. Necessary legislation to this effect may be enacted.

47. At least 50 per cent seats in pre-service courses in all teachers training institutions should be reserved for women. Spatial planning to ensure that women from rural areas are selected as teachers is essential.

48. Provision of composite teacher training courses for women who have had insufficient education to improve their educational qualifications along with their training, should be made.

49. The existing Integrated Rural Development Programme, National Rural Employment Programme, Development of Women and Children in Rural Areas, Training of Youth in Self-Employment Programme, Integrated Child Development Programme, etc., should have a component of literacy for their women beneficiaries. Training should be provided to the functionaries of various development departments by Directorate of Education in the States.

50. The State Resources Centres should produce suitable learning material for women on a priority basis. Literature for neoliterates should be suitably devised by experts, keeping in view the needs of different groups of learners.

51. Decentralization is the key to the successful application of the strategies outlined above in this decentralized approach, the village cluster or the block level is seen as most appropriate for the delivery of programmes. It is, therefore, necessary that the block is allocated a flexible budget so as to make funds available to village clusters/ villages for innovative educational activities and for equalization of educational opportunity.

52. An overall coordination of health, welfare and educational inputs would be most desirable. This would entail (a) Convergent policies in these sectors; (b) Coordination of delivery mechanisms; and (c) Pooling of allocations.

53. The strategies spelt out in the National Policy of Education, 1986, the Programme of Action for its implementation and the National Literacy Mission and the successful achievement of the goals, imposed in these documents, would be important for improvement in the status of women.

11

Deprived of Education

As centuries rolled on, Aryan culture was firmly entrenched in this land. Indian women were trapped more and more in the web of myth and lost their sense of self and will. The goddesses were robbed of their glory even though they were still seated on a high pedestal. Men's obsession was to pull them down to earth by having the women sing their praises and do their will. Only when the women pleased them and satisfied their ego-needs, did they call them the goddesses of the household (Girhya Lakshmi). The moment women defied male idiosyncrasies, they were called devils. Men took upon themselves the responsibilities of protecting and feeding the women who were consequently destitute and completely dependent. The women were not allowed to move outside the household without male company since it was taken for granted that they were incapable of defending themselves. Women became frail and weak creatures and believed that if any man other than their husbands touched them or cast a lustful glance towards them they were defiled and dishonoured. Hence, their only path to an honourable existence was to give the men unflinching loyalty, submit to their care and deny their own self and will.

Mythically Placed

Perhaps in no other culture does such a duality exist where women have been mythically placed upon a high pinnacle while at the same time pulled down to dust in reality. In no other civilisation the women's status in the social milieu has been raised so high and simultaneously, so brutally lowered as in the Indian culture. In other cultures women are usually labelled as either saint or sinner, while in India she is both. Years of being enmeshed in the many strands of this web have deeply affected the position of the Indian women.

Women of the early Aryan civilisation were highly respected. This society, however, as patriarchal, therefore, the birth of a girl was generally an unwelcome event. As early as in 2000 BC charms and rituals ensured the birth of a son in preference to that of a daughter. These charms are reported in the ancient Atharva Veda. Even though a son was desired and preferred, the birth of a daughter was a source of great pleasure to the family. Alteker points out that some scholars of this period were of the opinion that a gifted and well-mannered daughter might be a source of pleasure to the family. No restrictions were placed on girls in performing religious rites. The marriage of a daughter was not a difficult problem since she was free to choose her husband.

Freedom of Movement

The marriage of girls used to take place at the age of 16 or 17 years. The women were not restricted and were allowed freedom of movement within the society, even in the company of their lovers. The wife occupied the honoured place in the family as the mistress of her household. Marriages were mostly monogamous. Widow remarriage was usually permitted within the family. Parents desired their daughters to marry the husbands of their choice. During the early Vedic period, the prayer of an anxious father used to be "May Saviter lead and bring to thee the husband whom thy heart desires". Pinkham notes: It is important for us to note that a wife was on a level of equality at the hearth which was the altar of sacrifice.

Around 1500 BC, the education of the daughters confined to the family. Religious and secular training was given only to girls from rich and cultured families. Men performed functions in the religious sacrificial rites, which had previously been the wife's domain. Girls were married at about the age of sixteen years, and divorce and widow remarriage were, still permitted.

Gradually circumstances changed. As ancestor worship gained popularity, sons alone were permitted to perform religious rites. Women became "valued only as the vehicles for bearing sons, and when they were unfit or unwilling to perform this function, they were considered useless". The value of the sons increased further, and they began to be regarded as investments for the future. Without a son, no man or woman could hope to go to heaven. The position of the daughter was greatly undermined. Still the women were not debarred from the study of the Vedas and there existed very few taboos regarding the rearing of girls.

Prevalence of Marriage

During the Epic period in India, the birth of daughter became an exceedingly negative event because of the prevalence of marriage customs, which subordinated the position of women. Still, a daughter was regarded as a prized possession, and family took a keen interest in her rearing. In Mahabbarata, Draupadi is described as the common property of the five brothers. She was put at stake in a gambling bout. Sita, the ideal woman character of Ramayana, was put to fire ordeal to prove her chastity. She was denounced by Lord Rama to prove himself as an deal king. Draupadi did not accept her subordinate position and fought in an open assembly when Duryodhana the winner of the bout, sought to derobe her. Sita, on the other hand, took her humiliations with fortitude and goodwill toward her husband. However, by this time the right of the husband over his wife or a man over a woman has generally accepted by the society irrespective of whether women acknowledge it willingly or not.

This willing acceptance, even today, is considered as the ideal of womanhood. Sita is worshipped in most of the devout homes for her absolute obedience to her husband. Everywhere in India her example is exalted to be followed by all women. Sita had great strength of character and virtue. She pursued what she considered to be right. Her love for the husband was limitless. Her character was of utmost purity and chastity. If we for the sake of argument forget for the time being the divinity of Rama and Sita there arises a doubt in our minds that such a character might have been drawn to satisfy the male ego by the male poets. It might be possible that Sita's character was enfolded in the myth of male supremacy and female subordination so that the women's sole aspiration in life became the loyalty and the service to her husband who was put at the level of God to her. This emphasis on chastity and service to the husband may lead to the conclusion that the women of this period were put on pedestal as goddesses only if they lived the ideal and the virtuous life according to the most rigid standards set by a male dominated society.

The witch type of the nature of women is demonstrated in the Ramayana through the story about Kaikeyi and Manthra. Kaikeyi tried through deceit to obtain the throne for her son. Manthra prompted her to do so. Hence both are branded as great culprits at the opposite end of the spectrum from Sita.

An aspect worth noticing in the character portrayal of Mahabharata heroines is the strong willed women. They are depicted as "resolute, full of fire, passionate in comparison with the often slackened, spineless men". Perhaps the Indians of this period were not in full control of their women and were frustrated enough to seek means of controlling them. One such means was to put an exceedingly high value on loyalty and chastity. Meyer points out that in Indian literature no ideal of a man is found; however, idealistic character portrayals of women are outstanding, especially in the Epic period". We may not entirely agree with this view as the portrayal of characters of Shri Rama, Shri Krishna and other heroes of Epic period cannot be ignored and yet there seems to be truth in this observation that women of this period were certainly of strong will.

During the post-Vedic period the age of marriage of girls was nine or ten years. Since the marriage was performed at such a young age, the choice then was not that of the girl but of the parents or other elders. A woman was debarred from revoking her marriage but the husband was free to throw his wife out of his household if she was not submissive. Widow marriage became unacceptable and was banned by 500 AD. The dictum that "the wife ought to revere her husband as a god even if he was vicious and void of any merit was accepted as applying to all women". The Law of Manu became the accepted way of life. It stated that the father should protect his daughter while she was young, her husband when she was married, and her son when her husband was no longer there. This law contributed to woman's inferior status in society and denied her all decision making rights.

Kautilya was in favour of marrying girls at a tender age. He advocated the marriage of girls when menses appear. He advocated the punishment of parents who did not marry their daughters at proper time. According to Jha: "Probably Kautilya advocates early marriage with a view to maintaining the chastity of girls, preventing 'women' from joining nunneries, check love marriages, utilising the fertile period of girls for bringing forth offspring, and increasing the population at a time when frightful wars of conquest reduced Hindu population by one-half". Kautilya propagates the subjection of women in married life. The wife must remain under the control of her husband. As the girls were to be married at an early age their education was totally neglected. Kautilya considered that a wife must be fully devoted to her husband and blindly follow him. The woman's freedom of speech was totally curbed and since her individuality was denied she was kept ignorant.

At this time, Buddhism developed in India as a revolt against Brahmanism, a too formal ritualistic religion prevalent about six centuries before the birth of Christ, Buddhism soon spread throughout India and dominated the nation until about 800 AD. Buddhists still maintained women in an inferior position through an emphasis on celibacy for men who made women appear unclean or as objects simply for men's pleasure. Women were admitted to the Buddhist order as a gradual change occurred. According to Altekar, "this change was the beginning of a movement, which led to new attitudes about female education among ladies in commercial and aristocratic familes". Several ladies from Buddhist families led lives of celibacy with the aim of understanding and following the eternal truths of religion and philosophy. Some women like Sanghamitra went to foreign countries to propagate Buddhism. Also, many women of the Jaina faith devoted their time to learning and became famous scholars. However, these were early exceptions. For the majority of women, no educational gains were made between 300 AD and 800 AD because of either Buddhism or Jainism. The celibate Jaina monks considered women as the temptresses that perpetuated the misery that was life. This attitude certainly did not deter in general the Jainas from marriage or begetting of children. Women were given place of honour in the household. However, the monkish tales about celibacy did contribute to ambivalence among the Jaina men in their behaviour pattern with their women. Jaina men enjoyed their women in spite of the religious discourses about their evils.

Educational Equality

The road back to educational equality was slow and difficult. By 500 AD the religious influence had obligated all education for women. The model women were exposed to re-modelled. Women were exposed to such literature, which highlighted dependence and punishment for breaking the norms of conduct imposed on them by indifferent priests. A blind faith developed among the women through a process of awe and forced reverence. The Puranic literature cites examples where the husband was carried on his wife's shoulders to the house of a prostitute. The wife's willingness to put her husband's needs above hers' proved that she was a sati.

This literature which seems to have been developed by male Hindu priests completely subjugated the will of women. It emphasised husband worship along with the notion that a woman's salvation was possible only by doing that which her husband desired. An abundance of stories about Pativarta Nari or the husband worshipping woman influenced women to perform every kind of unnatural act for the sake of their husbands. Women started taking pleasure in their morbid existence. Eventually they became even greater fanatics than men in opposing their freedom. Perhaps they were so removed from the idea of an independent existence that even the thought of such responsibility frightened them. It may be said that it is human nature that one wants to stay with the familiar even if it is destructive because the unknown is scary.

Muslims considered marriage as a contract. In certain respects the Muslim law gave woman a higher position in the society than the medieval Hindu law. However, the purdah or veil as well as the women's ignorance of the law diminished this small difference. The Muslim men believed that their women would remain safe only if they were not exposed to temptation. Thus the women were denied the right to make choices.

The Muslims like Hindus believed that the women's only path to salvation lay in the service to their menfolk. Divorce was shunned and many myths were woven about the dutiful wife who was prepared to sacrifice her all for her husband. Muslim had put all types of restrictions on the movement of their women outside their households and by and large they were restricted from having any contact with men who did not belong to their immediate family. Chastity was valued and the husband considered it his conjugal duty to keep his wife away from temptation.

According to the Holy Quran women were respected because they bore children. Progeny was very important to the Muslims as defenders in warfare against unbelievers. Hence among Muslims there also developed ambivalent feelings towards their women. Women were respected for being mothers but at the same time they were restricted from having any freedom of action. They were completely subjugated by the dominant males. Due to a number of environmental factors affecting the Indian Muslims the feelings of respect were overcome by the need or restriction. Most of the legal rights of the women were virtually subjected to the male will.

The early Muslim period was one of great instabilities. Local feuds and conversions were dominating the social life. The fanaticism and religious intolerance closed the doors to rationality. The women were the worst sufferers of the irrationality of the ignorant priests and religious fanatics. Their spirit of inquiry was crushed, as they were not allowed any interaction with learned or open minded persons. The women were left with no option but to submit to their submissive role and suffer indignities and cruelties in silence. Dubey describes the personality and the character of the women that emerged during this period: They had no status in society; none in their own estimation. They were more like puppets, which move when someone pulls the strings than individual human beings with minds of their own.

Patriarchal Type Family

At this time the patriarchal type of family in its perfectly developed state was generally in existence. The senior male in the family was the undisputed head. Hindu women could not claim any patronage since the law of succession did not give them independent right of inheritance. The inheritor of the property was made responsible for looking after the widow of the deceased. However, in spite of their low social status, women were still the ideal of conjugal devotion, and the family was the most intimate and enduring social relationship. Dubey considered that "the Hindu family was an ideal family, the Hindu parents .... Mothers were not equalled by any people on the earth in tenderness towards their progeny and attachment to the family ties".

This attachment to their families was not an exercise of free will for the women. They only knew to be dutiful wives and loving mothers. No other options were open to them. In most cases, motherhood was the only solace for them in their subordinate existence. As mothers, they elicited respect, and through their sons, they ruthlessly made attempts to dominate their daughter-in-laws and other poor and dependent relatives. The condition of the women in the Indian society continued to remain low. The disruption of the Mughul Empire in the eighteenth-century and the consequent confusion throughout the country added to the women's miseries. At the beginning of British rule, the marriage age was lowered to three or four years. Since hygienic conditions were poor and disease and famine were common, a large number of girls became widows in their early childhood. These child widows were ill treated and considered a curse to their families.

The use of the veil became popular, particularly among the Muslims. The higher-class women were kept away from the males by means of purdah even a glimpse of a woman's fully clothed and veiled body by a stranger was not tolerated. While travelling, dark clothes also covered the vehicle, and when the women entered it and left it, the male servants or the carriers had to be removed from their presence.

The observance of purdah was not only to safeguard the honour and chastity of women, it also kept them for special pleasure of the men. Certainly, the veil produced a special type of feminine beauty, which was pale and passionate with mystic eyes, and the mind of a child. Such women seemed to appeal to the morbid taste of the pleasure lovers. When a woman is unlimited and has free social interaction with the opposite sex, her sexual impulses are toned down. Perhaps those who put their women in purdah do so to obtain more sexual pleasure out of them.

During the period of Muslim rule, quite a number of upper caste Indian widows burned themselves on the funeral pyres of their husbands. This was known as the sati system. The Sanskrit word sati means "true wife" or "good woman." Thus a woman was considered true to her husband when she burned her body with him after his death. Akbar, the Mughal emperor, made efforts to stop this practice about 1600 AD. He, however, was unsuccessful. When the British became the rulers, they found this practice so firmly entrenched that they also had no luck in disrupting it. The magnitude of the tradition is further understood by noting that in the year 1803, 275 women were burned at their husbands' funeral pyres within 30 mile radius of Calcutta. Within six months of the year 1804 in the same area, the number was 115.

The British passed an Act in 1829 to stop the burning of widows. However, the practice continued in rural parts of India as late as 1905 when a few people participated in a sati ceremony in Bihar and were condemned to prison. The Hindu priesthood strongly resisted the British India law. They argued that Vedas, their holy text, sanctioned the practice, therefore, alien rulers could not suppress this practice. When the religious texts were examined, it was found that the Hindu priests had falsified them to support this rite. The prevalence of the sati system and the opposition of its abolition by the orthodox priests show the extent to which a society can degenerate in the name of religious law. It also shows the strong influence of myth which the men and women came to believe. The honour of a family became so strongly linked with the widow burning that the kinsmen of a widow could cruelly push her into the fire. Unfortunately, the abolition of sati system did not end the miseries of the Hindu widows. Their burning was stopped, but they were still treated worst than the pet animals of the household. They were not allowed to remarry and had to pass their lives depending on the charity of their kinsmen and serving them like domestic servants. The plight of the young widows was extremely bad. They were not only tortured but also many times sexually exploited by the unscrupulous males in the family or the neighbourhood.

Unfortunately sati system is still not completely wiped out. In September 1987, a young widow of 18 years Roop Kanwar was burnt at the funeral pyre of her deceased husband, a bare seven months after her wedding. The burning took place before a large gathering of people. The illiterate village folk endorsed the sati pratha and the rural women developed worshipful attitude toward the burnt widow. She became a deity. The myth woven centuries ago around the virtuous wives and self-destroying satis as goddesses seemed to persist in the minds of the people. It is worth noticing that all those women and men who supported and organised the burning of Roop Kanwar were not totally illiterate. They were some that were educated. Yet the type of education which they had received did not result in opening the vistas of their minds. This has in fact opened the question of quality of education, which these persons had received. In the case of these persons education which they had received had completely failed in developing in them a positive attitude towards modernity and a will to fight against orthodoxy perpetuated by a corrupt and ill formed priestly class.

The institution of prostitution continued to flourish as a respectable way of life and the dancing girls were patronised by the nobles and landowners of their villages or towns. Chakraborty writes that in 1853, the Chief Magistrate of Calcutta reported that his town with its 416,000 people supported 12,419 such women. Of these upwards of 10,000 were Hindus including several daughters of the Kulin Brahmins.

Existing along with the customary form of prostitution, which was quite common in large part of the country there was another form of prostitution that of Devdasi cult or temple prostitution. In early times, the practice of offering virgins to the deity was common. Some examples can also be found in the temple precincts of Sumerian culture in Mesopotamia. In India, the Dravidians who may have borrowed it from Egypt or Mesopotamia probably introduced this custom. In the Rig Veda there is a clear reference to the dancing girl. Usha, the goddess of dowri, is compared to a dancing girl wearing embroidered garments and baring her bosom. In the Atharva Veda there is also a reference to the existence of women called Gandharva grihtas (possessed or owned by Gandharvas). They do not marry and exist for the pleasure of gods and men.

The cult of Devadasi originated in the early civilisation and became prevalent in South India between the sixth and the thirteenth centuries AD. During the reigns of Pallavas and Cholas all big temples recruited girls for temple prostitution. The temple dancers were married to the temple deity at a young age. They were taught music, dancing and the classical literature. After seven years of practice, the rite of worship of anklets (gajjai puja) took place. This was the first wearing of the anklets for the dancer. It has been traditional for families to offer their daughters as Devadasis or servants of the gods. In spite of the Devadasi Protection Act of 1934, some families still continue with this tradition in Maharashtra and Karnataka. In most other parts of India, this practice has been abolished.

The courtesan in India has filled a need for the men, which the wives were unable to meet. It seemed normal to a wealthy male that wives are kept for progeny and prostitutes for pleasure both sexually and aesthetically. The high-class courtesans throughout most of India's history were the most learned women in the country. Santosh Chatterjee in one of his articles has observed that "Be she of heaven or this earth, the courtesan in India had dual purposes in her life. She was in one way an object of lust for men, in another way she was the repository of all the delightful acts of music, dancing and personal decoration'.

The cult of Devadasis supported the envelopment of women in the web of myth regarding self-sacrifice and negation of will for men's pleasure. Women lost their individuality partly due to the contrivance of men and partly due to their need for the advantages they gained by being submissive.

Many factors contributed to women's dependent state. Numerous pregnancies during their most active years left her unfit and unable for engaging themselves in any type of employment except in the case of very poor or destitute women. Men accepted the responsibility of looking after the material needs of the women but in return for this they demanded from them unflinching loyalty and devotion. They denied them any opportunity to develop them physically or mentally or to develop their own will power. Thus women became weak and inferior to men as human beings. This degeneration of the women in India was at its peak by the end of the eighteenth century. By the beginning of the nineteenth century the entrapment of the women in the mythical web was so complete that in almost all the spoken languages of India women were, described as evil, an appendage of men, and always open to temptation.

And so such sayings were quoted:

> "To educate a women is like placing a knife in the hands of a monkey".
>
> "Where there are women, there is trouble".
>
> "Woman is a poisonous creeper, avoid her company; her love destroys faith, caste, wealth and money".
>
> "He who is guilty of sin easily begets daughters".

12

Scene in Free India

Modern methods of production, marketing and planning call for a higher level of knowledge and those skills that are required by a traditional economy. The increasing complexity and interrelationship among production, investment and the process of competitive selection, increases the importance of education and dissemination of information.

Though educational opportunities did expand in the post-Independence period, it was relatively slower among women, particularly at the primary and secondary levels. The rate of expansion was much faster at the level of higher education, and was the virtual monopoly of the middle-class. In the case of women, both secondary and higher education was practically confined to the urban middle-class. On the other hand, the number of illiterates, who remained outside the reach of the educational system also increased the women outnumbering the men. This pattern of educational development, coupled with the changes in the economy, has, inevitably affected the economic opportunities of women.

The work participation rate by educational level shows that while employment opportunities for educated women have increased, there has been a negative trend in the participation rate of illiterate and semi-literate women, whose share in employment has declined.

During 1981-91 the participation rate for illiterate women had declined substantially from 71.1 per cent to 55.3 per cent in urban areas, but showed marginal variations in rural areas. As pointed out in section II B and III A, the employment of women has declined significantly both in unorganized nonagricultural occupations and in organized industry. Our review indicates that there is a large-scale displacement of illiterate and semiliterate women workers from organized industry and non-agricultural occupations in the unorganised sector. This is also evident from the fact that the drop has been more marked in the urban areas. A superficial conclusion that could be drawn from this data, is that the decline in the numbers of illiterate or semi-literate women workers, indicates a rising level of education.

The pattern of women's educational development in the years since independence, however, indicates that it has failed to penetrate, in any significant manner, the large mass of illiterate adult women, whose numbers have increased over the years. Since they also come from the poorest section of the population, where employment is a dire necessity, this change in the composition of the women workforce has to be regarded as, an indicator of the displacement of this section of women from the workforce, a consequence of the changing levels of technology, and methods of business organization. The increase in the participation rate of the technical diploma holders from 0.6 per cent to 2.3 per cent, indicates the growing demand for modern technical skills in new industries like electronics, pharmaceuticals, electricals, etc., and in new services for technical personnel. The distribution of degree holders and technical female personnel by labour-force status and level of education indicates that the majority of them were employees and only 2.1 per cent being self-employed.

Among the educated women, the worker rates for women who have received a technical degree and diploma (mainly in teaching and medicine) were substantially higher than those who had received non-technical degree or diplomas or had studied up to the Higher Secondary level. The differential according to fields of specialization of technical degree and diploma holders are smaller among males than among females. The distribution of women degree holders and technical personnel by sector of employment show that 58 per cent are employed in the public sector, 36.6 per cent in the private sector and 5.4 per cent are selfemployed.

The extent to which persons of different educational levels undertake productive roles in the economy is an indicator of the nature of utilization of the investment in their education. Women with degree or diploma in medicine and teaching generally pursue a career. The differential participation rate between such women and their male counterparts in not more than 20 per cent.

The rising participation rate of educated women is also witnessed by the Employment Exchange statistics. Since 1963 the number of female job seekers with matriculation as well as higher education on the live Register has increased more rapidly than for males. Between 1964-68 the number of female job seekers registered with Employment Exchange increased by about 81 per cent while that of male job seekers increased by only 14 per cent. For matriculates and higher educated job seekers the corresponding increases were 72 per cent and 116 per cent for males and females respectively (Visaria, 1971). In 1973 the percentage increase of women work seekers over the previous year was 25.7 per cent for those with qualification below middle school, 39 per cent for matriculates and undergraduates and 95.4 per cent for graduates and postgraduates. This phenomenon assumes importance in view of the relatively rapid spread of women's education in urban India and the paucity of employment opportunities. Taking different subject fields together, the average duration of unemployment is higher for women than for men.

According to the Census of 2001, the average waiting period for a male graduate before getting employment was 9.9 months as against 11.6 months for a woman graduate. The only exception to this is the field of medicine and nursing where the average waiting period for men with postgraduate qualification and with doctorate is higher than for women. This sometimes acts as a strong deterrent for many a woman without specialization from seeking employment.

The total stock of degree holders and technical personnel by subject field, level of education and sex, and the distribution of degree holders and technical personnel who were found unemployed, was obtained by CSIR on individual enumeration slip in 2001. The study revealed that out of 7 lakh women degree holders only two and a half lakh were employed which is only 5 per cent of the total working women in the country. Of these employed women, 52 per cent earned less than Rs. 1000 and 20 per cent earned between Rs. 1000 and Rs. 2000. Of total number of unemployed women graduates only 160,000 women were seeking jobs and the largest number of this component were holding degree -in Arts and Humanities and the next were those holding degrees in Science. Of the women who were not seeking employment, 65 per cent had degrees in Arts and humanities, 60 per cent in Science, 20 per cent in technical or engineering and 10 per cent in vocational courses.

Problems of Literate Women

The paradox of women's employment is that while illiteracy drives many out of employment, education does not necessarily lead to their employment.

> That participation ratios are not higher has at least as much to do with considerations of status and prestige as with the absence of jobs for those who seek but cannot find them. It is of course conceivable that a more progressive and expanding society could elevate the position of women and change attitudes towards female work. But an economy whose capacity to absorb men of working age is strained, does not encourage the elimination of traditional forms of discriminations against economic activity by women. G. Myrdal (Asian Drama).

Idleness can both be voluntary and involuntary. Since our labour market does not provide full, productive and freely chosen employment and jobs are at a premium, many women prefer to avoid the competitive pressures. Utilization of labour in any society depends to a certain extent on social institutions, taboos and inhibitions related to status and work which affect women more than men. These attitudes are reflected in social institutions, and the relationship between institutions and attitudes is mutually reinforcing.

The development of education has been mainly confined to middle-class families, among whom the attitude to women's employment outside the home had been most restrictive. This attitude however has been changing rapidly under economic pressure and the changing social scene. The real difficulty lies in the failure of the economy to absorb all its labour power and to appreciate the need for an institutionalized pattern of labour utilization that takes note of women's roles as housewives and mothers. So far, in spite of occasional lip service to the idealised image of women in these roles, little attempt has been made to assess its productive value. Still less attention has been given to providing the necessary infrastructure to remove women's disabilities in the labour market. Education alone cannot remove these disabilities.

Professional Training

The need to relate education and particularly vocational training to actual employment opportunities has been repeatedly emphasized by various expert bodies like the ILO, the National Commission on Labour, the All-India Council for Technical Education, the Institute of Applied Manpower Research and the University Grants Commission, Committee on Coordination of University Education with Manpower Requirements.

In view of the current social prejudices against employment of women and their large-scale displacement from employment as a result of structural and technological changes taking place in the economy, vocational training for women requires special attention and priority. This has been emphasized by the International Labour Conference in 1965 and the UN Commission on the Status of Women in each of its reports. In India, the National Committee on Women's Education, had pleaded strongly for better and more extensive facilities for vocational training for women particularly since the general educational system paid little regard to the needs of industry and commerce.

The inadequacy of vocational training opportunities for women, widens the productivity gap between men and women at all levels and makes them unwanted by the economy. Training facilities when they are provided, display the existing social bias regarding the suitability of particular occupations for women which leads to over concentration in a limited group of subjects.

Our examination of opportunities for vocational and technical education for women is based on the following: (a) on the job training; (b) pre-employment training—technical and professional; (c) training programmes undertaken by different Government Departments and Voluntary Organizations for developing skills and human resources. We have not included professional training at the university level because, as will be discussed in the next chapter, there is no real evidence of discrimination or any substantial wastage of training at this level.

The major factor limiting women's contribution to the modern industrial sector is lack of adequate opportunities for on the job training. We have already pointed out that women have been greater victims of rationalization and modernization in industry. Some of the new industries like electronics, simple engineering, telecommunications, etc., provided in-service-training to women with comparatively higher educational qualifications. In spite of opportunities provided by these few industries, however, the disparity in opportunities available to men and women is glaring. Under the Apprentices Act, 1961, 161 trades with 87,000 places have been located for apprentices in 101 industries. 52,500 apprentices have actually been engaged against these places of which only 104 are women. The bias for confining women trainees to limited group of trades is clearly visible.

Representatives of trade unions informed us that the training provided to workers for handling new machinery in different industries, seldom extends to women except in the few specific industries like machine tools, telecommunications and electronics in which women's greater aptitude for particular operation has already been recognized.

In the non-engineering trades where women constitute 64.6 per cent of the total number of trainees, the most popular, trades are cutting and tailoring, embroidery and needle work, knitting, and stenography. Of these, the first two are completely monopolized by women even in co-educational institutions. The situation is very different in the engineering trades where they form a mere 2.7 per cent of the total trainees. The most popular courses are for draftsman, instrument, mechanics, radio and T.V. mechanics, electronics, surveyors, carpenters and painters.

On the recommendation of the National Committee on Women's Education, the Ministry of Education took up a scheme to establish women polytechnics for post-matriculation training in various skills in industrial, commercial and public service occupations in accordance with developing needs of the national economy and to promote awareness of new opportunities and needs for women workers in such fields as social welfare, nursing, chemical and pharmaceutical industries, etc., in which women could be gainfully employed'. The total admission capacity of all these polytechnics is over 3000 for courses which require 2 to 3 years for completion. According to the Ministry of Education in commercial practice, stenography, catering and food technology, the admissions exceed the sanctioned capacity, while in other trades they fall short of the available number of seats. The out-turn for all the courses is considerably lower than the admissions. The total out-turn during 2000 amounted to only 1820 against an admission figure of 4500. This points to both wastage of available facilities as well as a failure in the realization of the objectives of this scheme. In the absence of inadequate assistance in placement, quite a few women on completion of these courses remain unemployed. The second reason for this is that the courses are not designed with any particular consideration for the employment potential of the locality. For example, during the Committee's tour of Andhra Pradesh we were informed by officials of the Industries Department that though there was an increasing demand for women in the telecommunication and electronic industries, none of the women's polytechnics in the State were providing training in these subjects. On our asking why nothing has been done, the officials replied that the control of polytechnics rested with the Department of Education and not industries. In Himachal Pradesh we received a number of requests from women's groups for training in food technology so that the products of their orchards are not wasted but no training facilities of this type exist in that State. Courses introduced are not always in relation to the demands of the region, e.g., dress and costume designing, a significant avenue for employment of women in bigger cities, hardly constitutes an important or a significant source of employment in the interior of the country. A heavy concentration on the same course, e.g., tailoring, also leads to minimization of job opportunities.

In 1968-69 the All India Council for Technical Education had reviewed the functioning of women's polytechnics and came to the conclusion:

1. A direct relationship should be established between course of training provided and employment opportunities available. For this purpose, for each polytechnic, there should be an advisory Committee including representative of employing organizations. Before any new course is started, close consultation should be held with the prospective employers to determine available job opportunities.

2. Each polytechnic should establish a production centre in the relevant field to provide practical training and improve standards and content of the courses. Such production centres might be started with the assistance of small-scale industries departments of the State concerned.

3. Polytechnics should offer short term job-oriented courses in selected fields where employment opportunities exist.

4. Start an employment advisory service for its students.

5. Service units should be established in these institutions to cater to the needs of the local public in such matters as providing practical, services blueprints, model estimates, etc.

Earlier 75 per cent of the non-recurring expenditure and 75 per cent of the recurring expenditure was borne by the Central Government. Since the commencement of the 4th Plan the Central Government stopped direct financial assistance for implementing specific development programme and now it is for the State Government to implement these recommendations.

Unfortunately while the Ministry of Education supplied information regarding the list of sanctioned courses and admission capacity in each of the 24 polytechnics, we were unable to obtain actual information regarding the teaching facilities available in the different institutions. Unofficially information received from different sources suggests that in many of the institutions some of the courses exist only on paper, particularly since the stoppage of central grants. Many of the State Governments find it difficult to provide adequate support to these institutions for their general maintenance. This could account for the very poor number of admissions against the courses for the country as whole. The second reason is the failure to implement the recommendations of the All India Council for Technical Education regarding the opening of production centres and provision of employment advisory service. Technical training for women is a relatively new field in India. In the absence of greater assistance in the placement of successful trainees, parents will be reluctant to send them to these institutions.

It is to be noted that some private institutions providing similar types of training to young women in the large cities, including a placement services, which connect training to the actual employment potential of the area, have proved to be highly successful. Mention may be made here of two institutions in Delhi. The Secretarial Training School, started by the Young Women's Christian Association some years ago has proved to be so successful as to justify its expansion to other types of vocational courses during the last few years. A similar unit started by St. Thomas Girls Higher Secondary School has also expanded rapidly, and is attracting students with even university degrees. Their success lies in their placement assistance and in the liaison that they maintain with employing agencies.

In the present socio-economic set up, self-employment of women requires much more than training in a particular productive trade. Without knowledge of the market mechanism, and capital resources, training alone cannot help women to face the competition. The production centres recommended by the All India Council for Technical Education as a part of polytechnic training have remained conspicuous by their absence. In our view, without supportive assistance in the way of training in organization of production and marketing and in procuring capital and raw materials, it will not be possible for the majority of these young trainees to utilize their training in self-employment.

The officials of the Industries Department in Andhra Pradesh informed us that in spite of the existence of a Government scheme to provide financial assistance for generating self-employment, the Department has been unable to assist many women to obtain the required help from banks. Even when such projects are sanctioned by Government, banks hesitate to provide the loans as they feel that the life of the projects may terminate when these young women get married.

Role of Various Agencies

Unlike the more formal programmes of pre-employment training, in the sphere of informal training programmes, a great deal of emphasis has been given to training women by various agencies in charge of development and welfare. All agencies specifically concerned with women's welfare and development, both government and voluntary, have always attached the highest priority to improving women's earning capacity.

Programmes have been developed to solve the economic needs of women hard pressed by the processes of social change and break-down of familiar obligations to support needy women widows, deserted and aged women as well as women from lower income groups.

(i) The Central Social Welfare Board is the most important agency providing assistance for these programmes operated by autonomous and voluntary organizations. It provides financial assistance for setting up production units in small-scale industries, handicrafts and ancillary units for larger industrial undertakings. In 1999-2000, 54 handicraft units were functioning with an employment potential of 2000. Apart from this, 31 handloom training-cum-production centres are being assisted by the Board. Some training centres have also been set up in association with the All-India Handicrafts Board. There are 30 institutions running production units for handlooms under this programme in various States with an employment potential of 1900. According to information available, a total of 240 units are in existence under this programme providing employment to 7500 workers.

(ii) Training of development cadres: Under the insistence of various developmental agencies, particularly the Central Social Welfare Board, training courses have been developed for village level workers (Gramsevikas, Gramlakshis, Mukhya Sevikas, Balsevikas, etc., by agencies like the Kasturba Memorial Trust, Visva Bharati, Jamia Milia and various schools of social work. They are mostly pre-service or in-service training for these cadres, fully financed by Government.

(iii) The programmes by the Kasturba Memorial Trust, Visva Bharati and Jamia Milia, have displayed considerable innovative acumen in developing new types of cadres for working in rural areas.

(iv) The Indian Council for Child Welfare also runs 45 centres in different parts of the country for pre-service and in-service training for Bal-sevikas. The training is financed by the Government.

(v) The Ministry of Health has training programmes for Health Visitors and auxiliary nurse midwife for developing health services in both rural and urban areas.

The Ministry of Food and Agriculture has also organized 43 community canning and food preservation centres. There are four institutes of catering technology and applied nutrition in the country. Though not exclusively for women, they train some women. Under the co-ordinated programme for community development, training is given in selected productive activities like kitchen-gardening, poultry keeping, dairy science, etc.

The Ministry of Home Affairs has a scheme for training of women and children of Central Government employees belonging to the low income groups. There are 80 centres under this scheme. Training is provided in cutting, tailoring and embroidery. Students are recommended as private candidates for the diploma courses of the Industrial Training Institutes. Some home employment is provided to these women through Government contracts.

Similar programmes have been initiated in few of the States by the Department of Welfare, Labour, Industry and Education for training mainly in sewing, embroidery, handicrafts and tailoring.

We visited a number of these training centres. In our view, much of these well-meant efforts end in futility, because they are not linked to production and marketing. The bias for traditional or home crafts limits their scope since the indigenous markets for these products are now on the decline, and marketing, both internal and for export, is mainly in the hands of intermediaries. Strangely even the Government Emporiums are also dealing through middlemen and do not buy directly through the production centres, even though the latter are financed by Government. Even without these handicaps, the scope of the programmes are so limited that they can only make a marginal impact on the employment needs of women. Another difficulty lies in the multiplicity of agencies engaged in this work, leading often to duplication and overconcentration in a few areas, leaving the large areas of the country completely untouched.

It is unfortunate that though the training programmes developed by welfare and other developing agencies have shown greater understanding of the employment needs of women, their efforts suffer from lack of adequate resources and coordination. In our view, better degree of planning, coordination and redistribution of responsibilities in these fields would prevent considerable wastage of resources and instil a greater sense of urgency and productivity in these schemes for improving women's earning power.

Bibliography

Abrar, S. Amir, *Issues of Female Welfare*, Peacock Books, Chennai, 2002.

Agrawal, Usha: *Indian Women Education and Development*, The Indian Publications, Ambala: 1995.

Anshen, R.N., (ed.), *The Family: Its Functions and Destiny*, Harper & Row, New York: 1959.

Asthana, P., *Women's Movement in India*, Vikas Publishing House, Delhi: 1974.

Baig Tara Ali: *India's Woman Position*, S. Chand and Company Pvt. Ltd., Delhi: 1976.

Bala, Usha: *Indian Women Freedom Fighters*, Manohar Publication, New Delhi: 1986.

Barot, Jyoti: *The Indian Family in the Change and Challenge of the Seventies*, Sterling Publishers, New Delhi: 1972.

Bebel, August: *Women in the Past, Present and Future*, ed. By Mukerjee, Subrata and Rama Swami, Sushila, Deep and Deep Publication, New Delhi, 1996.

Bhushan, Jamila Brij: *Muslim Women*, Vikas Publishing House, New Delhi: 1980.

Billington, Mary Frances: *Women in India*, Amarka Book Agency, Delhi: 1973.

Blalock, H.M. and Blalock, A.B., *Methodology in Social Research*, McGraw-Hill, New York: 1969.

Bose, Moni Mohan: *Female Education in India*, B.B. Gupta Publication, Kanpur: 1921.

Carden, Maren Lockwood: *The New Feminist Movement*, Russall Sage Foundation, New York: 1974.

Carstairs, G. Morris: *The Twice Born*, Indiana University Press, Bloomington: 1958.

Chakrapant, C. Kumar-S. Vijaya (editors): *Changing Status and Role of Women in Indian Society*, M.D. Pub., New Delhi: 1994.

Chattapadhya, Kamladevi, et. al: *The Awakening of Indian Women*, Everyman's Press, Chennai, 1939.

Chaturvedi, Geeta, *Women Administration in India*, RBSA Publication, Jaipur, 1985.

Cormack, Margaret: *The Hindu Women*, Asia Pub. House, Mumbai: 1961.

Deckard, B.S, *The Women's Movement*, Harper and Row, New York: 1979.

Desai, Neera and Patel Vibbuti: *Indian Women*, Popular Prakashan, Mumbai 1975-85.

De'Souza Alfred: *Women in Contemporary India and South Asia*, Manohar Pub., Delhi: 1980.

Drucker, P.F., *An Introductory View of Management*, Harper College Press, New York, 1977.

Engineer Asghar Ali: *Islam and Liberation Theology*, Sterling Pub., New Delhi: 1990.

Everett, J.M.: *Women and Social Change in India*, Heritage Pub., New Delhi: 1979.

Friedan, Betty, *The Feminine Mystique*, W.W. Norton, New York: 1963.

Gandhi, M.K., *The Role of Women*, Bhartiya Vidhya Bhavan, Mumbai, 1964.

Ghadially, Rehana, *Women in Indian Society*, Sage Pub., New Delhi: 1988.

Good, W.J., *World Revolution and Family Patterns*, Collier MacMillan, London: 1963.

Goldstein, Rhoda L., *Indian Women in Transition*, The Scarecrow Press Inc., New Jersey: 1972.

Gorwaney, N., *Self Image and Social Change*, Sterling Publishers, Delhi: 1977.

Gullahorn, J.E., *Psychology and Women in Transition*, John Wiley, New York: 1979.

Gupta, A.K., *Women and Society*, Criterion Pub., New Delhi: 1986.

Hasan, Zoya (ed.), *Forging Identities, Gender, Communities and the State*, Kali for Women, New Delhi : 1994.

Hate, C.A., *Changing Status of Women in Post-Independence India*, Allied Publications, Mumbai: 1969.

Horney, I.B., *Women in Farly Buddhist Literature*, Buddhist Publication Society, Kandy: 1961.

Horney, Karen, *Feminine Psychology*, W.W. Norton & Co., New York: 1967.

Indra Prof. *The Status of Women in Ancient India*, The Minerva Book Shop, Lahore: 1940.

Inkeles, A. and Smith D., *Becoming Modern*, Heinmann Educational Books Ltd., London: 1974.

Jain, D: *Indian Women*, Publication Division, Government of India, Delhi: 1975.

Jain, P.C., Jain. Shashi and Bhatnagar, Sudha (eds.): *Scheduled Caste Women*, Rawat Pub., Jaipur: 1997.

Jain, Pratibha and Mahan, Rajan, *Women Images*, Rawat Pub., Jaipur: 1996.

Jayal, Shakambari, *The Status of Women in Epics*, Motilal Banarsidas, Delhi: 1966.

Jayashree, *India and Indian Women*, Granthayan, Aligarh: 1980.

Kalarani, *Role Coriflict in Working Women*, Chitra Pub., New Delhi: 1976.

Kapur, Promilla, *The Changing Status of the Working Woman in India*, Vikas Pub., Delhi: 1974.

Kapur, Promilla, *Marriage and the Working Woman in India*, Vikas Pub., Delhi: 1975.

Keeton Kathy and Basrin Yvonne, *Woman of Tomorrow*, Harvard Univ. Press, New York: 1985.

Kidwai, Shaikh M.H., *Women under Different Social and Religious Law*, Seema Pub., New Delhi: 1976.

Kirpal, Viney (ed.), *The Girl Child in 20th Century Indian Literature*, Sterling Pub., New Delhi: 1992.

Kishwar Madhu, *Off the-Beaten Track Rethinking Gender Justice for Indian Women*, Oxford, New York: 1999.

Kumar Ashok, *Women in Contemporary Indian Society*, Anmol Pub., New Delhi: 1993.

Kuppuswamy, B., *Social Change in India*, Vikas Publishing House, Delhi: 1972.

Lateef, Shahida, *Muslim Women in India*, Kali for Women, New Delhi: 1990.

Lederer, Wolfgang, *The Fear of Women*, Arun and Strattan, New York: 1968.

Mehta, Hansa, *Indian Woman*, Butala & Co., New Delhi: 1981.

Mehta, Rama, *Socio-legal Status of Women in India*, Metropolitan Book Co., Delhi: 1982.

Mehta, Raman Lal, *The Western Educated Hindu Woman*, Asia Pub. House, New York: 1970.

Mehta, Raman Lal, *Thesis on the Legal Rights of Women under Different Communal Laws in Vogue in India*, The Advocate of Indian Press, Mumbai: 1933.

Mehta, Sushila, *Revolution and Status of Women in India*, Metropolitan Book Co., Delhi: 1982.

Menon, M. Indu, *Status of Muslim Women in India*, Uppal Pub. House, Delhi: 1981.

Misra, R.S., *Women Education*, Chugh Pub., Allahabad: 1993.

Mittal Mukta (ed.): *Women in India. Today and Tomorrow*, Anmol Pub., New Delhi: 1995.

Moddie, A.D., *The Brahamanical Culture and Modernity*, Asia Pub. House, London: 1968.

Mohanty, Jagannath, *Education for All*, Deep and Deep Pub., New Delhi: 1994.

Moneil, Elton B. and Rubin Zick, *The Psychology of Being Human*, Canfield Press, San Francisco, 1977.

Montagu, Ashley, *The Natural Superiority of Women*, The Macmillan Co., New York: 1968.

Myrdal, A. and Klien, V., *Woman's Two Roles*, Routledge & K. Paul, London, 1968.

Nanda, B.R., *Indian Women*, Vikas Pub. House, Delhi: 1976.

Pal, B.K., *Problems and Concerns of Indian Women*, ABC Pub. House, New Delhi: 1989.

Pandey, Rekha, *Women from Subjection to Liberation*, Motilal Pub., New Delhi: 1989.

Phandis, Urnifla, *Women of the World*, Vikas Pub. House, Delhi: 1978.

Pinkham, Mildreth Worth, *Women in the Sacred Scripts of Hinduism*, AMS Press Inc., New York: 1941.

Prakash, G., *After Colonialism: Imperial Histories and Post Colonial Displacements*, Princeton University Press, Princeton, 1995.

Pujari, Premlata and Kaushik, Vijay Kumari, *Women Power in India*, Kanishka Pub., Delhi: 1994.

Rajgopal, T.S.: *Indian Ideal of Womanhood*, Ramakrishna Mission, Kolkata: 1969.

Ramabal, Saraswati Pundita, *The High Caste Hindu Woman*, Jas. B. Podgers Printing Co., Philadelphia: 1888.

Ranganathan, Sarala, *Women and Social Order*, Kanishka Publishers, New Delhi: 1998.

Rani, K., *Role Conflict in Working Wives*, Chetana Publications, New Delhi: 1976.

Rege, Y.M., *Whither Women*, The Popular Book Depot, Mumbai: 1938.

Rehman, M.M. and Biswal, Kantala Kanta, *Education, Work and Women*, Commonwealth Publishers, New Delhi: 1993.

Roby, Pamela, *Women in the Work Place*, M.A. Schenkrnan, Cambridge, 1981.

Rohibaugh, Joanna Bunker, *Women: Psychology's Puzzle*, Basic Books Inc., New York: 1979.

Ross, Aileen D., *The Hindu Family in its Urban Setting*, Univ. of Toronto Press, Toronto: 1961.

Sachidananda and Sinha, Ramesh P., *Women's Right: Myth and Reality*, Printwell Pub., Jaipur: 1984.

Sengupta, Padmint, *The Story of Women of India*, Indian Book Co., New Delhi: 1974.

Sharma, Anuradha, *Women and Work, Human Resource Management Perspective*, Gyan Pub., New Delhi: 1999.

Sharma, S. Ram. (ed.), *Women's Education*, Discovery Pub. House, New Delhi: 1996.

Sharma, Usha and Sharma, B.M., *Committees and Commissions on Women Education*, Commonwealth Pub., New Delhi: 1995.

Shridevi, *A Century of Indian Womanhood*, Rao and Raghavan, Mysore: 1965.

Sikkri, Rehana, *Women in Islamic Culture and Society*, Kanishka Pub., New Delhi: 1999.

Singh, Indu Prakash, *Women, Law and Social Change in India*, Radiant Pub., New Delhi: 1989.

Singh, Uttam Kumar and Nayak, AR, *Women Education*, Commonwealth Pub. House, New Delhi: 1996.

Srinivasan, M.N., *The Changing Position of Indian Women*, Oxford Univ. Press, Delhi: 1970.

Subbamma, Malladi, *Women, Tradition and Culture*, Sterling Pub., Delhi: 1985.

Suguna, B, *Working Women and Religion*, Discovery Publishing House, New Delhi: 1994.

Tandon, R.K., *Women, Nature, Education, Teaching and Rights*, Commonwealth Pub., New Delhi: 1996.

Thomas, P., *Women and Marriage in India*, George Allen and Unwin, Lord: 1939.

Thomas, P., *Epics, Myths and Legends of India*, D.B. Teraporevala, Mumbai: 1961.

Thomas, P., *Indian Women Through the Ages*, Asia Pub. House, New York: 1964.

Tikoo, Prithvi Nath, *Indian Women*, B.R. Publishing Corporation, Delhi: 1985.

Upadhya, Bhagvrat Saran, *Women in Rigveda*, S. Chand and Co., Delhi: 1983.

Usha, Rao N.J., *Women in Developing Society*, Ashish Pub. House, Delhi: 1983.

Vashishta, B.K., *Encyclopardia of Women in India*, Parveen Encyclopaedia, New Delhi: 1976.

Vitels, M.S., *Motivation and Morale in Industry*, Morton, New York: 1953.

Vyas, Anju and Singh Sunita, *Women's Studies in India*, Sage Pub., New Delhi: 1993.

Watson, T., *Management Organization and Employment Strategy*, Routledge and Kegan Paul, London, 1986.

Whyte, F.W., *Money and Motivation*, Harper and Row. Inc., New York: 1955.

Yaqin, Anwarul and Anwar Badr, *Protection of Woman under Law*, Deep and Deep Publications, New Delhi: 1982.

Index

C

D

G

H

I

O

P

R